D1529024

CATHOLICS AND UNBELIEVERS
In Eighteenth Century France

CATHOLICS & UNBELIEVERS

IN EIGHTEENTH CENTURY FRANCE

By R. R. PALMER

PRINCETON UNIVERSITY PRESS

Copyright 1947 by Princeton University Press

L.C. Card: 61-13266

I.S.B.N.: 0-691-00750-0 (paperback edn.)

I.S.B.N.: 0-691-05108-9 (hardcover edn.)

First Princeton Paperback Printing, 1967

Second Princeton Paperback Printing, 1970

Fourth Hardcover Printing, 1970

*Printed in the United States of America
by Princeton University Press, Princeton, New Jersey*

To CARL BECKER

PREFACE

THE purpose of this book is made clear in the opening pages, and is suggested also in the bibliographical note at the end. Here I wish only to acknowledge my numerous obligations.

To Professor Carl Becker I owe the debt of a student to a great teacher. It is to be wished that the qualities for which Mr. Becker stands—wisdom and tolerance, clarity and simplicity, the gift of seeing both the unique small fact and the universe behind it—were more easily passed from teacher to student, like knowledge of the French Revolution.

I am deeply indebted also to Professor Louis R. Gottschalk of the University of Chicago, who first introduced me to the study of the eighteenth century, and has given me help and encouragement ever since. Professor Ira O. Wade, of the Department of Modern Languages at Princeton, has saved me by his vigilance from many ill-advised assertions. I have profited greatly from a long friendship with Dr. Francis D. Wormuth of Indiana University. M. l'Abbé Joseph Dedieu, of the École Massillon in Paris, gave me freely of his wide knowledge of the eighteenth century, put his notes at my disposal, and set me on the track of many interesting discoveries. All these gentlemen except M. Dedieu have read the book in manuscript. The rigor of their criticisms is sufficient sign that they are not responsible for the opinions it contains.

The sympathetic interest of my associates in the Department of History at Princeton has been of great value to me. I am likewise indebted to the officials of the Princeton University Press.

The book could not have been written without the help of the American Council of Learned Societies, which made possible the year's stay in France from which the finished product has come.

To all these teachers, friends, colleagues and benefactors I express my thanks.

Princeton, N.J.   R. R. P.
June 1939

CONTENTS

I. The Conditions of Thinking   3

II. Nature and Grace   23

III. History and Tradition   53

IV. The Fact of Revelation   77

V. Some Modernizers   103

VI. Soul and Mind   130

VII. Creation and Causality   155

VIII. Obligation and Liberty   178

IX. Nature Again   206

Bibliographical Note   225

Index   229

CATHOLICS AND UNBELIEVERS

In Eighteenth Century France

CHAPTER I

THE CONDITIONS OF THINKING

THE French philosophers of the eighteenth century, the *philosophes,* are justly admired for the principles for which they stood. They asserted the right to speak freely what they thought, and claimed for the human intelligence the power to understand the universe in which it acted. They rose up against a state of society in which the liberties of an earlier day had turned into privileges, and privilege was accepted as a principle of social organization, dividing men, by birth or occupation, into classes fixed by the laws of the country. These philosophers, by using their reason, proposed to bring order to the old Europe where in the progress of a thousand years hardly anything had been abolished, where vestigial and functioning organs had grown almost inseparably together, so that feudal institutions existed along with absolutist institutions, intense localism with centralized authority, pure custom with deliberate policy, supernatural mysteries with beliefs established by science. Into this welter of contradictions the French thinkers brought the idea of a simple and universal natural law. And against men who held that their rights were special and peculiar, based on rank, or the favor of the Crown, or the custom of their locality, they affirmed that rights were human, inherent in the nature of man.

The ideas of the philosophers are well known. Much is known also of the conditions of society against which the philosophers protested. What is less known is the intellectual position of those who opposed the new thinkers. Everyone has heard of Voltaire and Rousseau, and everyone is likely to have an impression of the old France, with its court of Versailles, its nobles and its peasants, its censorship and its secret imprisonment in such strongholds as the Bastille. Few who are not versed in the subject could so much as name a conservative thinker of the time. There are good reasons for this fact, but, on the whole, it must be confessed that the thought of the Age of Enlightenment, more than that of any equally important period in modern history, has been studied chiefly from writings which express only one side of the question.

In the picture we usually receive, certain bold and progressive men, who are outlined with great distinctness, do battle with vague but powerful adversaries who are rarely described but are indicated as extremely unenlightened. Or, in another of the pictures offered, a "climate of opinion" pervades the scene, making all thoughtful men share in certain general ideas of the time, which, we therefore assume, could be subjected to no very searching criticism from contemporaries. Both these pictures have much to recommend them, but neither is complete, for neither takes account of what contemporary critics of the *philosophes* thought and said.

The purpose of this book is to examine the ideas of the opponents of the *philosophes*. Most intellectual opposition came from the church. Our study is therefore a study of the ideas of French Catholics from about 1740 to the Revolution. It deals largely, but not exclusively, with the conflict between the orthodox and the persons whom we shall call, as they were then called, philosophers, unbelievers, or infidels. To show that not all the ideas of Catholics were dictated by the interest of the Catholic Church, we shall consider also, from time to time, the opinions of French Protestants and of a few thinkers who were neither religious nor yet in agreement with the philosophers. The problem is complicated by much overlapping. All parties were affected, in varying degree, by two general systems of thought. The important task is to find, if possible, the most fundamental differences by which the two systems of thought were distinguished. Hence we treat at some length of the disputes between Jesuits and Jansenists, in which these differences are often clearly revealed. The two systems, so far as single words can describe them, may be called the natural and the supernatural; but these terms are ambiguous and troublesome; and more useful antitheses are suggested in the pairs of words used as chapter headings below.

This main subject is approached in the next chapter with a discussion of nature and grace. Meanwhile we wish to sketch a background against which the abstract questions that follow may perhaps be better understood.

The central fact was the existence of the church as a rich, powerful, and closely organized corporation. This corporation was a kind of government in itself; it raised and expended its own taxes, for example, and could not be legally required to pay taxes to the state. It used its great wealth to support its prelates in luxury, to maintain its elaborate worship, to educate the young, and to relieve the poor. It was backed by the leading families of France, and was entrenched in the whole family system; for it offered careers to able or to superfluous sons, and a place of dignified retirement for unmarried daughters. It disturbed the country by the intrigue, rivalry, and theological rancor of its clergy. A public power in its own right, it entered into secular politics, swaying the minds or demanding the aid of servants of the Crown. Through its parish organization, its schools, almshouses, and literary publications, it exercised over everyone in France an influence independent both of public opinion and of civil authority. These facts explain much of the opposition which it aroused in the eighteenth century. But they explain also, very largely, the policies of Louis XIV and the conflict of church and state that had gone on for five hundred years. In the crisis of the eighteenth century another element was added, in which issues even more fundamental were raised.

The church claimed the right to suppress all ideas of which its officials did not approve. It claimed to possess the truth and, unlike many others who have made the same claim, it had institutional authority behind it. It claimed also to be of supernatural ordination, to dispense upon earth the living word of God, to control the sole means by which men might be saved. "No salvation outside the church" was a doctrine to which theologians admitted qualifications; but for practical purposes it was the official teaching, since no ordinary person, living in Catholic France where the usual means of salvation were at hand, could reasonably expect to be saved without them. To belong to the church, to believe in its mission, and to accept its doctrines were requisite to a complete religious life. "Without faith, and a faith that embraces all the dogmas," wrote a minor apologist, *"it is impossible to be pleasing to God. . . .* He who believes as he should, loves God and his neighbor; he who does not, loves neither."[1] In these words breathes the spirit that makes for fanaticism. And among all the contrary tendencies that we shall presently discover, they should not be forgotten. Obedience to the church was fundamental. The church could forgive much: it could absolve from sin and countenance much latitude in thinking; but it could not forgive those who denied its ability to remove sin, or its right to propound the dogmas by which thinking should be governed. It could not tolerate those who questioned its authority.

It is unnecessary to review the consequences, the long tale of philosophers molested, ideas excoriated, books condemned to the flames. That story is well known. The warfare of science and theology has had many diligent historians; and it is to be hoped that the effects of the social control of ideas will continue to be remembered. In this warfare the church was not so much opposing reason and science themselves, which it had in fact done much to foster, as trying to discipline a reason which pretended that revelation was unnecessary, and a science which arrived at conclusions that made the revealed story seem improbable. Most scientists, from Galileo to Buffon, were willing to go through the motions of conformity; many, indeed, were at heart faithful to the church. The *philosophes* attacked directly and with scant disguise the very principles on which the whole ecclesiastical system rested. If they were intolerant, it was because on the questions they raised there could be no equivocation. Either the church expressed the will of God, or it did not. The revelation on which it based its authority either existed or did not exist. Its right to control the minds of men was either divine and immutable, or it was human, historical, and customary—and hence subject to denial.

In theory, the church had to be intolerant, for it was responsible to God for bringing the true faith to mankind. In theory, the philosophers stood for the toleration of all beliefs and the free expression of all ideas. In fact, however, the situation was less simple. The philosophers were by no means willing to allow liberty to their opponents, not even to those who were far from representing the formidable power of the church. Their method

[1] J. Deforis, *Préservatif pour les fidèles contre les sophismes et les impiétés des incrédules* (Paris, 1764), p. 358.

was not often the mild persuasion favored by liberals. They talked much of reason, but their sharpest instruments were ridicule and vilification, which enabled them to throw off a man's arguments by defaming his character or belittling his intelligence. La Baumelle went to jail, thanks partly to Voltaire, whose works he had ventured to criticize. Fréron, a conservative and Catholic journalist, was called by Voltaire, in a single work, a scribbler, scoundrel, toad, lizard, snake, spider, viper's tongue, crooked mind, heart of filth, doer of evil, rascal, impudent person, cowardly knave, spy, and hound. He found his journal gagged, his income halved and his career ruined by the concerted attacks of the philosophers. To silence him, at least two of these philosophers, Marmontel and d'Alembert, appealed to the censors whose very existence the enlightened thinkers are supposed to have abhorred. It is not possible, in short, to accept as characteristic of these thinkers the statement often attributed to Voltaire, that, though he disagreed with what a man said, he would fight to the death for his right to say it.[2]

To assert, on the other hand, that Catholicism in the eighteenth century was tolerant would be scarcely accurate, but would contain elements of truth. The point is made clearer by the distinction between toleration, which is a public policy, and tolerance, which is a disposition of mind. Catholics did not believe in toleration; they held, with the laws of the country, that a non-Catholic had no religious or civil status in France. Sometimes, however, they were inclined to a kind of tolerance, were willing to allow differences of opinion in which the authority of the church was not positively denied. Many of them, laymen and clergy, would think

[2] For examples of Voltaire's intolerance consult the index to his *Oeuvres* (Paris, 1883-85) under "Chaumeix," "Trublet," "Larcher," "Guenée," and especially "Juifs"; see also below, p. 210, n. 4. On La Baumelle see the *Biographie universelle*, "La Baumelle." On Fréron see Voltaire, *L'Écossaise*, from which the epithets cited above are taken, and *Anecdotes sur Fréron*; É. Fréron, *Année littéraire* (1760), Vol. IV, p. 114, (1772), Vol. I, pp. 1 ff.; F. Cornou, *Élie Fréron: Trente ans de luttes contre Voltaire et les philosophes* (Paris, 1922), pp. 164, 178, 219, 383-5, 455-6; J. Delort, *Histoire de la détention des philosophes* (Paris, 1829), Vol. II, p. 175; Grimm, *Correspondance littéraire* (Paris, 1877-82), Vol. II, p. 372, Vol. IX, pp. 62-3; S. Linguet, *Annales civiles, politiques et littéraires,* Vol. IV (1778), p. 293. Fréron's relative impartiality may be seen in many places, e.g. *Année littéraire* (1756), Vol. VIII, p. 273, where he vigorously defends Voltaire's poem *La religion naturelle* against the criticisms of A. Thomas, *Réflexions sur le poème La religion naturelle.*

it somewhat exaggerated to say, with the apologist quoted above, that without faith in all the dogmas no man could be pleasing to God. Orthodoxy held, then as now, that there was a legitimate natural morality apart from revealed religion.

More important than orthodoxy in producing this tolerance was the gradual cooling of religious ardor. By and large, the religious did not believe in their doctrines with the intensity, the sense of personal discovery and conviction, with which the *philosophes* believed in theirs. The implications of this fact are many. On the one hand, it made Catholics often more reasonable than *philosophes,* more willing to persuade, examine, or remonstrate, less given to sarcasm, mockery and abuse. On the other hand, this same fact, making religion less an experience of life, made it more an acknowledgment of authority. And with the decline of intolerance, the policy of "intoleration" came to be less the faith of a community than an administrative convenience, useful in some ways to the government, but chiefly benefiting the clerical bureaucracy.

This attitude among the religious—whether it be called indifference, formalism, tolerance, or receptiveness to new ideas— had developed gradually through several generations. It was not brought on by the writings of eighteenth century unbelievers. In searching for causes we must not exaggerate the importance of books, or ascribe too much influence to the ideas of radical thinkers. Why did Voltaire and Diderot become militant infidels, though born Catholics and brought up in Catholic surroundings? Why were they successful in spreading their opinions, convincing many readers even when they shocked them? The most general answer to both questions is that the Catholic religion was no longer as vital to many people as it once had been. It no longer seemed as essential either to public order or to a satisfactory understanding of the world. The causes for the change must be looked for in the general history of Europe.

Probably the most important of these causes was the growth of the state. There had been a time in Europe when the state, for practical purposes, did not exist. A man at that time, say in the twelfth century and earlier, had had little government and no country; his loyalties, rights, and obligations were local, personal, and concrete, running from himself to some other particular men.

So far as he belonged to anything else he belonged to the universal Catholic Church. So far as he was more than a villager, he was a Christian. Only by the church was he joined to men outside his own nexus of rights and duties; only the church gave him a public status, an abstract existence, an impersonal system of law, a body of administrative superiors whose powers inhered in their offices. By the eighteenth century this situation was radically altered. It was the state now, more effectively than the church, which made a man more than a villager, and regarded law as more than a body of personal relationships. This triumph of the state was not to be assured until the French Revolution, but nowhere in Europe in the eighteenth century had the process gone farther than in France.

In France, therefore, at the time we are dealing with, it was widely felt that the state was a more proper agency for ruling men than the church. Public authority now meant chiefly the civil power. And men whose connections were with one abstraction, the state, did not always look with favor on the other abstraction, the church. These men included the army of administrators attached to the King's Council, and the host of judicial functionaries attached to the supreme law courts, or parlements, of the country. They were professing Catholics, though in the law courts tinged with Jansenism; they detested unbelievers and radicals of every kind; but their work, like that of the *philosophes,* helped subordinate the church to the state. The government for more than two hundred years had appointed all the bishops. Twice in the eighteenth century it sought, unsuccessfully, to tax the clergy. In 1762 it expelled the Jesuits, whose most fatal offense, beneath the other charges made against them, was espousal of the principle that the spiritual power stood higher than the temporal. With scores of schools left vacant by the Jesuit teachers, the government embarked on a new policy of education, which was hardly different in principle from the policy of the revolutionaries a generation later. In the various projects drawn up at the invitation of the authorities, we find it asserted that "the state has an imprescriptible right to bring up its members," and that "a man in religious orders has no spirit of country." Despite the protests of the clergy, the number of lay teachers was greatly increased. Even the University of Paris, a fortress of clerical independence,

had to submit to a measure of secular control and secular standards.[3] On another occasion, when the archbishop of Paris forbade the decrees of the Parlement of Paris to be read, and declared that civil judges could not require priests to give the sacraments unwillingly, the civil judges solemnly burned his order.
In 1765, when the Assembly of the Clergy arranged to take meas-
ures against infidel writers, the Parlement of Paris pronounced
its acts illegal, odious, fanatical, and void. Though this decree of
the Parlement was annulled by the king on complaint of the
clergy, the provincial parlements took the same stand when similar acts were passed by provincial assemblies of the clergy.[4] The
trend to secularization was clear. The last step under the monarchy
was the toleration of Protestants, provided for in 1787.

All these developments were greeted by the *philosophes* as the
fruits of reason and enlightenment; and toleration, at least, has
often been attributed mainly to intellectual advance. The growth
of the state offers a more likely explanation. The state had so
far replaced the church as the chief authority in society, had so
centered allegiance, hopes, and values upon itself, and had so
improved its administrative technique and its means of dealing
with individuals however numerous or remote, that the rival
administrative machinery of the church was no longer useful to
it, and the religious views of private persons became irrelevant
to practical politics. The government could henceforth deal with
people most effectively, not as Catholics, Protestants and Jews, but
as citizens of France. Religious toleration was granted at the time
when national patriotism was becoming the chief loyalty of most
Frenchmen.

Another of the general causes in the withdrawal of religion
from the forefront of men's consciousness was a manner of thinking hard to name. It was a feeling of confidence in and content-
ment with the world. When even a peasant or journeyman tailor
could travel hundreds of miles, know where he was going, and
arrive; when people habitually planned and calculated for the future in their practical affairs; when everyone knew, if not the

---

[3] C. Jourdain, *Histoire de l'Université de Paris* (Paris, 1888), Vol. II, pp. 322-4.
"Un religieux n'a point l'esprit de la patrie."
[4] M. Picot, *Mémoires pour servir à l'histoire ecclésiastique pendant le dix-
huitième siècle* (2nd ed., Paris, 1816), Vol. II, pp. 313, 479-90.

facts of geography, at least that the world had been pretty thoroughly explored, and, if not the facts of history, at least that the past was not entirely a world of giants, wizards, saints, extraordinary heroes, and men five hundred years old—then a kind of thinking had arrived which, in contrast to some others, we recognize as our own. There was less feeling than formerly of terrible and capricious forces, less feeling that life was precarious and beset with evil. The unknown henceforth was not to be propitiated but investigated. For the educated there were the findings of science. All but the most humble by the middle of the eighteenth century knew that the earth moved about the sun. Most of the educated after 1750 accepted the physics of Newton.

As more was learned of the world, from science, exploration, history or the wider daily experience which a settled society could give, the old dualism between the natural and the supernatural became more acute. Ordinary matters could be dealt with by the concept of "nature." Religion thus became more definitely "supernatural"—a word whose content no one could rationally describe, but which signified that religion was somehow different from everything else. Thus the mysteries became more inscrutably mysterious, the dogmas more incomprehensibly dogmatic, and faith itself, for many people, the acceptance of authority in certain moments of life.

Not long before the middle of the eighteenth century, hardly noticed, an important word passed from learned into general use in the French language. This word was "civilization." Its promotion into common speech reveals nothing less than a revolution of ideas. A little reflection will show that civilization is one of the things that modern men have really respected. It is spoken of in the terms in which an earlier age spoke of Christendom or God. Civilization is now "outraged" by acts of brutality, divides the faithful from those who sit in darkness, gives men a common purpose, makes individual life worth living, stands contrary to ignorance, uncleanness, and disorder. It is civilization, if anything, that undergoes the processes of progress. To improve and extend it has been the ideal of Western men since the eighteenth century. This ideal, though the religious have usually shared in it, is rather different from the older ideals of religion. It has aimed at making this world comfortable, whatever might happen in the next.

Civilization had also a lighter side, especially in France before the Revolution. This meaning was expressed by the word "sociability," coined at about the time when "civilization" became current. Civilization in this sense was the life of the town. It meant gregarious and busy living, conversation and visiting about, a certain formality of speech and behavior, an agreeable manner toward equals and an easy gallantry to persons of the other sex. Those best succeeded who cultivated the personality rather than the soul, and who were witty but not disconcertingly profound. The civilized man was oriented toward the social world. He looked to its standards as those of correct taste, its morals as those of a gentleman, its judgment as a proper test of achievement.

Such an atmosphere was not very favorable to religion as traditionally understood. Love of solitude and meditation was likely to seem eccentric, self-denial rather useless and morose. The poet Saint-Lambert, for example, serving in the army in 1749, found himself billeted with a family of Jansenists, whose austerity he regarded as a kind of barbarism, and whose stern beliefs prompted him to write a bit of society verse. He appealed to *Indulgente société!* and ended by asserting that his tastes and desires were given by God.[5] There were many people in France who, though shocked when infidels questioned revelation, thought with Saint-Lambert that pleasure was a right, that the good man was the amiable one, that good morals were a form of good taste, and that the art of living was to mix smoothly in refined company.

The "world," the world of men and manners, was pleasant in the civilized century and in France, the civilizing nation, at least for those classes who in increasing numbers could acquire the

---

[5] C. Collé, *Journal* (1868), Vol. I, pp. 59-60, March 1749.

> "Indulgente société!
> O vous, dévots plus raisonnables,
> Vertueux sans férocité,
> Le goût polit vos moeurs aimables,
> Vous vous occupez sagement
> De l'art de penser et de plaire;
> Aux hymnes de votre bréviaire
> Vous entremêlez prudemment
> Et du Virgile et du Voltaire. . . .
> Je sens, j'ai des goûts, des désirs;
> Dieu les inspire ou les pardonne;
> Le triste ennemi des plaisirs
> L'est aussi de Dieu qui les donne."

rudiments of civilized living. The world in this sense was undoubtedly more attractive, more ordered, safer and more satisfactory than at any time in the troubled history of Europe since the long-gone Age of the Antonines which the men of enlightenment frequently extolled. But a world of this kind, tamed and made livable, was a challenge to the historic Christian religion. Christianity had arisen in the ruins of a civilization, in a time of uncertainty and despair; it had given comfort for affliction, offered a retreat to those who found the world too rude, curbed the passions of fierce barbarians who would have laughed at the ethics of a gentleman; it had brought order to a continent in anarchy, raised an ecclesiastical authority where no civil authority existed; and above all it had turned the eyes of men to another and a better world, a serene world of harmony and rest. Christianity, with good reason, was fundamentally unworldly. The people of the eighteenth century, with reason also, were admirers of the world.

Fewer people than a century earlier were choosing to enter the celibate and priestly life. The number of clergy in France on the eve of the Revolution is not definitely known, but in all probability it was smaller than when Louis XIV became king, although the population had considerably increased in the meanwhile.[6] Among those who had taken the vows there were ominous signs of discontent. In 1765 twenty-eight Benedictines of Saint-Germain-des-Prés in Paris petitioned against their rule. They declared that night services and fasting kept them from useful work, that their costume made them ridiculous in the streets, and that they wished to be known as scholars rather than as monks. The petitioners were disavowed by the majority in their convent, and were forced to retract before the archbishop, but a few returned into civil life, where they were protected from church discipline by the philosophers. In the same year Brienne, archbishop of Toulouse, a friend of d'Alembert and himself well disposed toward philosophy, was appointed head of the committee on monasteries of the Assembly of the Clergy. He abolished religious houses that had dwindled to less than fifteen members, and decreed that

---

[6] The number of all clergy in France was estimated in 1667, under Colbert's direction, at about 260,000. Some writers have put the figure for 1789 as low as 130,000; but the best estimate seems to be about, or just under, 200,000. See E. Levasseur, *La population française* (1889), Vol. I, pp. 228-9.

no order should have more than one house in the same city. The exile of the Jesuits and the decline of the Oratorians still further weakened the intellectual efficiency of the church.[7]

Outside the cloister the signs were at least equally alarming. Some preachers had to make an effort not to appear too philosophical, and to use sacred quotations to adorn arguments purely rational. Students of theology, it was said, often showed themselves more familiar in their examinations with the objections raised by unbelievers than with the correct reply to be made to them. Brienne, the future archbishop, a student at the Sorbonne in 1751, offered a thesis implying that the world was uncreated, a belief untenable by Christians. The young Turgot, at the Sorbonne in the same year, delivered a notable Latin address on the progress of the human mind. Other bachelors followed his example, choosing to hold forth in their public orations on history and politics rather than theology, while many of the elder professors wagged their heads and deplored the decay of religion. There was trouble at Saint-Sulpice, where aristocratic young men destined for high position in the church were sent to acquire a smattering of theology, and where they rioted and almost set the building on fire when told to give up their elaborate wigs. At Toul, in Lorraine, a deacon, as he walked in the church procession, was observed to be reading Helvétius. At La Flèche, in Anjou, seat of a great Jesuit school where Descartes had been educated, one of the professors wrote a poem in praise of freedom of the press. At Toulouse, in the 1760's, a professor of history named Andras had his students read Voltaire's *Essai sur l'histoire générale,* with only moderate expurgations. He was protected from his critics by Archbishop Brienne, who at last, however, had to consent to his dismissal.[8]

Sometimes the effects of worldliness were more subtle. Le Franc de Pompignan, bishop of Puy, a man of impeccable orthodoxy, included among his numerous writings in defense of religion a work called *La dévotion réconciliée avec l'esprit,* in which

---

[7] Picot, *op. cit.,* Vol. II, pp. 476, 503-5; A. Bernard, *Le sermon au dix-huitième siècle* (Paris, 1901), pp. 367-78.

[8] Bernard, *op. cit.,* pp. 73, 138, 364-5, 397, 403-5, 490, 497; Jourdain, *op. cit.,* Vol. II, p. 371; A. Sicard, *Éducation morale et civique avant et pendant la Révolution* (Paris, 1884), pp. 137-48.

he argued that piety was no obstacle to wit and intelligence, that a man might be devout and still shine in society, and that a priest who had a gift of *esprit* would more easily win souls to religion, since he would "capture their attention and overcome their distaste by the harmless attraction of eloquence." The sermon itself was in danger of becoming a rhetorical exercise. Encouraged by the Academy, which gave prizes for religious eloquence, some preachers turned their sermons into formal harangues, hoping rather to impress their hearers by elegance in discourse than to move their souls by the doctrines of religion. The Abbé Boulogne is said to have taken lessons from the actor Talma.[9]

In this atmosphere of worldliness, which is another name for a primary concern with the mundane values of civilization, it would be surprising to find French Catholics very fanatical. Fanaticism, indeed, was a word often used by the orthodox to describe Jansenists, Methodists, and others whose religion they thought too personal and intense. To Linguet, who liked neither the church nor the philosophers, it seemed that the philosophers were the only dangerous fanatics of the time. Catholics, far from being fanatical, were more likely than *philosophes* to countenance real skepticism. One of the few French skeptics of the time was Louis de Beausobre. The *philosophe* Raynal was short and severe in condemning his ideas as worthless; Fréron, a sincere if not passionate believer in the church, while stating that he disagreed with Beausobre, gave his book close attention and even praise, and wished the young author success in the future.[10]

Except for the ruthless suppression of Jansenists, the persecution that still went on was mostly sporadic and local, arising from mob excitement or from individuals with private ambitions to satisfy. The best known cases of persecution that ended in death are those of the Protestant Calas and the half-witted youth

[9] J.-G. Le Franc de Pompignan, *Oeuvres* (Paris, 1855), Vol. I, p. 453; Dupréaux, *Le Chrétien parfait honnête homme, ou L'Art d'allier la piété avec la politesse et les autres devoirs de la vie civile* (Paris, 1750); Bernard, *op. cit.*, pp. 31-3, 113-15, 155, 215, 309, 333-5, 390.

[10] Linguet, *Le fanatisme des philosophes* (Londres, 1764), a rather feeble pamphlet; for better statements of the same views, *idem, Annales civiles,* Vol. I, pp. 63, 249-50, Vol. II, p. 85, Vol. III, pp. 437-8 (1777), and Vol. XVII, pp. 357-9 (1790). On Beausobre's *Pyrrhonisme du sage* (Berlin, 1754), see Raynal in Grimm, *Correspondance littéraire,* Vol. II, pp. 190-1; Fréron, *Année littéraire* (1754), Vol. VII, p. 170.

La Barre. The new and significant feature of these affairs was not that they occurred but that numerous persons calling themselves Catholics could be aroused in favor of the victims.

In the Calas affair the circumstances were not clear. There is reasonable ground for believing that Calas was implicated in the murder of his son with which he was charged, that the court of Toulouse followed only the usual procedure of criminal justice, and that Calas and his family were ultimately exonerated, not so much because of literary propaganda (which the government would be likely to resist with all possible stubbornness) as because a certain nun in the convent where one of Calas's daughters had been temporarily lodged took an interest in the distress of the family, and communicated with a cousin high in the government at Paris, who then saw to it that the decision of the court of Toulouse was revoked.[11]

As for La Barre, who was put to death for desecrating a wayside cross, Linguet was active in his defense; and he concluded not only that the church authorities had been unjust but that La Barre would never have got into trouble had his mind not been turned by reading the vicious propaganda of the infidels. Grimm states that the books found in La Barre's library were pornographic rather than philosophical, but there was a dubious borderland in which these two fields of literature then merged.[12]

It should be noted also that the philosophers, though they talked commonly of burnings, were really in no danger of life or limb. The last important imprisonment for irreligious opinion took place in 1749, when, according to d'Argenson, "a quantity of *abbés, savants* and *beaux-esprits*" were arrested, including Diderot, some university professors and doctors of the Sorbonne. Diderot, says d'Argenson, "received the magistrate with the loftiness of a fanatic," but he was soon released, as were the others.[13]

[11] L. Labat, *Le drame de la rue des Filatiers: Jean Calas* (Paris, 1910), a very circumstantial book, argues that suicide was impossible, and that the younger Calas was killed by his father, though not intentionally. See also F. H. Maugham, who, in his *Case of Jean Calas* (London, 1928), believes that the younger Calas committed suicide.

[12] Grimm, *Correspondance littéraire*, Vol. VII, p. 77.

[13] d'Argenson, *Mémoires* (Paris, 1859-67), Vol. VI, pp. 10-11, 15, 26. After 1749 the most noteworthy cases of imprisonment were as follows: La Baumelle, who spent six months in the Bastille in 1753, for having written his *Notes sur le siècle de Louis XIV*, a work which offended Voltaire. Desforges, seven months

Among persons of intellectual pretensions the anti-philosophic Linguet seems to have suffered the most. He had to take refuge in England in 1777, and from 1780 to 1782 spent twenty months in the Bastille, an experience of which he has left a record worth reading by those inclined to minimize the hardships.[14] The *philosophes,* on the other hand, had much in their favor. A ferocious law was indeed passed in 1757, condemning to death all purveyors of irreligious and subversive opinions, but it was not enforced and the policy of Malesherbes, the head of the censorship after 1750, was exactly contrary to it. From his experience in office, in which resisting the demands of the *philosophes* for the suppression of their enemies was one of his burdens, Malesherbes came to believe that freedom of the press was the only fair or practicable policy. The granting of *permissions tacites* for illegal books became a usual procedure in his department and allowed some of the most radical books of the epoch, notably Helvétius's *De l'Esprit,* to slip through with the *Privilège du Roi* on their title pages.[15] It was such weakness and confusion in the law, rather than rigor, which produced injustice under the old régime.

That the philosophers had less to endure than is often thought, and that many of the clergy, when not abnormally aroused, were more enlightened than some historians have supposed, is often apparent in the attitude of the Jesuits. The Jesuits were opposed

in the Bastille in 1758-59, for a book advocating the marriage of the clergy. Marmontel, in the Bastille eleven days, 1759-60, for offending the Duc d'Aumont. Morellet, in the Bastille seven weeks in 1760, for a reply to Palissot's comedy *Les Philosophes,* in which he incidentally offended the Princess of Robeck. The elder Mirabeau, at Vincennes ten days in 1760, for having offended certain financiers in his *Théorie de l'impôt.* The younger Mirabeau was imprisoned later at the request of his father. Fréron was at Vincennes seven weeks in 1746, and in the Bastille six weeks in 1757. Most such imprisonments after 1750 were made for trivial reasons at the request of persons with private grudges to satisfy, and had little to do with the expression of general ideas. Delort, *op. cit.,* Vol. II, pp. 162-5, 180-4, 275-85, 298-307, 327-43, Vol. III, pp. 119-23.

[14] *Annales civiles,* Vol. X (1783), pp. 1-160. Also printed separately, *Mémoires sur la Bastille* (Londres, 1783).

[15] For the law of 1757, see Isambert, *Recueil des anciennes lois françaises* (Paris, 1822-33), Vol. XXII, pp. 272-4; on Malesherbes and the disintegration of the censorship after 1750, H. Robert, *Malesherbes* (Paris, 1927), pp. 61-73; J. M. S. Allison, *Lamoignon de Malesherbes* (New Haven, 1938), pp. 12-32; J. Belin, *Le commerce des livres prohibés à Paris de 1750 à 1789* (Paris, 1913), pp. 18-35; A. Bachman, *Censorship in France, 1700-1750* (New York, 1934), pp. 146-56.

to the encroachments of civil authority upon the faith, but in
other respects they were men of their time, men of the world
skilled in civilized living, and intellectually the most able in the
church. They published a monthly periodical, the *Journal de
Trévoux,* addressed to the general educated public. To all appearances this journal was among the most disinterested publications
of its time. More than most unbelievers and most religious apologists, the editors possessed the qualifications for a critical treatment of ideas: the ability to give an objective analysis of a book,
to represent opposing views fully and fairly, to disagree without
losing one's temper, and to make suggestions without seeming
oracular.

If we examine the issues for the year 1751, we find slight evidence to support the claim of the *philosophes* that the Jesuits from
the first were jealous and fearful of the superior enlightenment
of the *Encyclopédie.* What we do find is rational criticism. In the
early months of that year the *Journal* notes the prospectus of the
forthcoming Encyclopedia. Berthier, the editor, compares its classification of branches of knowledge to that made a hundred and
fifty years before by Francis Bacon. In some details he prefers
Bacon's, but makes no attack on the Encyclopedia, veiled or open.

In July the first volume of the Encyclopedia appeared. Berthier
(meanwhile praising Duclos's *Moeurs* and Rousseau's first *Discours*) waited until October to deliver his opinion. He then
greeted the first fruits of the new enterprise with expressions of
good will, and gave a full and careful synopsis of d'Alembert's
Discours préliminaire. Occasionally we may detect a note of irony.
To d'Alembert's observation that the current age was remarkable
for the number of its great geniuses, Berthier answers drily:
"It is a philosopher that gives this praise; it is to be supposed,
therefore, that he is not exaggerating, but speaks with full and
entire knowledge, and would not dream of saying, like the *Femmes
Savantes,* 'No one shall be clever but ourselves and our friends.'"
Further on, without apparent intention of sarcasm, he suggests
that the Encyclopedia might indicate its sources, when reproducing
passages from other works; and he advises the use of quotation
marks. The next month, November, Berthier notes further borrow-
ings from older works, disagrees, in passing, with the demand for
freedom of press among the learned, and observes that the articles

on heretics ought to point out their errors more distinctly. He declares, however, that the Encyclopedia is a noble and mighty enterprise, and that the Encyclopedists, after finishing their work, will be able justly to repeat the words of Horace, *Exegi monumentum ære perennius.*[16]

Following the clue of his chance observations, Berthier went on to search systematically for sources of the Encyclopedia, and he published three articles on this subject in the first three months of 1752. He showed, citing exact references, and with long parallel quotations, that over a hundred articles and parts of articles in the first volume of the Encyclopedia, some extending to several columns, had been copied almost word for word and without acknowledgment from earlier works, notably from the Jesuit *Dictionnaire de Trévoux,* certain technical dictionaries of commercial and nautical terms, and the philosophical writings of the Jesuit Buffier, who had died in 1737.[17] Such borrowing was not then thought very culpable, and if Berthier's discovery was embarrassing to Diderot and his colleagues, it was because they had announced themselves emphatically as pioneers.

Of dissent from the fundamental philosophy of the Encyclopedia, more is to be found in the *Journal des Savants* than in the *Journal de Trévoux.* The former journal took no notice of the new enterprise until October, being thus several months behind the Jesuits, and then printed a summary of the preliminary discourse, much more cursory than Berthier's. It devoted several pages to defending the philosophy of innate ideas against the empiricism expressed by d'Alembert, and pointed out that the sensationalist psychology was dangerous to religion. The next month it published an anonymous article on the metaphysics of the Encyclopedia. The author, a French Protestant living in Holland, objected to d'Alembert's aspersions on Descartes, and represented the Ency-

[16] *Mémoires pour l'histoire des sciences et des beaux arts* [generally known as the *Journal de Trévoux*] 1751, pp. 302-27, 708-37, 2250-95, 2423, 2592-623. See also two letters from Diderot to Berthier, in Diderot, *Oeuvres* (Paris, 1875-77), Vol. XIII, pp. 165-70, and Berthier's reply, *Journal de Trévoux* (1751), pp. 569-78.
[17] *ibid.* (1752), pp. 146-89, 296-322, 424-69. Most of these articles were brief, many of them mere definitions. The plagiarism from Buffier was apparently the work of Yvon, on whom see below, p. 119.

clopedists as men who had been carried away by the fashions of their day.[18]

In the first reception of the Encyclopedia by the Jesuits there was little, in short, that an American university professor might not have said. The specifically Jesuit view is revealed in only a few occasional phrases. It is true that these relatively peaceful relations did not last long. The year 1751 was an eventful one, and it soon became clear that the Encyclopedists were not simply gifted writers of whom educated Catholics might approve, though with reservations, but were determined and implacable enemies of the church who must be tirelessly combated. The Encyclopedists raised the question of church authority. On that question men had to take sides.

Enough has been said, however, to show that the conflict was not simply between enlightened and backward thinkers. Nor was it a dispute between skeptics and men of faith. The work of the *philosophes* was not to destroy a faith; that would have been a barren accomplishment. The great work of the *philosophes* was to supply a new faith, which more fully than traditional Christianity took account of the facts of the new age, giving a supreme significance to the rise of science, the growth of the state, the improvement of civilization, the increasing attractiveness and livability of this nether world. The new faith, involving the conceptions of nature, liberty, and progress, has been criticized since, and it was criticized then, with what success the reader may judge at the end of the book. It is evident that for practical purposes the criticism failed, for the ideas of the *philosophes* shaped the society of the nineteenth century. The old faith was attached to institutions whose evils were known and could be opposed. The ideas of the *philosophes* did not yet suffer from this handicap.

The upholders of the old faith were a motley host, exceedingly numerous, and varying from the dubious champions whom Fréron thought a menace to the cause, since they discredited religion by

[18] *Journal des savants* (1751), October, pp. 198-223, November, pp. 404-31. This November article was by Boullier, and was later printed separately, with some revision. See below, p. 139. For further criticism of the Encyclopedia see Fréron, *Année littéraire* (1758), Vol. II, p. 109; Linguet, *Annales civiles,* Vol. XI (1784), pp. 363-8. A. Chaumeix, *Préjugés légitimes contre l'Encyclopédie* (8 vols., Paris, 1758) was the most ambitious work written against the Encyclopedia.

their clumsiness in defending it, to a few men of undeniable critical talent, Fréron himself, Bergier, Gauchat, Pluquet, to name but
a few. In the following chapters we shall deal chiefly with the men
of ability, and with arguments that had a significant bearing on
the questions in dispute. This process of selection, by which the
trivial and the irrelevant are thrown into the background, may
well give a false view of the real ideas of the time, but it is a
method necessarily employed in most histories of human thinking, and one from which the philosophers have themselves already
profited. It is not partiality but fairness to set aside the more
absurd productions of the orthodox. Little need be said of writings that were only cries of horror, wild assertions and promiscu-
ous calling of names. In these writings expiring philosophers are
appalled by the prospect of hell, valets steal their masters' clothes
to vindicate their equality, servants crawl on all fours to prove
themselves natural, and young bucks disembarrassed of prejudices
teach philosophy to the girls they plan to seduce.[19] Such writings
were no more unreasonable than some compositions of the philosophers. They reflect popular feeling, and are important for that
reason. But from such writings alone we learn hardly more of
the critics of the philosophers than we should learn of the philosophers from *Les bijoux indiscrets* or *La pucelle*.

The best of the orthodox writers had some qualities of mind
commonly esteemed in discussion, if not very useful in violent
dispute. They sometimes had a sense of humor and irony; they
ranted less than their opponents; and they often expressed themselves with the grace, force, and precision of classic French. And,
on the whole, they were less fiercely intolerant. The faith of the
philosophers was new and burning; it was their own, their personal creation and discovery; it sprang from recent and contemporary history; it was offered as a program to cure the specific
ills of the age. The faith of Catholicism had none of this timeli-

[19] Much criticism of the philosophers was put in the form of fiction. For the
drama, see I. O. Wade, *The Philosophe in the French Drama of the Eighteenth
Century* (Princeton, 1926). A similar study might be made of novels, romances
and fictionized memoirs. In this class fall J. N. Moreau, *Nouveaux mémoires pour
servir à l'histoire des Cacouacs* (Amsterdam, 1757); J. Gros de Besplas, *Le rituel
des esprits-forts* (Paris, 1759); J. Vernes and Claparède, *Confidence philosophique* (Londres, 1771); L. Crillon, *Mémoires philosophiques* (Paris, 1777);
G. Gauchat, *Le philosophe du Valais* (Paris, 1772).

ness or this urgency; it was more casually held, as an hereditary possession; it was further removed from immediate issues of the day. The philosophers could hardly approach any question without their whole paraphernalia of argument: nature, humanity, the enlightenment of the age, the prejudice of their opponents, the bearing of the particular question on the general perfectibility and ultimate happiness of man. The orthodox in the age of reason, on the other hand, were in truth often reasonable—perhaps stodgily reasonable. Their dogmas, even when firmly believed in, were not forever obtruding into consciousness. When they approached a particular question they could deal with it concretely, without bringing in the whole apparatus of Christianity. So far as religion was only a special part of their thought, held in one corner of their minds, they were free to discuss other issues in a matter-of-fact way.

And yet—to reverse the tenor of the preceding pages, and return to the point with which we began—behind all this mildness and reasonableness there still stood the claim of the church to absolute domination in its sphere. It could still be said that only he who believed as he should loved God and his neighbor. A man did not have to believe much to be accounted a Catholic; he could range widely and share deeply in the new outlook on the world; but he had to accept the most important of all the dogmas, the infallibility of the church. This primary dogma implied much else: that revelation was genuine, that Jesus Christ was really God, that the tradition of the church was an undeviating ray which shone from Christ upon succeeding ages. On these ideas the vast structure of church authority was built.

If apologists for the church were relatively liberal in countenancing the new system of thought, it was in the hope, so far as it was planned, that the authority of the church might be better preserved. Such was especially the policy of the Jesuits. The Jesuits, to convert the Chinese, let them pay their usual respects to their ancestors and to Confucius. To keep the *philosophes* Catholic, they turned to philosophy themselves.

CHAPTER II

NATURE AND GRACE

THEOLOGY nowadays is often regarded as a defunct mode of thought, which used a method now discredited and dealt with problems which no one any longer thinks vital. Ethics also has declined as a subject of serious inquiry. Moral beliefs and practices are widely supposed to be matters of taste or custom, which reputable thinkers may describe but not presume to judge. Actually, of course, even the most reputable thinkers have their ideas of right and wrong, even when they can find for them no intellectual foundation.

The trouble is that modern men, like men of the Middle Ages, are bound by the limitations of their own method, and that, using a method which consists in ordering or measuring observed facts in time, they have no means of dealing with specifically moral questions and are sometimes tempted to dismiss them as unreal. These questions are, indeed, intangible and invisible. They are not observable facts in any scientific sense. They have to do with such matters as personal responsibility, the meaning of individual identity, the relation between self and circumstance, the source and significance of human acts, and the ends and purposes for which action should take place. With these questions theologians have commonly dealt, and their most heated controversies have often sprung from differences on these very matters.

The eighteenth century in France, fortunately for the historian who undertakes to describe it, was not an age of prolific thinking in theology. The disputes that went on are nevertheless revealing, for they illustrate, fully as much as the lay philosophy of the time, the clash between old and new, between a medieval and a modern outlook on the world. In particular, theologians themselves, independently of influence from empirical science or infidel philosophy, were engaged in acrimonious discussions of the idea and meaning of nature. They carried on these discussions in the intricate and all but unintelligible controversies that raged over Jansenism. And since the idea of nature was undoubtedly a large one in all eighteenth century thought, it is important to know what Jansenism was.[1]

Jansenism—so labelled by its enemies, its adherents holding it to be Catholic truth—owed its name and one of its chief books to Cornelius Jansen, or Jansenius, bishop of Ypres, who died in 1638; but in spirit it had existed at least since the Reformation, and it grounded itself firmly in the writings of St. Paul and St. Augustine. It was an easy application of Christian ideas, congenial especially to the serious-minded, to those who felt most keenly the weight of moral obligation, who sensed their helplessness in determining their own nature, and yet could assure themselves of their own righteousness. During the Reformation, when the serious-minded of Europe protested against the rising tide of worldliness and laxity, this severe kind of Christianity became that of most Protestants, and in particular of the followers of Calvin. The church was obliged to pronounce it erroneous, since it was maintained most vigorously by persons who rejected the Roman communion, but similar ideas appealed to many people who remained Catholic, especially in France and the Netherlands.

Scarcely had the Council of Trent disbanded when Michael Baius, professor of theology at Louvain, produced a book suspiciously Calvinist in tone, from which the Roman authorities drew seventy-nine propositions for condemnation.[2] Baianism, thus named and denounced, existed precariously under the attacks of theologians, until in the middle of the seventeenth century it took on new life and spread rapidly in the far more formidable form

[1] An interpretation similar to that given in this chapter, viz. that Jansenism represented an older religious attitude and that the course of orthodox theology pointed toward the philosophy of the eighteenth century, is presented by B. Groethuysen, *Die Entstehung der bürgerlichen Welt- und Lebensanschauung in Frankreich. I Band: Das Bürgertum und die katholische Weltanschauung* (Halle, 1927). See also T. E. Hulme, "Humanism and the Religious Attitude," in *Speculations: Essays on Humanism and the Philosophy of Art* (New York, 1924), pp. 1-73.
[2] *Dictionnaire de théologie catholique* (Paris, 1903—), art. "Baius." The important parts of the bull *Ex Omnibus Afflictionibus* (1567), condemning Baius, may be most easily found in C. Mirbt, *Quellen zur Geschichte des Papsttums und des römischen Katholizismus* (4th ed., Tübingen, 1924), pp. 347-8.

of Jansenism. The pope condemned Jansen's book in 1653; the Jesuits campaigned actively against his followers; in 1709 Port-Royal, the center of the movement, was destroyed by order of Louis XIV; in 1713 Pope Clement XI issued the bull *Unigenitus,* condemning one hundred and one propositions drawn from Quesnel's treatise on the morality of the gospels, and so in effect pronouncing the whole Jansenist theology to be heretical.

The Jansenists in the eighteenth century were thus in the same position as some of the early Protestants. Seeking to reform the belief of the church, they found themselves excluded from it. Yet they never became Protestants. They neither accepted their exclusion, nor renounced the authority of the church that had condemned them. They contented themselves with appealing to a future pope or general council, and were henceforth known as appellants. Why did these appellants never become Protestants? Why has there been no major secession from the Roman church since the end of the sixteenth century? Jansenism was the greatest heresy to arise in the modern church. In many ways it was the same heresy as that of Luther and Calvin. It was fought actively by the church for two hundred years, and even today is not quite extinct. One might infer that if Protestantism had been possible after the sixteenth century the Jansenists would have been Protestant, and further, that the success of the sixteenth century revolt was caused, not by theological and moral convictions which the Jansenists shared, but chiefly by other influences which the Jansenists could not command.

No powerful group in France had much to gain by embracing the Jansenist theology. The lawyers of the Parlement of Paris did indeed have Jansenist inclinations, but their strength was relatively slight, and the combination thus effected could claim as its greatest triumph only the overthrow of the Jesuits in 1762 and 1763. The king and the French church had already won so many liberties from Rome that they had little to gain by further defiance. There were no longer any powerful feudal barons, as in the sixteenth century, who could resist royal authority more effectively by joining forces with a group of religious dissenters. The upper classes, in France more than elsewhere, had acquired habits of worldly culture, so that in polite society the Jansenists seemed harsh and by the intellectuals were regarded as fanatics.

Unable to maintain itself either in the church or outside it, Jansenism diminished in outward strength through the century. It produced no great leaders, and attracted no other genius like Pascal. In 1715 more than thirty bishops, together with the Sorbonne and other faculties of theology, were reluctant to accept the bull *Unigenitus* as it stood, but the Sorbonne capitulated in 1730, and by 1760 only half a dozen of the bishops of France, or 5 per cent, seem to have had any sympathy with Jansenist theology; one of these, however, was the primate, Malvin de Montazet, archbishop of Lyons.

More and more, as orthodoxy won out, the Jansenists were to be found only among the lower clergy and the obscurer orders of the laity. They became more definitely a party in church politics, opposed to the existing methods of church government. To an extent difficult to determine, since the whole movement was necessarily kept secret, Jansenism in the eighteenth century inclined to what was called *richérisme,* a little-known kind of presbyterian doctrine which demanded greater independence for the lower clergy. This *richérisme,* it is thought, after a long subterranean existence emerged as a decisive force in 1789, when the lower clergy joined the Third Estate in great numbers.[3]

The Jansenists were long hunted out by the authorities, forbidden to express their views in speech or print, made on occasion to sign "notes of confession" certifying that they had been absolved by an orthodox priest, and at times they were denied extreme unction on their deathbeds unless they could show such a note or would declare their acceptance of the bull that condemned them. It is noteworthy that the Jansenists, although they were the people most generally persecuted in France in the eighteenth century, never demanded liberty or toleration on principle, and that the philosophers of the day rarely said a word in their favor. They regarded themselves as Catholics and believed firmly in the church;

[3] On the bull *Unigenitus,* for the text, see Mirbt, *op. cit.,* pp. 395-9; for its reception in France, F. H. Reusch, *Index der verbotenen Bücher* (Bonn, 1883-85), Vol. II, p. 724. On eighteenth century Jansenism see A. Gazier, *Histoire générale du mouvement janséniste* (Paris, 1922); L. Séché, *Les derniers jansénistes, 1710-1870* (Paris, 1891); E. Préclin, *Les jansénistes du dix-huitième siècle et la constitution civile du clergé; le développement du richérisme, sa propagation dans le bas clergé* (Paris, 1929); A. Sicard, *L'ancien clergé de France: Les évêques avant la Révolution* (5th ed., Paris, 1912), pp. 462-81, 593-627.

the enemies of the church preferred to champion Protestants,
Jews, Chinese mandarins or the emperor Julian the Apostate. The
Jansenists were, in fact, of all groups in France the farthest removed from reason as then understood; they were more intolerant
in spirit than the officials who persecuted them; and they were the
only people credulous enough, or serious enough in their faith, to
produce a succession of miracles in the full light of modern Paris.

Made criminal and clandestine, Jansenism came to flourish in
darkness and ignorance. This was an unfortunate consequence for
the church and for France. It meant that stern morals could henceforth be explained as a product of superstition, and strict living
ridiculed as provincial and uncouth. It meant also that a solidly
religious element in the church, if not a highly intellectual one, was
estranged from the hierarchy at a time when united action was
needed against the infidels.

The Jansenists, if they had no great thinkers, had some competent critics in their ranks. About a hundred writings having to
do with the bull *Unigenitus* are named in the Papal Index, and in
addition all criticism of the bull was prohibited by the Inquisition in
1717.[4] Nevertheless the literature grew. The most important enterprise was the periodical, *Les Nouvelles Ecclésiastiques, ou mémoires
pour servir à l'histoire de la constitution Unigenitus.* It appeared
weekly from 1728 to 1798, printed on hidden presses, and was
circulated by devious and ingenious methods through agents unknown to each other who could tell the police nothing if they were
caught. The weekly issue consisted of a single sheet folded to
form four pages, each of which contained two wide columns
printed in very small type. Vast and formless, without literary
grace, a jungle of theology almost impossible to explore, it is as
forbidding as the grim readers to whom it was addressed. The
Jansenists also wrote denunciations of the Jesuits and many treatises on religious questions, duly reviewed and praised by the
Nouvelles Ecclésiastiques, but probably read only by sympathizers
and by the church officials commissioned to examine questionable
literature. The most widely read of all these productions was
probably a great three-volume compilation made for the Parlement
of Paris to use against the Jesuits in 1762, containing quotations

[4] Reusch, *Index*, Vol. II, p. 726. The Inquisition, however, had no jurisdiction
in France.

from Jesuit writers chosen to show the enormity of their doctrine; it was called *Extraits des assertions dangereuses et pernicieuses en tout genre que les soi-disants Jésuites ont soutenues*. This work went through at least five editions, and like Pascal's *Provinciales* of a century before, which in essence it repeated, was of influence in arousing public opinion against the Jesuits, who in the next year were expelled from France.

From all these writings emerges a very significant fact: the Jansenists, except possibly for a few skeptics like Grimm, were the only people in France at the time who seriously questioned the current belief in nature. They were the only group who consistently refused to see in natural law a standard of right and wrong, and which denied the existence of a natural religion. Both infidel philosophers and official spokesmen of the church accepted nature as a standard of right and justice. They differed chiefly on the question whether revelation was necessary in addition. There was another difference also, of which most thinkers were less conscious and which was perhaps not always very clear. For the theologians nature meant first of all a rational and ideal harmony dominating the universe, and for the *philosophes,* first of all, the actual and empirical order of the physical world. More will be said of this distinction in later chapters.[5]

The Jansenists, like most of their contemporaries, scarcely drew this distinction, and in all probability would not have thought it significant. They accused the Jesuits of subverting Christianity by teaching that natural virtues and natural religion were in themselves good and in some cases even adequate. They declared that the Jesuits recognized two legitimate religions and two ways of living a good life, the natural one based on human knowledge alone, and the supernatural one based on revelation. They added that the Jesuits thus made Christianity merely an alternative and better way of life, not the only possible good one, and prepared the way for unbelievers who did away with Christianity altogether, on the plea that natural morality was good enough for them. The Jansenists therefore classed the Jesuits with the *philoso-*

[5] See below, pp. 204-5, 207-8.

phes as enemies of religion, the more dangerous because they were more willingly listened to by the faithful.[6]

Some of this naturalist doctrine which the Jansenists tried to discredit as Jesuit, was in fact the approved teaching of the church. It had developed gradually out of medieval conceptions of natural law, and more particularly, since the Reformation, out of modern disputes over predestination and grace. Catholic theologians had worked it out in answer to Calvinists, Baianists, and Jansenists— in the process, that is, of defining their position against the most persistent of modern heresies. It is often said that the church narrowed its position in thus defining it. In many ways, however, it broadened and loosened it. It is commonly said, too, by historians who profess rationalism but inherit Protestantism, that the Calvinists were the most advanced of the important groups in the Reformation. In fact, however, in its ethical theory the Catholic Church seems to have accommodated itself to the modern world more completely. At any rate, in their controversy with the Jansenists the Jesuits were arguing the position which persons of modern opinions most readily accept.

The Jansenists were the Puritans of the Catholic Church. They were morally aristocratic, exclusive and severe. The better to exalt the greatness of God, they abased the powers of man. They attributed their virtues to God, their vices to themselves. They loaded themselves with responsibility, but denied that they could win any merit. The only goodness they acknowledged was God, and it was a goodness so absolute, so objective and inexorable, that every deviation from it was for them inexcusable and wicked. The goodness of man lay in absolute conformity to this absolute standard, that is, in purity or perfection. Man, however, could not attain such a standard. He was therefore corrupt. All he could do was to keep the standard always in mind, relating every act to God; if he did not, then there was no goodness in him, his pre-

[6] These ideas are to be found throughout the Jansenist writings, but see especially: *Nouvelles ecclésiastiques* (1766), pp. 166-7, (1769), pp. 201-2, (1770), p. 174; B. Rivière, Abbé Pelvert, *Lettres d'un théologien sur la distinction de religion naturelle et de religion révélée* (n.p., 1768), Vol. I, pp. 42 *ff*.; F. de Fitz-James, bishop of Soissons, *Istruzione pastorale contro gli errori de PP. Arduino e Berruyer* (Brescia, 1763), Vol. III, p. 144 (the French original of this important work is difficult to obtain); A. Blonde, *Lettre à M. Bergier . . . sur son ouvrage intitulé Le déisme réfuté par lui-même* (n.p., 1770), p. 113.

tended virtues were vices, and he himself was doomed. He could relate every act to God only if he knew God's revealed will; he could therefore be a good man only if he was a Christian, and indeed, the Jansenists added, only if he was a member of the Catholic Church.

But even a Christian and a Catholic could not choose his own destiny. He could not himself determine what character he should have. He must accept himself as given, see himself as the creature of the Almighty, who, being eternal, and having no past, present, or future, knew eternally what sort of man he would be, and willed eternally whether he should have grace or remain enslaved to his human nature. Those who had grace received it for no merit of their own. They were simply God's chosen people, the elect. The others were damned—for no fault of their own, except that they were human, the progeny of Adam, hopelessly inferior to Absolute Perfection.

Such a belief is best suited to men who feel themselves to be a righteous minority in a world of evildoers, like the Christians in St. Augustine's time, the sterner Protestant sects, and the Jansenists. It could be of little use to a long-established traditional church whose business was to save everybody. It had the effect of making irrelevant the old instruments of salvation, for, if this theory was true, the sacraments could not be relied on to convey saving grace, and all the pains taken by the priesthood in ushering a man through life were reduced to hardly more than an empty gesture. It was imperative for the church to adopt a philosophy in which human effort counted for something, in which men could arrive at their objective by following a definite method outlined in advance. Such a philosophy would be more satisfactory to the generality of mankind. It would be in harmony with the deep-seated modern belief that man by his own efforts may improve the conditions of his life. And it would also preserve the authority of the clergy.

The Jesuits, from the very foundation of their society, took the lead in elaborating this philosophy. To predestination they opposed free will, and against the doctrine of total depravity they argued that men are in large part the authors of their own virtues. They became, in short, the champions of human nature. Hence ensued long discussions of the precise significance and consequences of

Adam's fall, important in laying the theoretical foundations. The Jesuit position was stated in 1588 by a Spanish member of the order, Luis Molina, founder of the Molinism which for two hundred years was a word of sinister meaning for all enemies of the Jesuits. Among theologians Molina is notable for his theory of the "middle knowledge," by which God, besides knowing actual and possible future events, knows also those acts which freewilling agents may, but will not, perform. By this hypothesis Molina sought to harmonize the free will of man with the omniscience of God. This matter, however, need not detain us.[7]

Molina began by considering "the fourfold state of human nature and free will." To the three states generally admitted— the state of innocence in which man had been created, the fallen state into which he had lapsed, and the state of grace in which he existed through Christ—Molina added a fourth, the "state of pure nature," in which it would have been possible for man to be created, though in fact he had been created in the state of innocence. This hypothetical state of pure nature was no invention of Molina's. Medieval philosophers had discussed it, but Molina was the first to make it the basis of a theological system.

In the state of nature Molina conceived of man as being without grace or sin, but in full possession of his powers of knowing, willing and feeling. Reason was thus natural to him, and the power of rational living; the impulses of sense were natural, concupiscence was natural, and natural also were such weaknesses as hunger and thirst, sickness and death.[8]

This was a profoundly significant departure. It implied that these common qualities of man were somehow more fundamental to his nature than the glory in which, according to Christian tradition, he had been created. It meant that certain gifts that Adam had originally possessed—justice and integrity, freedom from unruly passions and exemption from sickness and death and physical evils—were to be regarded as accretions to human nature, privileges conferred by God in a second act of creation, in which

---

[7] On Molinism there is a recent work by F. Stegmüller, *Geschichte des Molinismus* (Münster, 1935), which, however, like N. Abercrombie's *Origins of Jansenism* (Oxford, 1936), will be of use chiefly to theologians.

[8] L. Molina, *Liberi arbitrii cum gratiae donis concordia* (Olyssipone, i.e. Lisbon, 1588), pp. 12-17. There is a modern edition of this work, Paris, 1876, but no translation.

man was raised to a level that was not necessarily his. As such, they might be removed, and man would still remain. He would be impoverished, but not essentially changed. For, said Molina, when man fell from the state of innocence he lost only his supernatural gifts. He now, after the fall, actually possessed those powers that he would have possessed if created in the state of pure nature. Thus Molina's state of pure nature, though ostensibly hypothetical, was really the condition in which he conceived men to exist before receiving the ministrations of the church. Man was now, after the fall and before regaining grace, such a being as divine wisdom might have made. He was still a legitimate, if rebellious, child of God. He could not therefore be radically vicious. Such natural powers as he had, reason and the power of rational self-control, remained to him intact, and were good so far as they went. His impulses and desires were natural, not wicked in themselves, but only bad when not controlled by reason.[9]

To account for the religious process of salvation, Molina drew the distinction between natural and supernatural. Man, he argued, was not merely a natural being, but might also become a supernatural one, regaining the supplementary qualities with which he had been originally endowed. He thus might arrive at what was denied to the natural intelligence but was nevertheless the chief object of human life: salvation, heaven, or the intuitive vision of God. His own effort counted for something in reaching this end; he must cooperate of his own free will; but he could do nothing alone, and special grace was necessary to effect the result. In merely natural matters, however, which were of no significance for salvation, men might perform acts that were morally good of their own free will, without the aid of grace, simply with God's "general concourse," which was given to all. Thus in effect, to the puzzle of free will and divine omnipotence, Molina answered that in natural matters men depend on themselves, but that in supernatural concerns they are dependent also on God.[10]

Molinism was censured by the church in 1607 for inclining too much to Pelagianism, that is, for conceding too much to human

[9] M. J. Scheeben, *Natur und Gnade* (Mainz, 1861), pp. 1-2.
[10] Molina, *op. cit.*, pp. 22 *ff*. For a thorough Jansenist criticism of Molinism see C. Guyon, *Apologie des jésuites convaincue d'attentats contre les lois divines et humaines* (n.p., 1763).

independence.[11] Nevertheless it represented the direction in which
Catholic theology had been moving since the Council of Trent.
It was firmly defended by the Jesuits, whose ethical teaching
cannot be understood without it. Contrary propositions were re-
peatedly condemned at Rome. Before Molina began to write,
Baius had been found in error for maintaining that "the integrity
of the first creation was the natural condition of human nature,
not a gratuitous exaltation of it." He was also condemned for the
opinion, "Free will, without the aid of God's grace, produces
nothing but sin." The Quietist Molinos, a century later, met the
same fate for teaching that "natural activity is the enemy of grace,
and is a hindrance to true perfection and to the action of God, because God wishes to act in us, but without us." The second of the
hundred and one propositions condemned in *Unigenitus* was this
statement: "The grace of Jesus Christ, efficacious principle of good
of whatever kind, is necessary to every good work; without it no
good work either is or can be performed."[12] The church, in short,
did not officially believe that human nature, left to itself, was
powerless for good.

To show how far the church had committed itself to Molinism
we may well fortify ourselves with the testimony of an expert,
the wholly orthodox Scheeben, who was a papal theologian at the
Vatican Council of 1870. The church, he says, to oppose the heresy
of Jansenism, maintained "that by original sin man had lost only
his capacity for works bearing on his supernatural destination;
that there was, however, another field of activity, namely the natural, for which the necessary faculties and powers remained in
nature, potentially at least, if not in their full development. This
distinction between natural and supernatural fields of activity,
between a natural and a supernatural ethical order . . . was the
double-edged sword by which the church opposed both errors

[11] L. Pastor, *History of the Popes* (Eng. trans., London, 1891—), Vol. XXV,
pp. 229-52. The bull which condemned Molinism in 1607 was held by the
Inquisition in 1654 to be of no binding force. This concession to the Jesuit influence followed immediately on the condemnation of Jansen in 1653. See *ibid.*,
p. 249, n. 1, and Reusch, *Index*, Vol. II, pp. 306-7.

[12] Mirbt, *op. cit.*, pp. 347, 395.

[Pelagianism and Jansenism], and not only struck them down but destroyed even their roots."[13]

The layman may well wonder whether the "double-edged sword" was not extremely dangerous to Catholicism itself. The distinction of natural and supernatural had always existed in Catholic thought, but in the great ages of religion matters of primary concern to mankind were not regarded as natural. The natural was by definition that which was not specifically Christian and not known exclusively through the Christian revelation. In the Middle Ages men felt that they understood the supernatural better. By the seventeenth century the tendency was the reverse. By nature, men were coming to mean that which they understood best, and as they came to understand more and more things, they enlarged the boundaries of the natural. Nature was the intelligible and rational order of things, and the supernatural was correspondingly reduced to the unintelligible and the arbitrary. God was still thought of as the mind or force behind both, but he was most closely associated with the supernatural, and so was becoming mysterious and ineffable.

Theologians who conceded that most matters in human life were natural only yielded to this modern tendency, and pointed the way to the infidel philosophers of the Age of Reason. The more they attributed to nature the less they attributed immediately to God, the less to special theological information, and the less to the operations of the clergy. Making nature itself a standard of good they tended to separate morals from religion; they weakened the meaning of the Christian revelation, representing it as in part a restatement of natural law, different only in being more precise and more binding, and in part as a supplement to natural law, providing in addition certain positive rules on the procedure of worship.

The Jansenists were the one group who in the eighteenth century most resolutely opposed this kind of modernism. They were intelligent enough to perceive the logical coherence of their oppo-

[13] Scheeben, *op. cit.,* p. 4. Scheeben was an expert on the theory of the state of pure nature, and edited a treatise on the subject by the eighteenth century theologian Cassini. Scheeben receives extraordinary commendation from H. Hurter (S. J.), *Nomenclator literarius recentioris theologiae catholicae* (3rd ed., Oeniponte, i.e. Innsbruck, 1903-13), Vol. V, Part 2, pp. 1511-14.

nents' system, and attacked with great vehemence the whole conception of the state of pure nature. They denied that man was a natural being. The question at stake between them and the Jesuits, whom they regarded as their particular foes, was the great question that agitated the whole epoch. What is the nature of man? Is he the image of God? Which of his various qualities make him specifically human? Which are so essential that without them he would not be man?

All Christians admitted that, in point of fact, man had been made in God's image. The question, however, was one of metaphysical necessity: was it in keeping with divine wisdom or human dignity that man should have been made in any other way? On this point the Jansenists took the more exalted view of human nature, and the Jesuits the more modest one. The Jansenists regarded man as a noble being whose only proper function was to unite himself with God. To them it was unthinkable that this sublimest of God's creatures, in "the integrity of his nature," should be rocked by passion, benighted by ignorance, tormented by pain, and mocked by the prospect of death. The Jesuits could well enough imagine these afflictions as natural and normal, and regard Adam's original exemption from them, as well as his original ability to unite himself with God, as special privileges supernaturally conferred.

It was not inconsistent that the Jansenists, seeing in man a mass of corruption, should exalt human nature to the skies, and that the Jesuits, thinking men capable of some good, should regard humanity as essentially poor. Puritans and idealists are generally the severest judges, since they form the most flattering picture of what men should be; worldlings and realists are more lenient, keeping in mind the limitations of the species. The Jansenists saw a vast difference between man as he was and as he ought to be, or, in Christian terms, between man after the fall and man before it. The Jesuits, placing the ideal less high, had managed, by their doctrine of the state of pure nature, to show that man before the fall had not been very different, in his specifically human qualities, from the poor creature that they had to deal with every day. They minimized the consequences of sin, which the Jansenists emphasized in all their enormity.

The two parties fully understood and clearly stated each other's positions. From the theory of the state of pure nature, said the Jansenist Blonde, "the Jesuits and their partisans conclude that original sin produced no great wound in our nature. The only change was to strip us of free and supernatural gifts with which God enriched Adam at the moment of creation. These free and supernatural gifts were a garment of glory in which Adam had been clothed. The devil, jealous of this prerogative, set a trap and caused Adam to fall and lose this honor. Adam found himself stripped of his garment; and the difference between the state in which he would have been before receiving these supernatural gifts and the state in which he was after being deprived of them, is simply the difference between a man stripped and a man naked: *sicut spoliatus differt a nudo.*" Jesuits and Molinists acknowledged this belief, and branded as heresy the contrary view that sin had vitiated man's nature. "According to this system," said the Abbé Galien of Jansenism, "it follows that when man lost charity through sin, the loss was a wound, a disease, a corruption of his nature, not simply a stripping away [*dépouillement*] of a precious robe in which he had been clothed. The robe, however, is not of the integrity of his nature, but is something added to it."[14]

In short, the Jansenists maintained that, because of sin, man's actual nature was radically different from human nature "in its integrity." Man had suffered the "great change" that Pascal speaks of. His present nature impelled him irresistibly to seek pleasure in worldly objects; it was all sin and concupiscence. His

[14] Blonde, *op. cit.*, p. 70; J. Galien, *Lettres théologiques touchant l'état de pure nature, la distinction du naturel et du surnaturel, et les autres matières qui en sont la conséquence* (Avignon, 1745), p. 23. The Latin words are from Jansen's *Augustinus*. For further dispute see note 6 above; Guyon, *op. cit.*; F. Fourquevaux, *Catéchisme historique sur les contestations qui divisent maintenant l'Eglise* (5 vols., Paris, 1750-68); J. Fumel, bishop of Lodève, *Instruction pastorale sur les sources de l'incrédulité* (Paris, 1765), pp. 203, 221, 332, 375; *Nouvelles ecclésiastiques* (1766), pp. 157-8, 166-7. The bishop of Lodève accuses the Jansenists of aiding the infidels by denying free will, weakening the force of the sacraments, and representing Christian morality in so austere a light as to make it "odious and intolerable." The Jansenists reply that the bishop believes, like the infidels, that man is master of his own fate and that God is the spectator of events, not their cause. Both arguments were in frequent use by their respective sides. "Toute doctrine selon laquelle *le sort de l'homme de dépend point de lui-même*, selon laquelle *l'homme n'est ni le maître ni l'arbitre de son sort*, voilà l'hérésie que poursuit l'écrivain de M. de Lodève." *Nouvelles ecclésiastiques* (1766), p. 158.

true nature, now lost, was to be the image of God. His duty was to realize his true nature. But such was his present corruption that he could realize his true nature, and attain the sole end for which he existed, only by an impulse from outside himself independent of his own ego.

This seemingly external impulse the Jansenist called grace. Today we should probably say that it existed in himself. According to our way of understanding personality, in which the individual is given a kind of private property in his own being, the impulses that theologians called grace and concupiscence would be regarded as obscure energies somehow belonging to the self, yet of which the conscious self has no knowledge and no control, and of which conscious life, with its wishes, tastes, and inclinations, is simply an expression. The Jansenists, being the serious minded and the morally earnest, took full responsibility for the part of themselves whose effects they disapproved. They acknowledged it as their own, and under the name of concupiscence made it the substance of human nature in its actual state. The part of themselves that prompted them to disapprove they detached from their own ego, and, calling it grace, attributed it to God. They thus preserved the belief in God as the unique source of good. They held that every person was dominated by one or the other of these two drives. He was the child either of sin or of grace. They judged men as good or bad according as one or the other ruled him, according to the kind of nature that dictated his particular and conscious acts.

In Jesuit ethics, as we shall presently see, only conscious life had any moral significance, and moral judgment tended to fall more on particular acts than on total personality. The Jesuits would hold a man responsible only for what he did deliberately in full knowledge. They would not blame him for what he could not help. They could not regard as evil a force of which he might be unaware and which in any case he could not himself control. Hence they rejected the Jansenist conception of original sin, and denied that man was corrupt in the depths of his being. At the same time, they saw nothing creditable in good acts that a man was forced to perform. Hence they taught, in opposition to the Jansenists, that man must cooperate of his own will with the action of divine grace. They made man, as well as God, a source of good. The moral problem for them was not to annihilate and replace actual nature, but to add to and develop it. Similarly the religious problem was not to transform one kind of nature into another by miraculous infusions from without, but, while retaining and perfecting actual nature, to acquire in addition the supernatural graces that were highly honorable but not absolutely essential to human personality.

The softening of the dogma of sin was a fact of the utmost importance, for the idea of sin, the belief that man has both insulted God and betrayed his own nature, was fundamental to historic Christianity. The idea of sin, when intensely believed in, carried a strong sense of guilt. It implied that the troubles and difficulties of life arose from an inborn human fault, and that, being of supernatural origin, they could be removed only by supernatural means. Such was the Jansenist contention. To mitigate the idea of sin meant to change the theory of human trouble, implying that trouble was not a result of hereditary fault and that it might be remedied by natural effort. The Jesuits took this position. A good example is offered by the Jesuit Collet, in his *Tractatus de gratia,* which formed part of a textbook written for students of theology. Collet first laid down the theory of the state of pure nature. St. Augustine, he then argued, had gone astray in attributing the evils of life entirely to Adam's sin and fall. For, he said, citing Augustine himself, our afflictions are "natural and primordial." They antedate the fall; they arose positively from Adam's natural constitution, not negatively through the loss of supernatural gifts. Far from being a punishment for guilt, these afflictions "may be an incentive to advancement and a beginning of perfection." In these words Collet stated a principle that underlies modern thinking on a variety of topics, among them the idea of progress; for he saw in trouble not a visitation for guilt but a cause and stimulus to natural achievement.[15]

When compared to the Jansenists, the Jesuits were humanists. Their work in moral theology was to make a place for man's powers in a world which the Jansenists would reserve exclusively for God's.

[15] P. Collet, *Institutiones theologicae quas e Tournelyanis praelectionibus ad usum seminariorum contraxit Petrus Collet* (Paris, 1756), Vol. II, pp. 178-85. The Tournély to whose lectures this title refers was professor of theology at the Sorbonne in the early part of the century.

Even their spirituality, says Henri Bremond, was anthropocentric.[16]
They set themselves up as champions of human nature—against the
claims of God himself, so the Jansenists thought—but always with
the idea that man should be independent, his human faculties respected, and his achievements credited to himself. M. P-M. Masson,
in his admirable study of the religion of Rousseau, has noted how
both in Catholic France and at Calvinist Geneva many clergymen
anticipated Rousseau in favoring the idea of the natural goodness
of man.[17] M. Masson has expressed himself, if anything, too mildly.
The trend of Catholic theology, from the Council of Trent through
the bull *Unigenitus* and on into the eighteenth century, was to
enlarge the boundaries of the human, to extend the world of nature
and circumscribe the world of grace, to regard man in his mundane
and fallen state, not as "good" in Rousseau's sense, but as a legitimate and respectable inhabitant of the universe.

This development had no doubt long been implicit in the doctrine
of the church. It would be a mistake to attribute the high valuation
of man entirely to the humanism of the Renaissance, or the emphasis on nature entirely to scientific discovery. Both had arisen, in
part, from a belief in a natural law which could be known to men
per lumen naturale; and this belief, coming from the Greeks, had
existed in Catholic thought since the time of Thomas Aquinas.
Natural law, in this sense, was different from the laws of nature
later formulated by science. It was a moral and logical conception. It
signified a right reason which existed both in the human mind and
in the eternal structure of things. It was the ultimate rightness and
rationality which men could glimpse even without revelation, and
which, running through the world of appearances, held together
this world, so seemingly diverse, in one system of understandable
relationships. It was the harmony of the universe to which men, as
rational beings, should conform.

According to the most orthodox theologians this natural law was
an aspect of the law of God. It existed because God existed, and
because God was essentially rational and just. This belief was

[16] H. Bremond, *Histoire littéraire du sentiment religieux en France* (Paris,
1921-36), Vol. III, pp. 31, 113-17, 134-8; *Revue d'ascétisme et de mystique*
(1922), pp. 420 ff.
[17] P. Masson, *La religion de Jean-Jacques Rousseau* (Paris, 1916), Vol. I,
pp. 273 ff., Vol. III, pp. 165 ff. On the humanism of the Jesuits see also A.
Schimberg, *L'éducation morale dans les collèges jésuites* (Paris, 1913).

frequently stated by the theologians of the eighteenth century. But by the eighteenth century, in the minds of many, a subtle shift of attention had taken place. Some men, in believing that the world was rational, seemed to be moved not so much by faith in a God who was the essence of reason as by faith in reason itself, or by admiration for the natural faculties of human beings. Theologians who took this course were on the verge of being *philosophes*. Sometimes, indeed, since their intellectual training was more rigorous than that of the *philosophes* and their regard for logical consequence more entire, they laid down their principles with a candor at which even deists might be embarrassed.

The Jesuit Abbé Camier, in his textbook of philosophy for use at Toul, could reason God out of existence and yet keep his faith in moral distinctions and in moral obligation—a feat which only the most radical *philosophes* were able to perform. "Natural law," said Camier, "has binding force independently of the existence of God. . . . Reason dictates, independently of the existence of God, that good must be done and evil avoided, and man is bound, independently of the existence of God, to give obedience to the dictate of reason. Therefore, independently of the existence of God, man is bound to do good and avoid evil, or, what is the same thing, moral principles impose obligation independently of the existence of God."[18]

This was a more sweeping statement of absolute rationalism than a deist could allow, so long as he remained a deist. Professional theologians, to whom God is likely to be an intellectual abstraction, are perhaps less troubled than ordinary believers, or unbelievers, by emotional complications.

The Abbé Hooke, an Irish-born professor of theology at the Sorbonne, while implying the same dissociation of God from reason and right, was less the rationalist and more the empiricist, relying on the testimony of human faculties. "There is," he affirmed, "a certain sense of right and wrong placed by nature in the minds of men. . . . We know by conscience that this moral sense is in us, and it would be vain to try to demonstrate it by argument; it is analogous to the intuitive perception of truth which is the basis of

[18] Camier, *Institutiones philosophicae ad usum seminarii Tullensis* (Neocastri, i.e. Neuchâtel, 1769), Vol. III, p. 422. This work was reprinted in 1770, 1777 and 1781.

all knowledge, or to the sense of taste by which we distinguish foods; and just as we should have no notion of truth or falsehood if this intuitive perception of truth were taken away, nor any notion of flavors without this sense of taste, so, if this sense of right and wrong, of honorable and shameful, were removed, these words would have no force or meaning. This sense is so natural, so constant and uniform, that it can be stifled by no prejudices and extinguished by no passions; its sacred judgment can be corrupted by no bribes; it lives in the most wicked men, to whom virtue is so pleasing that they involuntarily admire their betters."[19]

This was exactly the doctrine of many *philosophes*. We can imagine Diderot writing these very words. Yet the principle was not unorthodox. It was hardly in keeping with a strict view of original sin, but neither was Catholic orthodoxy. If Hooke's statement inclines toward the new philosophy, it is because he compares the perception of right to a sensation, thus revealing the influence of the school of Locke, and because he puts great trust in the power of conscience, thus approaching the school of Rousseau.

From these principles of Camier and Hooke, which were not thought to be extreme (except by the Jansenists), it must follow that moral truth and revealed religion had no necessary connection. To separate the two was the great aim of the *philosophes,* who in this matter used arguments no different from those of the theologians. The difference was in intention. The *philosophes* felt that by detaching the moral world from the Christian revelation they were proving the church to be unnecessary. The theologians meant to strengthen the church; they intended, by arguing that reason imposed moral duties and that a natural faculty informed men of the wishes of God, to keep within the church, and coming to the confessional, the ever more numerous people who were losing their awe for the priesthood.

A significant doctrine, that of "philosophic sin," illustrates the distinction drawn between morality and religion, and shows also

[19] L. Hooke, *Religionis naturalis et moralis philosophiae principia, methodo scholastica digesta* (Paris, 1752-54), Vol. I, pp. 482-3. The second volume of this work was called *Religionis revelatae principia,* the third *Religionis naturalis et revelatae principia*; and the three volumes do not differ greatly from the author's *Religionis naturalis et revelatae principia* published in three volumes in 1754, and reprinted in 1774. See also Camier, *op. cit.,* Vol. III, pp. 404-7, for arguments to show the reality of good and evil much like those of the *philosophes.*

how the theologians, having set up natural or rational standards for moral life, sought to keep this moral life within the purview of the church by classifying delinquencies from it as a species of sin. The theory of philosophic sin, formulated in the seventeenth century and condemned by Rome in 1690, was especially favored by the Jesuits, and formed one of the principal charges brought against them by the Jansenists in 1762. Its meaning was simply this: If a man commits an act which he does not know to be prohibited by God, but which he does know to be contrary to right reason, he is guilty of no theological sin, but of a philosophical one, since he violates the code by which philosophers profess to govern themselves. The doctrine might as well have gone under the name of "philosophic virtue," since its adherents believed that acts in harmony with right reason had a moral value even when the agent knew nothing of God. What they believed, in short, was that right reason was something different from God. It was for this belief that they were condemned in 1690, though Camier, who certainly entertained the same belief seventy years later, seems not to have been disturbed.

The Jesuits formally abjured belief in philosophic sin, and always gave the correct explanation, namely that since right reason was itself the word of God no one who understood right reason was wholly ignorant of divine law. Nevertheless the idea kept cropping up through the eighteenth century. When nature was distinguished from God, and men assumed to know right and wrong by a natural faculty in themselves, "philosophic" virtues and vices were inescapable. The great Jesuit text on moral theology, Busenbaum revised by La Croix, in its edition of 1733, states the doctrine and rejects it as condemned by the pope. It proceeds immediately to reinstate it. "Although all knowledge of God were absent, yet a man could act morally for good or for bad, if only he chose of his free will to act in keeping with, or in contradiction to, the first principles of right reason placed in us by nature." The question is simply one of fact, whether men do exist wholly without knowledge of God. The significant point is that, while the authors can conceive that men may have no knowledge of God, they give no indication of doubting that all men possess a knowledge of right reason given by nature. Their final statement is very cautious: if it be possible for men to have no knowledge of God, then an act done consciously in violence to right reason "would have no formal theological badness," but "it would have some moral badness . . . because it is contrary to the right reason by which philosophers govern themselves. Whether this badness should be called sin can be only a question of terms."[20]

This cool question, "whether badness should be called sin," was itself, in the very asking, a separation of morals from religion, implying two standards of conduct. It was a question unthinkable to the Jansenists, to whom sound morals and Christianity were identical. "All the works of infidels are sins, and all the virtues of philosophers are vices."[21] This fierce proposition, condemned as a Baianist heresy before the Jansenists were heard of, was the uncompromising belief of the Jansenists, as also of Calvin, Augustine, and St. Paul. To the Jansenists there could be no philosophic sin, because all sin was theological; all good and bad were theological, because all good was the will of God. To pretend that all men possessed a natural faculty for knowing divine law was for the Jansenists a monstrous perversion of Christian truth, inspired by pride and presumption, which in effect identified man with God himself.

The Jansenist bishop of the tiny southern diocese of Alais, Buisson de Beauteville, "of revolting memory" according to a modern Jesuit writer, took issue with the archbishop of Aix on these questions. With some support from Fitz-James, bishop of Soissons, he waged a war of pamphlets, vainly argued before the Assembly of the Clergy, and composed, but never published, an appeal against the bull *Unigenitus*. Beauteville, or his theological secretary Gourlin, one of the most active Jansenists of the day, pointed to Augustine and a long line of theologians to show that

[20] H. Busenbaum and C. La Croix, *Theologia moralis antehac ex probatis auctoribus concinnata* (Coloniae Agrippinae, i.e. Cologne, 1733), Vol. V, pp. 44-6. A more positive rejection of the doctrine is made by the Jesuit P. Antoine, who was regarded as inclining to "rigorism," *Theologia moralis universa* (ed. Rome, 1783), Vol. I, p. 98: "Hoc repugnat, quia qui peccat contra rectam rationem, simul et indivisibiliter peccat contra legem Dei. . . ." For examples, chosen by the Jansenists, of the way in which the doctrine of philosophic sin was used to extenuate serious offenses, see *Extraits des assertions dangereuses et pernicieuses en tout genre que les soi-disants jésuites ont soutenues* (5th ed., Paris, 1763), Vol. I, pp. 290 *ff*. On the subject in general see the *Dictionnaire de théologie catholique*, Vol. XII, pp. 255-72, art., "Péché philosophique."
[21] Mirbt, *op. cit.*, p. 347.

all outwardly good acts not done in the Christian faith were vitiated by the supreme sin of pride—by "the vain satisfaction that a man takes in the natural beauty of an act, so that when he does not glorify the Lord for it he glorifies himself." The sin of the rebellious angel Lucifer, observes the bishop, expounding Augustine further, "consisted in his regarding himself with satisfaction, in contemplating his own excellence, and not referring to God the love and admiration that this excellence aroused. This defect, this failure to refer to him who is the source and principle of all good, vitiated, corrupted a thing good in itself, namely the love of his own being and of the gifts he had received from God."[22] To this point the Jansenists held ever fast, that all good things have their goodness only in God.

Some of the Jesuits, on the other hand, maintained that men need not worry too much about God. Jesus, indeed, had said, "Thou shalt love the Lord thy God with all thy heart." But there were ways of modifying even so explicit a command. A certain Professor Cabrespine of the College of Rhodez gave it out as his opinion, by refusing to sign a statement denying it, that "a man fulfils this precept in contenting himself with not hating God."[23] The Jansenists, who naturally heard of the affair, reported it forty years later in their *Extraits des assertions dangereuses.* They also quoted as a Jesuit proposition, from a seventeenth century student's thesis at Louvain : "Those who teach that men must love God with a predominant and constant love, and that all acts must be referred to him, have seemed to the faithful to be unjustly severe, and to burden the souls of men with a yoke more likely to lead to ruin and insanity than to salvation." This was no isolated opinion or meaningless thesis set up merely for disputation. In 1763, at the moment of crisis, when the Jesuits were striving to show the purity and

[22] Buisson de Beauteville, *Lettres en réponse à celles de Msgr. l'Archevêque d'Aix* (Toulouse, 1764), pp. 26-7. The modern Jesuit referred to is A. Jean, *Les évêques et les archevêques de France depuis 1682 jusqu'à 1801* (Paris, 1891), p. 257. Beauteville objected to the distinction made by Brancas, archbishop of Aix, between morally good acts and acts useful for salvation; the former, according to the archbishop, were useless for salvation except when "elevated to the supernatural plane by the grace of Jesus Christ and the views which faith unfolds." See J. Brancas, archbishop of Aix, *Lettre à l'Evêque d'Alais* (Aix, 1764).

[23] *Extraits des assertions dangereuses,* Vol. II, p. 100. No reply in the Jesuit *Réponse au livre intitulé Extraits des assertions . . .* (n.p., 1763-65).

orthodoxy of their teaching, they replied to the Jansenist *Extraits* vigorously defending the proposition, declaring it to be the true doctrine of the universal church, which, they said, had put its members under no such extravagant obligation as to require "predominant and constant love of God."[24]

The Jesuits were charged also with the strange idea that a Christian need not always be Christian in his conduct. Le Moyne, professor at Auxerre, was censured in 1725 by the bishop for this opinion : "A Christian, acting deliberately, may act simply as a man, and lay aside the character of a Christian in those actions that are not specifically Christian." The Jansenists insisted that by this outrageous principle the Jesuits allowed all crimes to be committed with impunity.[25]

Such ideas were indeed radical enough, but they were not necessarily as immoral as the Jansenists imagined, or as many modern critics may too hastily suppose. They were not immoral, so long as morality was separate from religion. They were not immoral, if nature itself was good, and if men had a natural faculty for distinguishing good and evil without reference to God. If the Jesuits had believed, like the Jansenists, that man's only good lay in identifying himself with God, then it would have been highly improper for them to teach that he need not always keep God in mind. If they had believed, like the Jansenists, that man, without grace, was a being capable only of evil, then it would have been criminal for them to announce that he might at times "lay aside the character of a Christian." If they had believed, with the intensity of the Jansenists, that every instant of existence was a portion of eternity, and that every act a man performed and every thought he entertained were significant of his deepest character and of value to his immortal soul, then they would not have found so much that was "theologically indifferent," or implied that certain acts were not "specifically Christian." Actually, they reserved such ideas as these for mystics and the genuinely religious. For the world at large they preached a mundane morality not essentially different from that of the infidels of the day, except that they left room for a supernatural

[24] *Extraits,* Vol. II, p. 80; *Réponse,* Vol. II, pp. 46-7.

[25] *Extraits,* Vol. II, p. 100; no reply in *Réponse.* See also the arguments of two Jesuit professors that men are not obliged to act always *ex motivo honestatis moralis* in the *Extraits,* Vol. I, pp. 356-8, and Vol. II, p. 98.

addition to it. This supernatural addition, by which anyone might
be saved, consisted for the most part in the ceremonial and sacra-
mental practices superintended by the clergy.

To vindicate their orthodoxy, the Jesuits maintained that, in
teaching what looked to their opponents like philosophic sin and
related errors, they were in reality teaching only the authorized
doctrine of the church on *ignorantia invincibilis* and *conscientia
erronea*—the doctrine that no act is reprehensible if done by a man
"invincibly" ignorant of the law on the subject, or honestly mistaken in his interpretation of it. Around these two Latin terms the
controversy raged, for, whether or not orthodox, the explanation
seemed to the Jansenists no more plausible than philosophic sin
itself.

In the eyes of the Jesuits, no one was free to obey the divine law
who did not know it, and no violation of this law which a man
committed unconsciously could be held against him. "To take a
position as far removed from Calvin as possible," wrote the Italian
Jesuit Casnedi, "it is to be affirmed that there can be no sin without
awareness of evil, or with intention of good." Jesuits everywhere
held to this principle. For example, at the College of Bourges in
1760 a student presenting a thesis on the old question of invincible
ignorance argued that no guilt attached to a person who unknow-
ingly transgressed either a divine or a natural law.[26]

Much that followed from such teaching was distasteful to the
Jansenists. It followed that well-meaning infidels who had never
heard of Christianity were not guilty of sin, and did not suffer the
full pains of hell.[27] It might even follow that Protestants were not
altogether damned. The Abbé Bergier, the most prominent champion of Catholicism in the latter half of the century, inclined to
this opinion, and made use of it in arguing against Rousseau, incidentally provoking the wrath of the Jansenists by his concessions.[28]

It might even follow from the great importance set upon conscience that honest doubters should not be prematurely blamed.
"Nor is the opinion condemned," say Busenbaum and La Croix, "of
those who say that if the reasons for our faith ceased to be probable

[26] *Extraits,* Vol. I, pp. 320, 400; Busenbaum and La Croix, *op. cit.,* Vol. I,
p. 302.
[27] Busenbaum and La Croix, *op. cit.,* Vol. I, secs. 71, 75.
[28] *Nouvelles ecclésiastiques* (1770), pp. 198-200, where Bergier is quoted.

to a man, and if the reasons for the opposite error became morally certain, and if this change were invincible, such a man might for a time suspend his assent to the faith, until he should again comprehend its truth."[29] How far the priests of the time used this amazing principle to combat the crisis of the Age of Reason, although a question of the greatest importance, is one to which not even an approximate answer will ever be possible. It is likely that they used it unwillingly, and as rarely as they could.

It followed also that, according as a man had an easy or a difficult conscience, he might practise a slack morality or a strict one. The Jesuits, like all theorists who emphasize conscience and intention rather than fulfilment of objective standards, tended on the whole to make conscience less exacting. Modern psychologists will approve of much of their teaching—their views, for instance, on *conscientia scrupulosa*. By this term they meant an anxious conscience, one that searches itself interminably for faults and magnifies trifles into serious offenses. For Jansenists and Puritans an anxious conscience might be a sign of holiness, but the Jesuits regarded it as a spiritual disease, which the confessor should do everything in his power to cure.

For example, if a penitent believed it a sin not to raise his hat in passing a priest on the street, he was to be strongly urged to pass with his hat on his head. He was to be made to forget such trivial fears. He was especially to remember that "neither God nor the church requires what involves too much difficulty to perform, that he may do what he sees upright men do without fear of sinning, and that he is excusable in omitting what the law prescribes, if in good faith and without contempt of it he thinks the law does not exist, and would be willing to observe it if he knew that it did exist."[30]

Most cases were not so simple, nor were all methods of quieting consciences so unobjectionable. For more difficult situations there was the system known as probabilism. Since the time of Pascal, probabilism has received more attention from critics of the Jesuits than it deserves, for it was at best only a means to an end. It was essentially a method for setting doubtful consciences at rest. It was

[29] Busenbaum and La Croix, *op. cit.*, Vol. I, p. 130, n. 5. See also *Extraits,* Vol. II, p. 122, and *Réponse,* Vol. I, p. 226.

[30] Busenbaum and La Croix, *op. cit.*, Vol. IX, p. 848; see also Vol. I, pp. 287-307.

based on the maxim, *lex dubia non obligat,* "a doubtful law imposes no obligation." The probabilists thought that the divine law might be doubtful; that was how they differed from Jansenists and all persons of intense moral conviction.

According to probabilism, a confessor, considering a given problem of conduct, might declare it equally likely that the law did and did not apply. If he advised the person concerned to regard the law as inapplicable, he was a probabilist. If he took the "safer opinion," *opinio tutior,* recommending that the law be considered binding, he was a tutiorist. There were further complications, according as probabilities varied from equality; and in the hands of some practitioners the theory became a means of excusing any crime; but in 1679 Innocent XI condemned such extensions, notably the idea that non-observance of the law might be risked even when the greater probability showed it to be binding. It does not appear, however, that the system was widely abused in eighteenth century France.

But the Jesuits remained, almost to a man, the avowed enemies of the tutiorists. By this grotesque term they classified the Jansenists, who, being severe moralists, maintained that men were bound to observe the divine law when there was any shadow of probability that it applied—and they added that it did apply in all the affairs of life. The Jesuits held, with some justice, that tutiorism was literal-minded insistence on legal precepts, that it was impracticable in real life, taking no account of the perplexities which men of the world could not escape, and that, stifling conscience under a dead burden of obedience, it deprived human life of true moral value.[31]

Probabilism could exist only along with the more fundamental doctrines of invincible ignorance and mistaken conscience. Only with these doctrines to excuse him, could a man take the risk of not observing the law. Granted these doctrines, if he acted on a mere probability that the law did not apply, and if he was in fact mistaken and did objectively violate it, he was guilty of no offense, for

[31] Among the propositions condemned in 1679 were: "2. Probabiliter existimo iudicem posse iudicare iuxta opinionem etiam minus probabilem. 3. Generatim dum probabilitate, sive intrinseca sive extrinseca, quantumvis tenui, modo a probabilitatis finibus non exeatur, confisi aliquid agimus, semper prudenter agimus. 4. Ab infidelitate excusabitur infidelis non credens, ductus opinione minus probabili." Mirbt, *op. cit.*, p. 387. For a good statement of the Jesuit position on probabilism and tutiorism see the *Réponse au livre intitulé Extraits des assertions,* Vol. II, pp. 99-120.

"moral good depends on the judgment of the agent." Thus acting, he did not intend to fulfil the law, but neither did he intend to break it; his act was therefore good, since, as the archbishop of Aix said, "it was not directed by an intention wholly bad." The whole system depended also on the Molinist conception of human nature, in which ignorance and error were regarded not as punishment for sin, but as essential and original in the human mind. And it implied the principle, ultimately disintegrating to moral responsibility, that no obligations exist where none are felt.

The Jansenists waved aside all such apparatus of extenuation. To them, ignorance of good was itself bad, was in fact the original sin that enslaved man to the world and the devil. The *Nouvelles Ecclésiastiques,* year after year, reechoed with denunciations and cries of horror. The editors particularly disliked the methods used by the Jesuits in their numerous schools, which they regarded as centers for the systematic debauchery of youth. To choose one example from many, they complained that the Jesuit schoolmasters at Rouen were going from bad to worse by adding dancing to dramatics. "The Jesuits this year, at their great Tragedy, have had the students *dance* a (so-called) *Moral Ballet,* in which they mean to show how PLEASURE, when *wise and regulated* [in their manner] becomes an EXCELLENT teacher for the young."[32]

So we arrive at the charge often brought against the Jesuits that they excused and encouraged loose living. The Jesuits, being conspicuously successful, made many enemies, usually for other reasons than the complexion of their moral teaching, but these enemies generally selected this moral teaching for special attack, as the means by which they could best scandalize the world.[33] Hence

[32] *Nouvelles ecclésiastiques* (1750), p. 181. See also the *Journal de Trévoux* (1750), p. 2100, where the Jesuit editors, while not disapproving of dancing, condemn the statement of the Jesuits of Rouen that "religion is not as much opposed to pleasure as it appears to be."

[33] The *Extraits des assertions dangereuses* is the best example for the eighteenth century. See also, besides Jansenist writings already noted, the *Instruction pastorale portant condamnation de la doctrine contenue dans les Extraits des assertions,* written by Roussel de la Tour, compiler of the *Extraits,* and issued officially in 1763 by Jacques de Grasse, bishop of Angers; and a compilation called *Institutio pastoralis de DD. Episcoporum Suessionensis, Andegevensis ac Alesiani epistolis pastoralibus . . . contra patres Societatis Jesu* (1766). These three bishops, those of Soissons, Angers and Alais, with Caylus of Auxerre and Malvin de Montazet, archbishop of Lyons, were the chief patrons of Jansenism

unfriendly critics of the Jesuits are very little to be trusted. The Jansenists, though the most sincere of all, often exaggerated and sometimes falsified the purport of the quotations that they liberally made from their enemies' books.

For example, the *Nouvelles Ecclésiastiques* in 1773 quoted with indignation from the contemporary Jesuit Camier, *indulgere sensuum voluptati et licet et expedit, natura ad hoc invitante,* which may be understood to mean, "it is both lawful and expedient to indulge in the pleasures of sense, because nature invites us to."[34] The reader is supposed to take this as a categorical endorsement of lechery. If, however, he turns to the original, he finds that Camier, in writing the words, was occupied with other thoughts. He was discussing, in its due order, the question of "the duties of men to the body," and what he wrote was this: "So great is the connection and relation between man's body and his soul, that the happiness or misery of the soul itself depends on various conditions of the body. . . . 1. The body must be supported with the necessary nourishment. . . . 2. The body should be neither pampered nor broken with labor. . . . It is especially to be noted that there is no fouler pest than moral softness [*mollities,* to which the old word 'lewdness' is perhaps the nearest we have], which pollutes the mind itself with contagion. . . . 3. We are required to exert ourselves to shut the road to vices . . . *Quod si nonnihil indulgere*—Although some indulgence of the pleasures of sense is both lawful and expedient, as nature invites us to it, it does not follow that in enjoying these pleasures there should not be moderation and discretion."[35]

This was only the teaching of eighteenth century common sense. It was not notably Christian, but neither was it, as a statement of principle, scandalously immoral. The Jesuits and many Catholics of the time were in fact as much naturalists as the infidels whom they denounced. They looked to rational rather than saintly living, and held that human nature should be cultivated rather than denied. Their supernaturalism accompanied, without contradicting or even modifying, the naturalism of their views of daily life. The very

in the episcopate of the time. The French bishops were overwhelmingly opposed to the expulsion of the Jesuits. See L. Cahen, *Querelles religieuses et parlementaires* (Paris, 1913), p. 68.

[34] *Nouvelles ecclésiastiques* (1773), p. 171. See also the issues for August 1771 and August 27, 1772.
[35] Camier, *op. cit.,* Vol. III, pp. 522-4.

theologians in the schools could believe in the innate goodness of man.

The Abbé Hooke of the Sorbonne, for example, whom we have already noted, published in 1752 a treatise on "Natural and Revealed Religion." It was written in Latin, and meant to be read only by the clergy. "Man's natural propensities," he said, "are in accord with inner sense, reason and conscience. If we consider all the duties of life, whether toward God, ourselves or our neighbors, there is none that is not commended to us by some natural propensity. There is in all men a general benevolence and freely given goodness, whose force is so great that we succor strangers in distress and are moved to help all unfortunates by a natural pity. . . . Thus there is no duty that is not commended to us not only by reason but even by appetite, and there is no natural instinct, inclination or passion which if it be moderate is not useful to human life." The author thus implies that man's tendency to goodness is not merely natural but even physical, that the love of virtue is a kind of appetite, and the fulfilment of duty a refined selection of pleasure. From this point to *sensibilité* and *bienfaisance* the distance is not far, and the abbé's Latin grows warm with the pathetic eloquence of Rousseau. "Yet the aptitudes and spontaneous movements of the body show what agrees with nature and what does not. What charm is given to the countenance by friendly cheer, by sociable merriment, by glad fellow-feeling and rejoicing! What beauty by a serene and placid mind, that knows itself in the right, and by its inner sense of self-approval! In the face of a friend or of one moved by gratitude for a kindness, what a pleasing, though gentle flame gleams benignly in the eyes!"[36]

So, as early as 1752, in the gaunt halls of the Sorbonne, nature no longer meant the pure rationality of the world, but the inner possession of human feeling. Theologians and philosophers were turning sentimental on principle. Men in these years, torn between doubt and faith, became altruists to assure themselves of their own virtue, and Diderot, great thinker that he was, could seriously declare, "I must indeed be a good man to afflict myself so sorely!"

To sum up, the idea of nature had made deep incursions into theology, and it produced, in those sacred precincts, sounds that strangely resembled those issuing from the more profane quarters

[36] Hooke, *op. cit.*, Vol. I, pp. 486-7.

of the philosophers. It was not the old nature of the Augustinian tradition upheld by the Jansenists, the nature that was the privation of God, and so evil. It was not the nature of science, without color of right or wrong, shorn, by a principle of method, of moral significance. It was the nature that meant what was right, fitting, and proper, the nature that existed by the reason and justice of God— except for those theologians who, like the most advanced unbelievers, could persuade themselves that this moralized nature might exist alone. Nature, for the orthodox, was one of the ways of God to men. It was a way by which men knew of truth, justice, and right.

For believers, there was another way, revelation, which opened up the world of grace. With so much transferred to the world of nature, with justice and right assigned to the sphere of reason, with man's inclinations to goodness, his feelings of compassion, his capacity for rectitude ascribed to the humanity in himself, only a mysterious part was left for revelation to play.

Revelation, according to orthodoxy, made man a supernatural being. But what was it to be supernatural, when justice and goodness were considered a part of nature? It might mean two things: to be saintly, aloof, and holy, living in a righteousness not of this world; or to be ritualistic, performing the acts that were prescribed by the church, and acquiring the grace which the sacraments imparted, and which, though not necessary to make a man just or good, promoted him into heaven. In either case, the chief function of revelation was not to establish the principles which theologians admitted existed by reason, but to confirm the supernatural powers of the Catholic Church.

CHAPTER III

HISTORY AND TRADITION

WHETHER or not Catholic thinkers were introducing anything fundamentally new into the teaching of the church, they could not let it appear that they were, for Catholic truth was by definition changeless. They were obliged, therefore, to give some account of the past.

Let us assume that there were two ways in which the past might be dealt with, and call these two ways history and tradition. Neither historians nor theologians are likely to approve wholly of the sense in which the two words are used here; yet the distinction may be valid, and at any rate there was much in the eighteenth century that it serves to make more clear. Tradition was the older of the two methods. In the eighteenth century history definitely took a place alongside it, and in this fact lay one of the great claims of that century to be the Age of Enlightenment. But then as now the two methods were not always kept clearly apart. The *philosophes* who rejected Christianity kept some habits of mind that went with traditionalist thinking, and their views were consequently in a sense unhistorical. Their religious adversaries, on the other hand, often used an historical method to defend the Christian tradition. Despite all the writings of Augustine and Bossuet, it was only in the eighteenth century that critical historical inquiry, based on evidence, became a foundation of religious apologetics. Therein lay a great weakness, for historical method was not really suited to Catholic theology, if indeed it was not irrelevant to all deeper problems of religion.

We may set aside as unproved the idea that history describes the real past and tradition only an imaginary one, and see the problem for what it is, namely how men, living always in the present, can retain anything of events that have slipped forever beyond their reach. Tradition may be said, then, to flourish best where written documents are few. It trusts the unaided human memory, and enters the past not by going directly to what we call sources but by appealing to a social memory which, because of the overlapping of generations, is continuous and unbroken. It is realist in the scholastic sense; it assumes the reality of society, to which it regards individuals as incidental.

The Abbé Gauchat explained the theory in 1758, citing Bossuet and Houteville. A great society, he said, whether a nation or a church, retained a knowledge of ancient facts that was "not only durable but always exactly the same." Any given age, besides the weight of its own authority, "has that of all ages that are in a manner interwoven with it." Why? Because there is never a time when all men cease to exist. To use Paris as an example: its population (says Gauchat) is 900,000, but only 30,000 die in any given year. Despite replacement of individuals, "the body remains precisely the same." There is never a time when the younger members can fall into error, for there is always present a majority of elders to correct them. The social memory remains intact and authentic; historical evidence serves only to confirm it.[1]

Originality, on which modern men have set a premium, was in this system of thought very much at a discount. To demand the evidence of one's own eyes, to profess to believe only in the dictates of one's own reason, were not states of mind of which it was proper to boast. Truth was the possession of the whole community. It was fundamentally the body of knowledge necessary to assure the survival of the community and the salvation of the individual, rather than a mass of information about particular facts and events. The lives of individuals, their opinions, discoveries, and achievements, were ephemeral and vain; the substantial reality was the communion of the faithful, in which the dead and the living were equally present, and all individuals fused in the mystical unity of the church. The individual lived by the experience of the group, in which as a Catholic he participated fully, and in which he trusted more confidently than in his own restricted powers.

"But have you yourself seen Jesus Christ rise from the tomb and ascend to heaven?"—so an apologist puts to himself a favorite query of the infidels. "Yes," he answers, "I have seen him by the

[1] G. Gauchat, *Lettres critiques, ou Analyse et réfutation de divers écrits modernes contre la religion* (Paris, 1755-63), Vol. IX, pp. 73-5.

eyes of the apostles, by the eyes of seventy-two disciples, and of more than five hundred brethren; through them have I spoken with him, eaten and drunk with him since the Resurrection; through their ears have I heard his promises and his threats."[2] This is the Catholic Idea, in the true sense in which catholic means universal. The eyes and ears of the first witnesses are the eyes and ears of the church, and so, by an intimate communion, the eyes and ears of every believer.

When the Catholic Idea breaks down, when the profound doctrine of the communion of saints gives way to the belief that individuals are separate existences mutually external and independent, then the first witnesses to the acts of Christ become simply the persons who happened to be present, who are now remote from us in time, and who perhaps had beliefs and purposes that are not our own. The gap thus opened by a new sense of time and individuality has to be bridged by history, and the defense of religion becomes a defense of ancient testimony, by which apologists seek to demonstrate that certain historical events did in fact take place seventeen hundred years before.

The Catholic Idea involved what seems to us to have been a confusion in dealing with questions of fact and of right, or at least it implied that correctness of fact and correctness of conduct are determined in the same way. Empirical facts were significant only so far as they threw light on the Christian destiny of man. The same authority which presided over that destiny might therefore also claim the power to decide whether a man's factual information was true. Prescription, or the theory by which continuous tradition establishes right and wrong in a legal sense, was used also to determine the rightness or wrongness of knowledge. Catholics were to believe certain facts about the past because they accepted the authority of the church in the present, much as if, because we accept the political authority under which we live, we were obliged to believe implicitly the history of the country prescribed by the government.

Tradition, as a means of knowing the past distinct from history, is perhaps no more than the development of this idea. In tradition, the "authentic" account of past times is the one that supports present ideas of justice and is accepted because these ideas are accepted.

[2] J. Denyse, *La vérité de la religion chrétienne démontrée par ordre géométrique* (Paris, 1717), p. 343.

In history, in which the facts are thought to have an authority of their own, the "authentic" story is the one that presumably emerges from the facts themselves.[3]

Tradition, as a form of social memory arising from the overlapping of generations, had to reach back to the beginning of the world if it was to be satisfactory. For this purpose the unusual longevity of the Hebrew patriarchs was of the highest importance. It meant that in early times society had always included not merely two or three but as many as a dozen generations living together. Knowledge of man's origin was thus particularly certain. The *Journal Ecclésiastique* gave statistical proof in 1761, by publishing a table to show how many years each of the patriarchs had spent in the company of others. It appeared that the father of Noah had lived during the last fifty-six years of Adam's life, and so had heard Adam's personal recollections, which he later handed down to Noah unchanged; and that the grandfather of Abraham had lived twenty-seven years with Shem, who in turn lived four hundred and forty-eight years with his father Noah. Thus Abraham was practically a contemporary of Noah, and only four persons stood between him and Adam himself. And Moses, when he wrote the whole story down not long afterwards, was separated from the creation by only a few lifetimes.[4]

The method of tradition rested upon confidence. It was highly social; it assumed that men could be trusted. It assumed that each generation would hand on unaltered the knowledge that it had received, because it assumed that all generations were interested in the same knowledge. It took little account of processes in time. It bound together past and present in a perpetual community in which men succeeded each other simply as fathers and sons, all sharing in the same beliefs and aims, at whatever point in the chronological sequence they might happen to fall. In this timeless world there was little sense of cause and effect, or of antecedent and consequence; human affairs were not thought to have risen so much from efficient causes working onward into the future as from final causes or

[3] cf. F. Para du Phanjas, *Les principes de la saine philosophie conciliés avec ceux de la religion* (Paris, 1774), Vol. I, p. 23.

[4] *Journal ecclésiastique*, 1761, 32-34; C. Le Gros, *Examen des ouvrages de J.-J. Rousseau et de Court de Gébelin* (Genève, 1785), pp. 48-9.

general reasons for existence that stood wholly outside the chronological sequence.

For an idea or an institution to be fully authentic and acceptable, it had to exist through the whole range of time. So long as it was known to have once been a novelty, so long as its origin could be referred to a definitely remembered date, it was thought to be a novelty yet, and of doubtful validity, for in this view of the world whatever had been introduced in time might perish in time, and could form no part of the perpetual knowledge by which the community should live. Hence the church traced itself back to Adam, and represented itself as the rightful successor to the Jewish Temple. Orthodoxy was defined as what should always have been believed, and heresy as an opinion that arose with a particular individual at a particular date. Paganism and polytheism were condemned as abuses, on the ground that they were not as old as the world itself. They were aberrations from the truth with which Adam had started, and which only the Jews, and after them only the Christians, had preserved entire. These mistaken forms of belief could thus be explained and assigned a place in the annals of Christendom, but Christianity could not be understood by reference to other religions. The Christian tradition was supreme: it explained the history of the world, but was not explained by it.[5]

Truth was thus understood to be the body of doctrines which either had been or should have been always believed. The past was not studied, as we say, for its own sake. Past societies and individuals were not thought to be really distinct from the present, of importance in their own right, worthy of respect simply as expressions of the human mind. There was no real significance in their differences, or special circumstances, or particular ways of meeting general problems. The important thing was to relate all known human beings to the received body of doctrines, to show how they did or did not align themselves with the perpetual body of knowledge which it was the duty of all men to entertain. The very infidels in the eighteenth century often found it necessary to place their truths in an original state of nature, and tended to regard any deviation from this state as a prejudice introduced by

[5] L. Hooke, *Religionis revelatae principia* (Paris, 1752-54), Vol. II, p. 799; C. Yvon, *Histoire philosophique de la religion* (Liége, 1779), Vol. I, pp. 55, 264; A. Paulian, *Dictionnaire philosophico-théologique* (Nimes, 1770), p. 285.

misguided individuals. To them, however, it was the Christian Church that was a novelty, which, having arisen historically, might also disappear, leaving men free to live by the perpetual laws of nature.

Tradition used the past as a storehouse of precedents and precursors. Men read old books less for information than for wisdom. Theologians studied Augustine as a predecessor of themselves. Voltaire conferred the same honor on Julian the Apostate, declaring him to have been "the greatest, or at least the second greatest of men," because he had sought to suppress Christianity. Voltaire could not believe that Jesus Christ taught the same doctrine as the professors at the Sorbonne, but he could readily persuade himself that a fourth century Roman emperor was only Voltaire differently placed in time. In opposition, he could be an historian; in supporting his own views, he looked for the authority of tradition.

Inconsistency of this kind was perhaps inevitable. Certainly it is common enough. History has by no means ousted tradition as a way of thinking about the past. Nor is it only conservatives who find the method useful. In America today, the most advanced collectivists will claim Emerson as their precursor, much as the Jesuit Suarez laid claim to St. Paul. If it is argued that Emerson, like later collectivists, was interested chiefly in human welfare and progress, so Suarez might have argued, with equal indifference to specific doctrine, that St. Paul, like himself, was interested chiefly in the salvation of the soul.

It may be said without paradox that belief in progress itself arises from traditionalist thinking, for it does not result from pure historical inquiry, but is an attempt to bind together past and present in one great society, to attribute to all mankind a constant effort and a single aim, and thus to show that men are engaged in a perpetual enterprise that has been the same since man became man.

Tradition is always in effect an instrument of present authority. It fortifies received opinions, whether conservative or progressive. Ostensibly, it fortifies these opinions by representing them as an outgrowth of the past; actually, it projects these opinions into the past, and gives the appearance of perpetuity by enlarging the present. Traditionalist reasoning, therefore, often seems to be a plain begging of the question. It could be argued, for example, that the existence of heresies proved the authority of the church, because heresies, which were "nothing else than a rebellion against the visible authority of the church," had in fact existed since the birth of Christianity. The traditional act of baptism proved the existence of the original sin which it was the function of baptism to remove; and the traditional celebration of Easter and of Sunday proved the Resurrection which these days had been instituted to commemorate.[6]

Or there was the more famous argument based on the existence of the Jews. It was an observed fact that the Jews suffered cruelly in the present. Either their suffering was a punishment for the death of the Messiah, or else it was only oppression, and other peoples were guilty of a crime. The Abbé Fangouse thus stated the alternatives boldly. But, he explains, the Jews themselves, by their holy books, assure us that the Christ whom they put to death was the true Messiah. How do we know that these books tell the truth? Because the Jewish people undoubtedly exists today. The existence of this people today, with all its wealth of law and faith and ritual, would be an unfathomable mystery without the historical explanation which the Old Testament provides. We are involved in fewer mysteries if we accept the Old Testament as it stands. "But if this history is true, the miracles reported in it cannot be false; the truth of a history depends on the truth of the facts it contains, and the miracles are facts." That is, once a history is accepted as true, it follows that all its statements of fact are also true. If the miracles are true, so are the oracles. "The oracles teach that the present state of the Jews is the just punishment for crime; the crime was the death of the King of Glory, the promised Messiah. The Messiah therefore has appeared." And therefore the Christian revelation is literally and factually true.[7]

Certainly there were many perversities in such reasoning, but the strangest is perhaps the method of conceiving the past. This method was a roundabout way of affirming the opinions held in the present. The truth of the traditional story is established by the supposed impossibility of understanding the past or present in any other manner; and the truth of the story then guarantees the truth of all the remarkable incidents, prodigies, and miracles that it

[6] N. Jamin, *Pensées théologiques* (Paris, 1769), pp. 125-6; N. Bergier, *Réponse aux conseils raisonnables* (1773), p. 60.
[7] Abbé Fangouse, *Réflexions importantes sur la religion* (Paris, 1785), pp. 77-89.

relates. Nothing could be more foreign to the true method of history. Historians, so far as they meet their own standards, do not suppose that contemporary belief provides the only means of knowing the past. They begin, that is, if not by defying the authority of the present, at least by setting it aside as irrelevant to the questions with which they deal. They test the truth of a written document by considering the circumstances and purposes of its author, trying to enter into the past itself, to place themselves mentally in the bygone age. And they do not feel that when they accept an old record as substantially true they must accept also every occurrence that it describes. In particular, most historians have a means of their own, based on faith in the regularity of nature and distrust in human testimony, by which they can deny that such things as miracles ever happened. Thus they can build up a story that is likely to be different from the story supplied by tradition, and which in any case is dangerous to tradition because it offers another method and another authority.

By the eighteenth century something of the historical spirit had entered the minds of many people who were not aware that it might undermine tradition. The accumulation of printed books in Europe, giving men a more distinct knowledge of their recent predecessors, had changed their outlook on the past itself, and made it harder for them to feel the passive and respectful awe for their elders that went along with belief in tradition. The Protestant Reformation had raised a prolonged and open discussion of ancient scriptures. The revival of classical letters, and the attempts of humanists to transport themselves into the pagan world of Greece and Rome, had shown that by no means the whole past was reflected in the tradition of the church. Technical criticism of documents had begun; from Lorenzo Valla to Bayle and Richard Simon and Spinoza, there were men who declared that writings hitherto held sacred had originated in credulity or fraud, or had been vitiated in transmission.

The clergy themselves turned to history. Jesuit followers of Bollandus, not content to leave the saints to oral tradition, bestowed upon them the doubtful advantage of historical investigation; and the Benedictines, using such new sciences as paleography, patiently deciphered forgotten old manuscripts, without worrying too much about the consequence for theology. It dawned upon men that little was known of the past, but that much could be learned; and the very realization was ominous for tradition, which had purported to tell them all that was vital for them to know.

So men were coming inevitably to think in historical terms, to consider the past as a sequence of facts and processes in time. They were coming to feel that truth should depend on the facts they could observe, rather than that the facts should take their significance from a truth received through other channels. They came to believe in the necessity of evidence. Christianity henceforth had to be proved by facts, if it was to be proved at all. All through the eighteenth century, as we shall presently see, the great aim of apologists was to prove religion by historical fact, by actual events which no rational man should be able to deny. Yet even before the eighteenth century began, there were men in the church who doubted whether such historical proof was possible.

The professors and students in the best theological schools were not so isolated from the world as their enemies the *philosophes* would have us believe. They were often aware of what was happening, and knew that the critical methods made popular by Bayle struck very deep. The result, for them, was much perplexity of mind. They were modern enough to accept the new method as valid, and yet not willing to dismiss the Christian revelation as false.

As early as 1693, at the Jesuit college of Caen, the whole matter was being freely discussed, as is shown in a student's thesis of that year. The Christian religion, according to this surprising document, "is evidently believable, but not evidently true. Evidently believable, for it is evident that whoever embraces it is a prudent man. Not evidently true, for either it teaches obscurely, or the things that it teaches are obscure." This reminds us of Pascal's search for grounds of belief free from the tyranny of proof. "Indeed," the thesis continues, "those who say that the Christian religion is evidently true are bound to admit that it is evidently false." This statement apparently means that those who seek to argue purely from common-sense evidence will be obliged in the end to confess themselves defeated. "Infer then that it is not evident: 1. that there is any true religion on earth. . . . 2. that the Christian religion is the most nearly true of all those that exist on earth; for have you travelled in all countries, or do you know those countries in which others have travelled?" Here we are reminded of the deists, who thought that they must consult the experience of strange and savage peoples, and analyze and compare the beliefs of all mankind, before arriving at religious truth. ". . . 4. [It is not evident] that the oracles of the prophets were announced under the inspiration of God; for what will you answer if I deny that they were true prophecies, or affirm that they were only guesses? 5. that the miracles reported to have been performed by Christ were true miracles, although no one can prudently deny them."[8]

Voltaire and the *philosophes* could hardly have asked more sweeping concessions. The author of the thesis accepts his adversaries' method. He concedes that truth must depend on the kind of evidence that the infidels demanded: the facts of history, the facts or supposed facts reported by travellers from societies outside the pale of Christendom. Using this test of truth, he concludes that Christianity is not demonstrably true, but only believable; and in the Age of Reason, for most churchmen as well as for most unbelievers, to believe what was not demonstrably true was to fall into superstition and credulity. The thesis therefore does not represent the views of most of the leading apologists in the eighteenth century. They, too, accepted their adversaries' method, but they thought that by using this method, by arguing strictly from facts, they could prove the truth of Revelation.

In all probability the author of the thesis himself, and the Jesuit teachers before whom he defended it, did not doubt the validity of Revelation. Probably they were only indulging in the kind of speculative radicalism that goes on in modern universities, and which was permitted even in the church in the obscurity of the Latin language and the classroom. They did not mean to undermine belief. They did, however, theoretically and for the moment at least, separate belief from what they recognized as truth. Presumably they meant to found belief on the tradition and authority of the church. If so, they implied that tradition itself was not, properly speaking, true, but only believable.

Catholic thinkers were caught, indeed, in an extremely embarrassing difficulty. As modern men, touched by the spirit of history, they were inclined to reread existing writings, and to search out and interpret others that had been lost. But tradition still stood, with its

---

[8] *Extraits des assertions dangereuses et pernicieuses que les soi-disants jésuites ont soutenues* (5th ed., Paris, 1763), Vol. II, p. 82. There is no reply at this point in the Jesuit *Réponse au livre intitulé Extraits . . .* (n.p., 1763-65).

perpetual stock of knowledge, telling them in advance what the old writings meant, and what hitherto undiscovered documents must reveal. The Abbé Gauchat grappled with the difficulty in 1761. He meant to found orthodox belief on the evidence of historical fact, but showed in effect that it could rest only on tradition.

The Bible, said Gauchat, was not a work of physics, and so could not be in conflict with natural science. It was a work of history; "it teaches us certain facts which bear on the designs and works of the Lord, and on our duties and true interests." But it was a history of a special kind. It was, and must remain, the *sole* historical source for the events that it described. "What would become of religion, if we were once to admit the principle, moderate though it is and hence the more seductive, that *for historical detail Scripture is not our sole and unique rule*? To admit this principle would be to leave our restless and carping critics the judges of the facts. They would check the chronology of Scripture against that of profane histories, or perhaps of the annals of China or the gods of Egypt. Soon they would deny the facts which they judged not to square with these dates, then the facts which seemed contrary to physical laws, and gradually they would reduce our sacred oracles to purely moral and symbolic books. That would be the end of revealed religion, which depends of necessity on facts."

Gauchat was surely right in maintaining that, to keep the Biblical story intact, it would be well to avoid the comparative method. But his argument was hardly historical. He wished to prove revelation by historical evidence, but, in selecting and weighing the evidence, he dismissed as irrelevant the historical criticism of documents, and appealed to the tradition of the church, and to the very belief in revelation which it was his purpose to justify.[9]

The question of the proper use of Scripture was further complicated by the decisions of the Council of Trent. The Council had decided that Catholic doctrine was contained both in Scripture and in tradition. To the Scriptures, then, men must go. They must compare and reconcile the various versions—Latin, Greek, and Hebrew. But the Council had decreed the Latin Vulgate to be "authentic." What then, someone was bound to ask, could be the use of reading the Hebrew and the Greek? Moreover, by the same decree, it was

[9] Gauchat, *op. cit.*, Vol. XV, pp. 91-2.

forbidden to interpret Scripture, in matters of faith and morals, in any sense other than that understood by the Catholic Church. What then, since this sense was known by tradition, could be the practical use of reading the Scriptures at all?[10]

As for the Vulgate, much depended on what was meant by "authentic." It was a known fact that the Vulgate was only a translation, made by St. Jerome four hundred years after the time of Christ, setting forth in Latin the truths that the inspired authors had expressed in Hebrew and in Greek. This being so, most theologians concluded that the Fathers at Trent, in declaring the Vulgate to be authentic, had intended to affirm only that it was the best of the various Latin versions, without errors of faith or morals. When its meaning was doubtful, the original texts were to be consulted, but no man was to regard his reading of these originals as the official doctrine of the church. "Authentic" therefore meant simply authorized as the teaching of the church. It was a question of legitimacy or right.

But others in the seventeenth century saw in authenticity a question of fact. Like modern historians, they argued that an authentic document was one that exactly expressed what its author had said. The Vulgate then, being authentic, must represent the true original Scriptures, and the Greek and Hebrew versions, when they differed from it, must be wrong. Not that Moses or Matthew had written in Latin; it was simply that, while we get our Greek and Hebrew texts only from medieval manuscripts, we know by tradition that the Vulgate has been in use in the church since the earliest ages, when it could still be compared to the true originals that have since been lost. Therefore, according to Suarez, Valentia, and others who took this view, it was the Greek and Hebrew that should be corrected to accord with the text of the Vulgate.[11]

In this way tradition was vindicated, remarkably enough, by the method of history. The theologians of this school used the new

[10] For the decrees of Trent see Mirbt, *Quellen zur Geschichte des Papsttums und des römischen Katholizismus* (4th ed., Tübingen, 1924), pp. 291-2.

[11] H. Griffet, *L'insuffisance de la religion naturelle* (Liége, 1770), Vol. II, p. 134; C. Frevier (S. J.), *La Vulgate authentique dans tout son texte, plus authentique que le texte hebreu, que le texte grec qui nous restent* (Rome, really Rouen, 1753); and the review of this work in the *Journal de Trévoux* (1753), pp. 2017-83, where the reviewer disagrees with the author's contention that the Greek and Hebrew should be made to correspond to the Vulgate.

science of the criticism of sources. They pointed out, what no one could deny, that all historical knowledge of the Bible depended on a few manuscripts of which none went back to the time of Christ or the apostles. They thus cleared the way for traditional knowledge, and were free to assert that the Vulgate was the oldest, most authentic, and only inspired text of Scripture. With one deadly stroke they cut down the Protestants who objected that the Vulgate was not the real Bible, and turned upon the infidels their own weapons of historical inquiry, criticism, and doubt. It required only audacity to apply the same tactics to all written records, to defend tradition by extreme skepticism, and maintain that there can be no historical knowledge of times antedating the manuscripts that we possess.

A certain Frenchman, Jean Hardouin, a Jesuit, had the necessary audacity, or the necessary gift for carrying the new principles to their logical extreme. Contemporaries thought him highly eccentric, if not positively mad; but he was mad, if at all, in the manner of Hamlet, knowing very well which way the wind was blowing. Church historians have dismissed him with a word; few lay historians have noticed him. He is worth attention, however, for *le hardouinisme* aroused much heated discussion within the church, and probably contributed to the downfall of the Jesuits in 1763. It shows, moreover, to what lengths men might be driven in their attempt to guard tradition against the new principles of history.[12]

Father Hardouin believed in two things passionately, the Catholic Church and the critical examination of documents. He was obsessed with the fear of atheism, which apparently he interpreted in the widest sense, suspecting even some of his Jesuit colleagues of being atheists in disguise, and seeing in history a long series of atheist plots against the faith. At the same time he possessed real acumen in dealing with the technical problems involved in the investigation of manuscripts. He was a prodigious worker, one of

---

[12] On Hardouin see, apart from his own writings, F. Reusch, *Index der verbotenen Bücher* (Bonn, 1883-85), Vol. II, pp. 804-8; Griffet, *op. cit.,* Vol. II, pp. 190-267; G. Berthier, "Observations sur les systèmes des PP. Hardouin et Berruyer" in the *Journal de Trévoux* (1761), pp. 3012 *ff.*; F. de Fitz-James, bishop of Soissons, *Istruzione pastorale contro gli errori de PP. Arduino e Berruyer* (Brescia, 1763), a work which in its French original seems to have disappeared from the libraries of Paris. Langlois and Seignobos, *Introduction to the Study of History* (Eng. trans., New York, 1898), p. 99, mention Hardouin briefly.

those pioneering scholars whose labors are all but incredible today. The collections of documents that he published were so numerous, so thorough, and so reliable that he was never able, said his contemporary Daniel Huet, to undermine his reputation as a scholar by the strangeness of his views.

Hardouin's views might well seem strange, for he maintained that all written records purporting to date from before the fourteenth century were forgeries, except the Vulgate and the works of Homer, Plautus, and a few minor profane authors. Everything else, the Greek and the Hebrew testaments, the bulk of the classical literature, the works of St. Augustine and the Fathers, the records of the early church councils, the books of St. Thomas and most of the scholastics—all was false, a pure figment of the imagination, a gigantic fraud perpetrated in the fourteenth century by plotting atheistical monks who wanted to invent a church history for their own sinister ends, and whose efforts soon bore fruit in the Protestant rebellion. As a matter of fact, said Hardouin, there was no *history* of the church, but only *tradition,* only the oral tradition, kept alive from age to age, without the use of records, by the perpetual presence of the Holy Spirit. So Father Hardouin, who spent his life preparing the materials for history, turned the new science upon itself, and, to protect tradition, argued on historical grounds that history was impossible.

He understood precisely what he was doing. "Piety and the Christian religion," he said, "demand that we free them from a greater danger at the risk of incurring a lesser. The lesser danger is to acknowledge the falsity of certain facts that have hitherto received credit; the greater danger, and in the long run by far the greatest danger, is that, while facts of this kind are kept safe, faith itself should be shaken or corrupted."[13] The choice is between facts and faith; we must choose faith, because faith is more precious, and because in any case the facts are vouched for only in the dubious manuscripts of unknown monks. It is a mistake to suppose that the church has any need of written authorities. "Away with the idea that the Church of God should need or use false witnesses and testimony! The church was able to stand without any divine scripture; and in fact it did so stand before the writing of the Gospel of

[13] J. Hardouin, *Ad censuram scriptorum veterum prolegomena* (London, 1766), p. 2.

Luke; it stood by Apostolic tradition alone, as it now stands by the institution of its pastors and by the communion with the Apostolic See shared by the greatest number of the Christian people. So much the more can it stand without the writings of those who are called Fathers, and whose meaning is so uncertain that even their Catholic defenders interpret it differently because of the difficulties in the words." What does it matter what these so-called Fathers thought? "Why should the church, to settle a controversy about the faith, ask the opinion of Ambrose, Augustine, Jerome and the others? Should the church then be taught by them? Did not they, if they were Catholic doctors, learn from it? . . . For the Roman Church its faith and its tradition are sufficient, without help from Augustine or any other private person whatever, since the church holds its authority and power of magistracy from no one, except Christ and the Holy Spirit granted to it; the church should be taught by no one, but should teach all as a mother and mistress."[14]

These sentiments, however abnormal, were certainly Catholic in spirit. They followed from the principle announced by Augustine himself, that Catholics believe in the Scriptures because they believe in the church, not in the church because of the evidence of Scriptures. The church does not hold that it needs any written authorities; it affirms that it does in fact possess them. It does not hold that its doctrine was developed by individual thinkers; it affirms that certain thinkers did in fact express its doctrine correctly.

Hardouin differed with the majority of theologians simply on the question of fact, the mere historical question whether, apart from the Vulgate, the church did possess any written authorities. He boldly denied that it did, on the ground that the living church was itself the only source of authority. Having thus dismissed the early Fathers and Councils as irrelevant, he proceeded by historical methods to prove them inexistent. He placed authority squarely in the present, in the affirmation of properly qualified church officials. In doing so he only stated openly what the Fathers at Trent had sought to disguise, perhaps even from themselves, when they set up Scripture as a source of Catholic belief and then forbade its interpretation in any other than the Catholic sense.

[14] *ibid.*, pp. 57-8, 11.

Hardouin's arguments might be embarrassing, but they were not to be too vigorously denied.

Hardouin's most famous follower was another French Jesuit, Isaac Berruyer, who, between the years 1728 and 1758, published a huge work in many volumes, called the *Histoire du Peuple de Dieu*. It was a kind of New History, designed to tell the story of the Bible in language that the eighteenth century could understand. Berruyer modernized all that he could, put imaginary conversations into the mouths of the sacred characters, dwelt on the love affairs of the patriarchs, presumed to know the thoughts and motives of all persons in the story, invented new incidents and circumstances, and introduced a good deal of comment to point the moral for his readers. He included in the set one volume of theological essays in Latin, which particularly scandalized the clergy. The book created a tremendous sensation, especially the Second Part, which appeared in 1753 and dealt with the New Testament.

The pope, the archbishop of Paris, the Sorbonne and the Parlement of Paris all condemned Berruyer's work, and it was solemnly burned by the public hangman. Christophe de Beaumont, the archbishop, assembled the high Jesuit officials in Paris, and put at their disposal ten thousand crowns with which to buy up all possible copies. Four thousand copies were seized by the police at the gates of Paris. But too many had been sold; nothing could stop the circulation; the scandal had to be faced. The Jesuits officially disavowed the book. The provincial announced that it had been published without his knowledge and contained much that he disapproved. Handbills were given out at churchdoors and other public places, stating that the Society had nothing to do with the affair, and had been unable to prevent Berruyer from publishing. Berruyer himself, though he acquiesced humbly in the condemnation of his Second Part, proceeded unhindered to write the Third, which he published four years later.

In view of the iron discipline of the Jesuit order, the official protestations were not entirely convincing, and many people believed that Berruyer really expressed the views of his colleagues, and was disavowed only because he had raised such an unexpected uproar. Certainly the Jesuits did what they could to protect him. They kept him as a member in good standing, and after the first

crisis they defended him against what they called Jansenist persecution. The pope deplored the condemnation of the book by the
Faculty of Theology, on the ground that since he himself had
already censured it further action could only give it more pub-
licity. When in 1764 seventy-eight parish priests petitioned the
archbishop of Rouen to suppress it in his province, the only reply
they received was a reprimand for their impertinence. There is,
in short, reason to believe that Berruyer had friends in high places,
and that many influential prelates did not disapprove of his opinions as much as they appeared to.[15]

Berruyer, like Hardouin, meant to strengthen tradition by
means of historical skepticism. His skepticism, however, was more
sophisticated than Hardouin's, and indeed more modern in tone
than the aggressive disbelief of the infidels. To dispose of ancient
writings which, if granted an independent authority, might be in-
convenient to the church, he argued that the circumstances in
which these writings were composed were so different from those
of the eighteenth century, and the sentiments of the authors and
true meaning of their language so difficult to ascertain, that modern readers could not really understand them, but were obliged to
interpret them in the light of their own purposes and beliefs. He
thus developed a theory of climates of opinion. Each age, he
thought, had its own intellectual atmosphere. Ancient writers, including the "Sacred Authors themselves," had written for men
who had the ideas and interests of their own time. They could
scarcely be understood by men of the eighteenth century, just as
writers of the eighteenth century would in time become almost

[15] On Berruyer, see the works referred to for Hardouin, note 12 above, and
also M. Picot, *Mémoires pour servir à l'histoire de l'église au dix-huitième
siècle* (3rd ed., Paris, 1853-54), Vol. III, pp. 248-51; d'Argenson, *Mémoires*
(Paris, 1859-67), Vol. VIII, p. 141; E. Regnault, *Christophe de Beaumont*
(Paris, 1882), Vol. I, pp. 360-5; C. Guyon, *Apologie des jésuites convaincue
d'attentats contre les lois divines et humaines* (n.p., 1763), Vol. II, pp. 258-9;
Requête de cinquante-six curés du diocèse de Rouen (En France, 1764); *Bref
de N. S. P. le Pape Clément XIII à la Faculté de Théologie de Paris au sujet
des censures de cette Faculté contre l'Émile de Rousseau et l'Histoire du peuple
de Dieu du P. Berruyer* (Paris, 1764). Berruyer was also accused of Arianism.
On this matter see J. Duhamel, *La vérité catholique sur le mystère d'un Dieu
incarné* (n.p., 1756); J. Gaultier, *Lettres théologiques contre le P. Berruyer*
(n.p., 1756).

unintelligible to future generations. The Bible therefore had to be interpreted in the light of contemporary belief.[16]

Berruyer did not pretend to have a perfectly objective understanding of the Bible. Old writings, he thought, were necessarily so interpreted as to conform to the opinions of the living. "Whether Catholics or Protestants, we all read Scriptures with the prejudices of our own dogmas. These dogmas being already in possession of our minds, we look for them in the Scriptures. . . . If I attack a Protestant by opposing his dogmas with a text, it may happen that I do not always confute him, for this text in its literal sense may not be relevant to his error."[17] It was therefore false, in Berruyer's opinion, to suppose that the Scriptures were an independent authority for the true faith. Nothing could be proved from them, because their meaning was not self-evident to modern men. "To speak properly, dogmas are not proved primarily and directly from the meaning of Scripture, but the true and legitimate meaning of Scripture, and the meaning that is adulterate and to be condemned, are known to us by the articles already believed by Catholic faith."[18]

This was the ultimate reply to all Protestants, who claimed to know the objective meaning of the Bible and to judge the church by its independent authority. In proportion, however, as the argument against the Protestants was perfected, it became more transparently illogical to believe, as the Council of Trent had ordained, that Catholic doctrine was derived both from Scripture and from tradition. It was impossible to regard the two as coordinate in authority. All that was possible was to believe, on the assurance of the church, that Scripture and tradition were identical in the general content of their teaching.

Berruyer, like Hardouin, became embarrassingly explicit in denying the necessity of written authorities. For him as for Hardouin, the oral tradition was supreme. It was useless to appeal to documentary records. "It would be an intolerable presumption to call back the church, charged essentially with preserving the deposit of faith, to what she taught in former times through her

[16] Berruyer, *Histoire du peuple de Dieu* (Paris, 1728-58), Third Part, Vol. I, pp. 8-10. Answered by Fitz-James, *op. cit.*, Vol. I, p. 108.
[17] Quoted by Fitz-James, *op. cit.*, Vol. I, p. 77.
[18] *Histoire du peuple de Dieu*, Second Part, Vol. VIII, p. 173.

Fathers—as if she taught it no longer. Those that she honors today with the name of Fathers and Teachers were her disciples and children while they lived." Thus are Augustine and other troublesome doctors disposed of : if they were Catholics they could not teach error; that they were indeed Catholics we know by the honor in which the church holds them today. "Always young and always virgin, despite her fecundity of seventeen hundred years, either from the first the church was not the true bride of Christ, or else she cannot for a moment have forgotten to teach what she learned from her bridegroom. The vast volumes and ostentatious quotations of rash reformers will never avail against this force of prescription. It is in the teaching of the Roman Church, and in its *present teaching,* that I find without risk and at small cost the tradition of all the ages; it is there that the Religion of Christ must be found, even by those who seek to combat it."[19]

The effect of Berruyer's whole philosophy, it will be seen, was to remove all possibility of historical argument against the church. Both his doubts and his affirmations served this end. Doubting that the writings of the past were intelligible in themselves, he looked to the present for a true knowledge of their meaning. Affirming that Catholic doctrine was changeless, he concluded that living Catholics must represent it in its full and timeless purity. The present thus became absolute. No argument drawn from the past could be valid against it. What the church believed at any given moment defined its belief in all ages past and future. However much it might change, it could never appear to change, for it carried its past and future with it. Tradition triumphed over history as a method of knowing the past; the idea of perpetuity over the idea of process, the authority of present belief over the authority of historical records.

Berruyer only made explicit what the whole theory of tradition implied. He showed that tradition, with all its seeming submissiveness to the past, really depended purely and simply on the affirmation of the present, and could be known only by the pronouncements of living men.

True Christian doctrine at any given moment was thus what the church asserted it to be at that moment, and it was hardly

19 *ibid.,* Vol. I, p. 263. Italics mine.

necessary for Berruyer to develop at length what was perhaps his most radical idea, namely that Jesus Christ had not attempted any definite religious teaching. All that Christ and the apostles had tried to do, according to Berruyer, was to convince their hearers that the Son of God had appeared among men. They could best convince the Jews by miracles and mysterious language, and they left points of ethics and dogma to be passed on by tradition through the church. "Hence it is that on innumerable matters which we, taught by the Catholic Church, firmly and fully believe, there is rarely any mention in the public speeches of Christ to the people." Christ's only public revelation was the disclosure of his supernatural powers. The Jews had been astonished into accepting him, and the church was founded on the palpable fact of his more than earthly origin. "Everything else, I repeat . . . having to do with matters of belief was left to a private institution, in order that men might perfectly understand Christian doctrine according to its particular mysteries, sacraments, decisions, dogmas and hierarchy."[20]

Thus the church in the eighteenth century was further liberated from dependence on the past. Persons disposed to read the Gospels historically, to find out what Christ had really meant to say, were following a false scent and could contribute nothing to the elucidation of religion; for Christ had not really said what he meant, but had only intimated his views to a few associates to be passed on by tradition, and in his public discourses had purposely shrouded himself in the unintelligible and the occult.

Both Hardouin and Berruyer, having reduced tradition to the pure dictum of the present, taught the modernized kind of Christianity which their opponents called Molinism. The central point in this doctrine, it should be remembered, was that man in his own nature was able to achieve a goodness pleasing to God, and that grace was necessary only for acquiring supernatural virtues and rewards. Man might have been originally created with the concupiscence and other imperfections which in the eighteenth century he actually possessed; neither in the eighteenth century, therefore, nor at any time since the Fall, was he wholly bad or totally depraved.

[20] *ibid.*, Vol. VIII, pp. 168-9.

Let us hear Hardouin commenting on 2 Peter i:4, where Christians, to become partakers in the divine nature, are enjoined to flee the corruption of concupiscence—*concupiscentiæ corruptionem* in the Vulgate. "It is not concupiscence that the Apostle condemns," observes Hardouin, "but the *corruption* of concupiscence. But if you consult the Greek codices, concupiscence will be seen to be in itself corruption."[21] He thus blandly admits that the Greek text confirms the view taken by the Jansenists and the Protestants, but the point is of no importance to him, since the Greek text is spurious. Reading the Latin, and construing an objective genitive, he can easily prove his own interpretation. Or again, commenting on Romans vii:24, where Paul cries out in anguish, "O wretched man that I am! . . . ," Father Hardouin remarks placidly that there was no need for such overwhelming affliction, "because a man is wretched only by his own fault; by the fault of another he is simply unfortunate, as are the descendants of Adam, because deprived of justice by his original sin."[22]

Such a reading of the text, besides doing scant justice to Paul, might well be dangerous to Christianity. It was a purely nominalist interpretation, in which Adam was regarded as an individual man, not as a representative of human nature. His fault was therefore his own. His descendants had no moral connection with him, or at least no share in his guilt. The way was open for the infidels who thought it preposterous that men should suffer for the misdoings of a deceased ancestor.

Berruyer was even more outspoken than Hardouin in declaring man to be innocent and inoffensive. Nature, he all but said, could teach men everything needful in morals and religion, except the manner of worship preferred by God, which was known by special revelation. The Jews, for example, had received only their ceremonial by the direct command of God; their ethical ideas, their belief in a Deity and in rewards and punishments after death, were drawn from nature, the common fund in which all peoples shared. Apart from ceremonial, therefore, there had been no essential difference between the Jews and other peoples of the earth. There was a spirit common to them all, "which, in whatever

[21] J. Hardouin, *Commentarius in Novum Testamentum* (n.p., 1741), *in loc.* 2 Peter 1:4.
[22] *ibid., in loc.* Romans vii:24.

time or place, made into children of God all those who wished
to be born of God, and which even to those too numerous and
almost infinite hosts who chose darkness rather than light, gave
the *power of becoming children of God* if they wished."[23]

Thus salvation, according to Berruyer, at least before the coming of Christ, had lain within the free will of every man to choose.
The Fall had not vitiated man's nature. Pagans were not necessarily wicked. Indeed, Berruyer went out of his way, in recount-
ing the Bible story, to explain that pagans might be very worthy
men. Describing the voyage of St. Paul to Rome, he told how
the party landed at the island of Malta, where they were received
most cordially. The natives, he observes, were regarded by the
Romans as barbarians—"but these barbarians, if not very pol-
ished, were at heart the most humane of man."

And he proceeds to generalize much like a *philosophe*. "Despite
the deprivation to which we are reduced by the sin of our first
fathers, we do not cease to be men, that is charitable, kind and
compassionate, except when, by art or education, we graft upon
the foundation of humanity the vices which dishonor it, and
which we do not bring with us from our mothers' wombs."[24]
Sin, that is to say, was an act of our first fathers, a mere historical
event, now happily remote; today we are blameless, and except
when education and society corrupt us, virtuous and good.

Such ideas of human nature were to many Christians extremely
unwelcome. The church, perhaps, might have countenanced them.
Except for the archbishop of Lyons, who was half a Jansenist,
the high ecclesiastical officials who censured Berruyer rarely referred to his views on nature, grace, revelation, scripture, or
tradition. They condemned him for having turned the Bible into
an up-to-date novel. The Jansenists definitely objected to his principles. For years the *Nouvelles Ecclésiastiques* campaigned against
him. Through the 'fifties and early 'sixties of the century, when
the writings of unbelievers were accumulating thick about them,
the editors of this journal never wavered in their attack. Berruyer
is easily the author they most frequently mention, even in the

[23] Berruyer, *op. cit.*, Second Part, Vol. VIII, p. 217. Italics Berruyer's.
[24] *ibid.*, Vol. VII, pp. 305-6.

momentous years 1762 and 1763, when Rousseau's *Contrat Social* and *Émile* were raising a turmoil in the world of letters.[25]

The most weighty attack, however, was delivered by Fitz-James, a Gallicized son of the Scottish Fitz-James who had come in exile to France with James II. This Fitz-James, who from 1739 to 1764 was bishop of Soissons, commissioned the Jansenist Gourlin, who also wrote for the bishop of Alais and for the *Nouvelles Ecclésiastiques,* to make a thorough examination of the doctrines of both Hardouin and Berruyer. The resulting work, issued as a Pastoral Instruction to the diocese of Soissons, filled four large volumes, and was translated into Italian.

Published in the early 1760's, this theological treatise formed part of the propaganda by which enemies of the Jesuits brought about their downfall. It was, however, a carefully written work, not inaccurate in its quotations. Its arguments were those of the *Nouvelles Ecclésiastiques* and of other Jansenist tracts of the time. We need not consider them at length. Briefly, Fitz-James (or Gourlin) accuses Hardouin and Berruyer and the Jesuits generally of preaching two true religions, the revealed and the natural, by either of which men may be justified before God. He charges them with perverting the doctrine of the Council of Trent on original sin. He reproaches them with undermining the authority of the church by destroying the validity of its written evidence. He scoffs at the notion that ancient writings, because of differences in intellectual background, may be unintelligible to modern men. If we must be Catholics in order to understand them in a Catholic sense, he asks, how can we ever hope to argue with heretics and infidels? He is scandalized at the idea that Christ rarely mentioned religious doctrine in his recorded utterances. Above all, he is aghast at the thought that tradition depends entirely on the present teaching of the church. "To assert, as Berruyer does, that it is in the present teaching of the Roman Church that the tradition of all the ages is to be sought, is, under a false appearance of respect for the teaching of the church, to take away the support which it finds in tradition; it is to represent this teaching as isolated, lost in a solitude, shut up in the present time; when on the contrary it is a chain, a perpetual continuation of teaching,

[25] *Nouvelles ecclésiastiques,* 1763, pp. 73, 75 and *passim.*

always sufficient and always uniform, which has lasted without interruption from the Apostles to us, and will last until the consummation of the ages."[26]

Certainly Hardouin and Berruyer would agree that Catholic tradition was perpetual, uniform, and unerring. They simply did not try to prove it by documents. They were in the way of being historians, and they knew that the documents in question did not irresistibly compel an unsympathetic mind to assent to the Catholic interpretation. They were aware that too much investigation of the past might lead men to doubt many things that were said about it. They therefore boldly affirmed that if Catholic authority was to stand, it could stand only by its sheer weight in the present. They held that belief in the church was a matter of faith to which historical argument was unnecessary and irrelevant. In their view, the claim of the church to be supernatural and divine needed no support from natural, historical, or documentary evidence, and should be emancipated from evidence of this kind. They distinguished questions of authority from questions of history, the supernatural from the natural, faith from reason. They carried on the traditions of the Jesuit order, for their most audacious speculations were intended to fortify the power of the Catholic Church.

[26] Fitz-James, *op. cit.*, Vol. I, pp. 17 *ff.*, 78 *ff.*, 108, 112, Vol. III, p. 144, Vol. IV, pp. 170-1; *Oeuvres posthumes* (Avignon, 1769), Vol. I, pp. 110-31, 282.

CHAPTER IV

THE FACT OF REVELATION

THE main problem for all Catholic apologists in the eighteenth century was to establish the authority of the church. Hardouin and Berruyer sought to establish it by historical skepticism. Most apologists took exactly the opposite course. They held that the revelation which the church claimed to possess was a fact of history, to be confirmed by the most rigorous historical method. Their attempts to rest the argument on this basis of fact were not entirely successful. They were often obliged to appeal to the authority of the church in evaluating historical testimony, particularly on the decisive question of miracles, and so slipped toward the position of Hardouin and Berruyer, who maintained, frankly and cheerfully, that the only ground for Catholic belief was faith in the Catholic Church itself.

Against unbelievers who had no such faith the argument of historical fact was undoubtedly the strongest that could be used. It was useless to invoke tradition against men who rejected it. It was useless to assert that established religion was necessary to society, or that Christianity gave the most satisfactory explanation of man's life, for both these contentions, whether or not true, could easily be questioned, and were in fact denied by the unbelievers. Such arguments were pragmatic, and pragmatic arguments could not establish an absolute authority. The dominant school of apologists therefore undertook to prove religion by facts alone, to demonstrate empirically that a supernatural world existed. They hoped in this way to meet their opponents on their own ground.

It is doubtful, however, whether the *philosophes* were really to be persuaded by citation of facts. They disbelieved in the supernatural with a conviction that no amount of evidence could shake.

Diderot stated the faith of a militant rationalist: "A single demonstration impresses me more than fifty facts. Thanks to the extreme confidence that I have in my reason, my faith is not at the mercy of every charlatan. . . . I am more sure of my judgment than of my eyes." He therefore defies the "pontiff of Mohammed" to display his wonders; though the blind see and the dead rise from the grave, still he will not believe the pontiff's teaching. "Why pester me with prodigies when all you need to convince me is a syllogism?"

Montesquieu, writing to his friend Warburton, bishop in the Church of England, delivered the opinion of a gentleman and humanist: "It is not impossible to attack a revealed religion, because a revealed religion exists by particular facts, and facts by their nature may be matter of dispute; but it is not the same with natural religion, for natural religion is drawn from the nature of man, on which there can be no dispute, and from the inner sentiment of man, on which again there can be no dispute."

Rousseau raised the cry of a Protestant and a democrat. Driven from France and condemned at Geneva for having published his *Émile,* he was hidden away in a little Swiss village, where, standing up at a pine board fastened to his wall, he wrote his replies to the spiritual powers that had condemned him. The one addressed to the Catholics he called, with a republican flourish, a letter from Jean-Jacques Rousseau, "Citizen of Geneva," to Christophe de Beaumont, "Archbishop of Paris, Duke of Saint-Cloud, Peer of France, Commander of the Order of the Holy Ghost, Provisor of the Sorbonne, etc." The letter was a plea for natural religion in place of revealed, or, more exactly, a protest against the kind of revelation which, having occurred in the remote past, was communicated to men through a long line of intermediate persons. "How many men between God and me!" "Is it simple, is it natural that God should have gone in search of Moses to speak to Jean-Jacques Rousseau?"[1]

To all such objections the leading apologists had one invariable answer, that whether or not it was reasonable, simple, or natural, revelation had in fact occurred. In an important sense the ortho-

[1] Diderot, *Oeuvres* (Paris, 1875-77), Vol. I, p. 149; Montesquieu, *Oeuvres* (1 vol., Paris, 1835), p. 672; Rousseau, *Oeuvres* (Bruxelles, 1827-28), Vol. VII, p. 31, Vol. XVI, p. 130.

dox were the skeptics and the *philosophes* the true men of faith. Like the great scholastics of the thirteenth century, the *philosophes* believed in the rationality of the ultimate nature of things. The rational and the real were for them the same, and they therefore thought that truth was to be known by processes of reasoning. Like Thomas Aquinas, they demanded that their beliefs should satisfy their intelligence, and that religion should express the true nature of man.

The dominant apologists, on the other hand, followed rather in the tracks of William of Occam. In the four hundred years since the time of Occam, faith in reason and natural law, broadly speaking, had passed from religion into lay philosophy. Now, in the eighteenth century, it was the *philosophes* who most actively held that faith. The orthodox, therefore, especially when consciously opposing the *philosophes,* as in the writing of apologetics, tended strongly to Occam's position. Like him, they were unable (except by religious faith) to affirm the ultimate rationality of things. The world in their eyes was less the product of God's reason than of his will. There was no ascertainable reason why anything should be as it was; everything might have been different, had God willed it so; and the only way of discovering what existed was by experience of the facts. Hence it was beside the point to ask whether it was reasonable for God to have made a special revelation, or whether the mysteries were in harmony with reason or with the nature of God or man. It was enough to know that the revelation had in fact been made, and that the mysteries had in fact been given to men to believe.

The danger in this way of dealing with the problem was that reason and faith might become totally divorced. Eighteenth century apologists hardly escaped the danger, but at the beginning of the century a means of avoiding it was offered by Leibniz. In his *Theodicy,* Leibniz included a "Discourse on the harmony of faith and reason," written in answer to Pierre Bayle. Bayle, citing numerous theologians, had argued that the Christian mysteries were inconceivable and contrary to reason, and hence could be believed only by an act of faith. Leibniz denied that the mysteries were contrary to reason. By reason he meant the objective relation between necessary truths, the logical and mathematical consistency of ideas. The regularities of nature were not necessary truths, since they might have been otherwise without logical contradiction; they were simply the observed order of phenomena, and as such had nothing to do with right reason in the strict sense. "Pure and naked Reason," he said, "as distinguished from Experience, has to do only with truths independent of sense." The Christian mysteries and miracles, therefore, when they clashed with the usual facts of experience, were by no means contrary to reason itself. Indeed, they must be in entire harmony with reason, for God, though he could suspend the contingent order of nature at will, could not suspend the laws of right reason which were of his very essence.[2]

The apologists of the eighteenth century generally made little use of this part of Leibniz' argument. They tended to slip rather into the position of Bayle. For it was Bayle's rather than Leibniz' view of reason which dominated the eighteenth century, which apologists therefore had to meet, and which indeed they understood better themselves. Reason in the eighteenth century meant not objective rationality but the critical faculty of the human mind. It judged the very facts of common experience from which Leibniz had sought to free it. The reasonable, in the Age of Reason, meant what was plausible to common sense.

The apologists were thus under pressure to put the mysteries, not only "above reason," but beyond the reach of rational study altogether, to shut up reason and faith in separate compartments, and to emphasize the very unintelligibility of the dogmas. To defend revealed truths they availed themselves of another part of Leibniz' argument, and at the same time avoided the pure fideism of Bayle, by maintaining that these truths were to be believed, not because in themselves they carried any conviction, but because their revelation had been accompanied by certain historical facts, namely the miracles and the fulfilment of prophecies.

The Abbé Houteville, in his *Religion chrétienne prouvée par les faits,* first published in 1722, struck out on the path that leading apologists through the century were to follow. His work became standard, and was many times reprinted. The problem, as he stated it at the outset, was to know whether the mind, in believing what it cannot conceive, may be sure that it is avoiding the traps of error. "Our mysteries, as such," he said, "are inaccessible to man living on earth; we confess it. Vainly does he try to bring

---

[2] Leibniz, *Essais de théodicée* (Amsterdam, 1712), pp. 1-104.

light upon them; a jealous night redoubles in proportion as he tries to remove it. The mysteries are the quicksand of reason and are matter of faith. That is the side of darkness. But the certainty of these same mysteries is bound up with evident and known truths, and is inseparable from them. That is the side of light. We believe, but our belief has solid foundations, and we demonstrate it to whoever wishes to hear. Do you ask what kind of proof it is that is so triumphant over rebellions of the mind? It is facts—that is, what is most palpable, most trenchant, and most persuasive."

The question was an historical one, and Houteville laid down rules of evidence of which any historian would approve. A fact, he said, before being accepted as true, must first of all be possible; it must be reported by two or more witnesses, who must be informed, sincere, and without reason to deceive; it must fit in with other known facts; and it must not be contradicted by contemporaries, or distorted by the intervening generations through which knowledge of it reaches the present.[3]

"Religion, facts, events, proved geometrically!" cried the Abbé Nonotte in amazement, when Diderot demanded a syllogism instead of a prodigy. ". . . Can any but fanatics and madmen speak like the author of the *Pensées Philosophiques*?" The words are significant. For Nonotte as for Houteville, "religion, facts events" all went together, and had little to do with the requirements of abstract reason. In place of reasoning the apologists offered the data of history. The Abbé Calmet explained copiously in twenty-two volumes how every statement in the Old and New Testaments could be literally true. There were many others eager to perform the same task on a less gigantic scale. Did the infidels ask how Noah and his three sons could have built the ark, even in the hundred years that Genesis allowed them? Father Fournier, a professor of hydrography, had an explanation: Archias of Corinth, with three hundred workmen, had built in one year the

[3] C. Houteville, *La religion chrétienne prouvée par les faits* (Paris, 1722), pp. 3, 18-20. See also the earlier work of J. Denyse, *La vérité de la religion chrétienne démontrée par ordre géométrique* (Paris, 1717), which despite its title argues purely from fact; and, as a curiosity, P. Rulié, *La religion chrétienne prouvée par un seul fait, ou Dissertation dans laquelle on démontre que les Catholiques à qui Hunéric, roi des Vandales, fit couper la langue, parlèrent miraculeusement* (Paris, 1766), reprinted in 1889 by the Société Catholique des Bons Livres.

great ship of Hiero of Syracuse; therefore three workmen in a hundred years could build a ship equally capacious. But the infidels objected that three men could not move the big trees used in so large a vessel. The Abbé Bullet advanced another hypothesis: Noah could have hired workmen, who, though not believing in the prophecy of the deluge, would be willing to help build the ark for wages.[4]

By such matter-of-fact explanations the sacred writings were to be proved credible. The faithful themselves could no longer understand the Biblical narrative without interpreting in the light of common sense. They hoped, by making most of it seem probable, to have the occasional miracles more readily believed. They assumed that the wonders would be accepted only if the writers told, on the whole, a sensible story. Indeed, the Abbé Bergier once let slip the suggestion that the miracles themselves might have arisen from natural causes, although, like all the apologists, he meant to use the miracles to prove supernatural intervention.[5] His suggestion, though made accidentally and in haste, betrayed a fundamental and very general difficulty.

Apologists had two tasks to perform: they must show that most of the facts in the Bible were easily possible, but that some of the facts were possible only by special action of the Almighty. The trouble was that the conception of miracles was itself ambiguous. It could be important only at a time when the physical world was thought to be generally regular. When, as in Biblical times, men have no clear notion of the regularity of physical phenomena, they can have no clear idea of the exceptional and the miraculous. Only in a sophisticated society do men distinguish between the marvellous and the natural, and only men who believe in laws of nature can use miracles as a convincing form of evidence.

All the leading apologists made great use of the miracles, because, like Houteville, they all began by asserting that the revealed doctrines were utterly mysterious and unintelligible. In this

[4] C. Nonotte, *Dictionnaire philosophique de la religion* (n.p., 1773), p. 350; A. Calmet, *Commentaire littéral sur tous les livres de l'Ancien et du Nouveau Testament* (22 vols., Paris, 1707-16), reprinted 1724-26 in 9 fol. vols.; J. B. Bullet, *Réponses critiques à plusieurs difficultés proposées par les nouveaux incrédules sur divers endroits des Livres Saints* (Paris, 1773), pp. 14-15. Bullet quotes Fournier.

[5] N. Bergier, *Réponse aux conseils raisonnables* (1773), pp. 58-9.

respect their tactics were different from those generally adopted in England, where such churchmen as Clarke, Butler, and Paley did all they could to harmonize Christian doctrine with eighteenth century reasonableness. The difference was perhaps ultimately a result of difference in the principle of authority in the churches of England and of France. In France and the Catholic world it was possible, and was indeed the part of wisdom, to attempt to prove only that revelation had taken place, and to leave its meaning to be interpreted by the church; the problem, above all others, was to prove the divine authority of an established institution.

The apologists who took such pains to argue from history, hoping to meet the doubters on the ground of fact, complained indignantly that their enemies refused battle on those terms. The doubters, indeed, entrenched themselves on the higher ground of abstract reason. The defenders of Christianity could with difficulty engage them, because there was a difference of opinion on the first of Houteville's principles of evidence, namely what kind of facts were possible. The unbelievers, with their faith in reason and nature, were persuaded in advance that they knew what was impossible. Diderot, for example, once declared that if every person in Paris told him that a dead man had just come to life, he would not believe it. The faithful, on the other hand, being on this matter Occamites and empiricists, would not presume to set bounds to the Almighty, or to judge what was possible before hearing the evidence.

Revelation, they kept repeating, has in fact occurred, and here is the historical testimony. "Revelation, say the Christians, *is a fact*; and hence they argue to prove that it exists. If this method were followed, they might have the advantage. But a subtle way of taking the advantage from them is to answer, *Revelation is a doctrine*. From this point the whole face of the thesis changes; the question of fact is abandoned, and the argument falls upon the doctrine." Or as the Abbé Trublet expressed it: "Whatever objections may be made to the mysteries of religion, we must believe them, say their defenders, if Christ and his apostles performed the miracles related in the New Testament. Now Christ and his apostles did perform these miracles. Hence, etc. What does the unbeliever reply to this? . . . He objects to the mysteries."

Or the archbishop of Lyons: "To sum up, revelation is the sole foundation of our faith, and the certainty of this revelation is based on facts which we consider to be as indubitable as any that history reports. If, then, there were a reasonable way to attack religion, it would be to undermine these facts and to overthrow the authentic monuments which bear witness to them." But the infidels only trifle; they use the method, "so unreasonable and inappropriate [*injuste*], of submitting the certainty of facts to the rules of probability, ancient usages to the customs of the present, the designs of God to the reason of men"—or they resort to anecdote, burlesque, and vulgarity to amuse the fops of Paris.[6]

It was not quite true, of course, that the infidels paid no attention to the facts cited by their opponents. They studied very closely the allegations that Noah had put two animals of every species into the ark, that the sun had stood still while Joshua finished his battle, that Jesus had walked on the waters, and that the apostles had spoken foreign languages with a remarkable facility. If they were impatient in dismissing such stories as childish, and rather obtuse in seeing no spiritual value in them, they were at least meeting the arguments of their opponents, who demanded a literal understanding of the texts and founded the truth of Christianity on the actual occurrence of physical prodigies.

But it was true, as the apologists complained, that the unbelievers were not arguing strictly from fact. They were arguing, as the archbishop of Lyons said, from the custom of the present and the reason of men, and above all from probability, *vraisemblance,* or what seemed true to them. Such arguments in themselves could not determine questions of fact in the past. They were useless without the assumption of a uniformity of nature through time, by which the probability of the eighteenth century became a test for events in the first. And to make this assumption was to beg the very question that the apologists raised.

The issue, as believers saw it, was simply this: given knowledge drawn from historical testimony and knowledge drawn from contemporary observation of nature, which of the two, when they con-

[6] G. Gauchat, *Le philosophe du Valais* (Amsterdam, 1772), Vol. I, p. 83; N. Trublet, *Essais de littérature et de morale* (1749), Vol. II, pp. 416-17; A. de Malvin de Montazet, archbishop of Lyons, *Instruction pastorale sur les sources de l'incrédulité* (Paris, 1776), pp. 58-9.

flict, are we to doubt? Can history certify facts which natural science pronounces to be impossible? The answer was evident to the infidels. "The testimony of men," said Rousseau, "is then at bottom only the testimony of my own reason, and adds nothing to the means that God has given me for knowing truth."[7]

The argument was much like that of Hume, who reduced human testimony and sense phenomena to forms of individual experience, and then argued that, in the experience of every individual, it was more likely that men should lie than that nature should be inconstant. Rousseau's reason, like Hume's "experience," found that nature was invariably regular. It was perhaps the testimony of Newton and other scientists that had planted this information in Rousseau's mind, but once implanted and germinated it became the dictate of reason itself, and made it necessary to reject, as mere human opinion, the contrary testimony of the Bible and general belief of Christendom. The reply given by the Abbé Gauchat was judicious. "The testimony of men," he said, "has a preponderant weight even in the objects of reasoning. . . . On matters of fact it is testimony that decides, and not only does testimony assist our reason, but without it it is wholly impossible for reason to know the facts. . . . The nature of the facts makes no difference. In this respect all witnesses have equal authority."[8] That is to say, we are never entitled, when we pretend to learn from facts, to reject those as false which seem to us extraordinary. Or, in more general terms, it is impossible empirically to disprove the supernatural.[9]

[7] *Oeuvres*, Vol. VII, p. 30.

[8] G. Gauchat, *Lettres critiques, ou Analyse et réfutation de divers écrits modernes contre la religion* (Paris, 1755-63), Vol. XIX, pp. 205 ff.

[9] On the belief that, since the content of the revealed doctrines is beyond the reach of the human understanding, their truth can best be demonstrated by the "extrinsic" evidence of historical fact, see almost any apologist of the time, but especially: Para de Phanjas, *Principes de la saine philosophie conciliés avec ceux de la religion* (Paris, 1774), Vol. II, pp. 64-9, where it is held that there can be no relevant argument against the mysteries since no one can possibly have any conception of them; Gauchat, *Lettres critiques*, Vol. XVII, p. 129, who declares that the church itself does not pretend to understand the mysteries and to demands for explanation answers simply, "Je ne sais rien. Ces objets sont certains, mais incompréhensibles"; Le Franc de Pompignan, bishop of Puy, *Oeuvres* (Paris, 1855), Vol. I, p. 364, where we are told that there are two uses of reason in religion, one to explain the objects of belief, the other the motives for belief, and that only the latter is legitimate; the *Avertissement du clergé sur*

The doubters were in a stronger position when, instead of dogmatically denying the supernatural, they sought to show how belief in miracles had naturally arisen. Their efforts in this direction were rather heavy handed, for, with the exception of Rousseau, they neither had nor wanted any understanding of religious minds. They therefore generally regarded the workers of miracles as impostors and the witnesses as fools. The founder of a revealed religion, in their view, was simply a man cleverer than his fellows, who, in the words of Voltaire's Mohammed, had "conceived a project" to "deceive the world" by "taking advantage of the errors of the earth." This theory, such as it was, served its purpose of making religion intelligible to rationalists of the time. It reduced the unknown to the known, the allegedly supernatural to the all too natural ignorance of uninstructed men. The theory was of course denounced by the faithful. Pope Benedict XIV, indeed, seems to have enjoyed Voltaire's *Mahomet,* or *Le Fanatisme* as Voltaire frankly called it, but on the complaint of certain of the French clergy its performance in Paris was stopped by the police.[10] It should have been evident enough that Voltaire and the other *philosophes,* when they said Mohammed, meant Jesus Christ.

The apologists, fully as much as the infidels, needed a natural and sensible explanation of the origin of belief in miracles. They represented the witnesses to the acts of Christ as men difficult to convince, little disposed to believe in the supernatural, carefully on their guard against irrational enthusiasms, withholding their assent until they had seen and judged the evidence, and at last yield-

les dangers de l'incrédulité (Paris, 1770), p. 16, where these motives for belief are enumerated as follows: "Il semble que la certitude de la révélation se manifeste à tous les sens de l'homme et à toutes les facultés de son âme. Faits extraordinaires et miraculeux, prédictions justifiées par l'événement, promesses de l'Ancienne Alliance accomplies, caractère divin du Messie, ébranlement de la nature au moment de sa mort, témoignages non équivoques de sa résurrection, choix des Apôtres, conversion éclatante de l'Univers, constance inébranlable des martyrs, enchaînement sublime de la doctrine, excellence des préceptes, perpétuité de l'enseignement." So definitely historical was much of the argument that it is not surprising that Henri Griffet, a prominent apologist, was the author of a technical manual on historical method, *Traité des différentes sortes de preuves qui servent à établir la vérité de l'histoire* (Liége, 1769), which was not a polemical work, and was praised by Grimm, *Correspondance littéraire* (Paris, 1877-82), Vol. IX, p. 217.

[10] See the letters exchanged between Voltaire and Benedict XIV, which Voltaire published as an introduction to *Le Fanatisme, Oeuvres* (Paris, 1883-85), Vol. IV, pp. 101-5.

ing to the overpowering pressure of the facts. Thus while the infidels regarded the first Christians as simple dupes, the religious
writers thought of them as distrustful intellectuals.

One of the earliest of the characteristic eighteenth century
school, whose book appeared in 1717, declared it axiomatic that
men are not easily credulous, and set up precisely the same alternatives as the infidels, arguing that the apostles either knew by
factual evidence that what they preached was a true revelation,
or else were "the most impudent liars and manifest impostors that
the world has ever seen."[11] Houteville laid down the same principles, and so did the other leading apologists. On this matter they
were as rationalistic as their adversaries. They were all willing to
accept the same statement of alternatives: either the miracles had
happened exactly as reported, or the first Christians were deliberate
frauds. And when poor misunderstood Rousseau, unable to take
either of the two choices thus offered, groped for a third explanation, and suggested that Jesus might have been lifted above common sense by the sublimity of his message, he was roundly denounced by all parties concerned.

The theory of martyrs worked out by the apologists confirmed
their arguments of fact. It perhaps did inadequate justice to men
and women who had died for religion, but it relieved them of the
odium of fanaticism placed upon them by the infidels. The infidels had pointed out that all religions had their martyrs, that men
had let themselves be tortured for Mohammed as well as for Christ,
and that martyrdom therefore proved nothing except the stubbornness of the victims and the cruelty of the persecutors. The apologists answered by defining a true martyr as a person who had died
purely for empirical facts.

Bergier set forth the argument fully. He explained why it was
only the Jews and the Christians who could claim true martyrs.
"Facts are the only kind of proofs on which witnesses can be admitted, whence it follows that Christianity is the only religion in
which the testimony of martyrs can prove anything, because, along
with Judaism, it is the only religion based on certain and incon-
testable facts. If a witness gives his life to attest that he has seen
and touched a man who had been pronounced dead, what court on

---

[11] Denyse, *op. cit.*, p. 12; Houteville, *op. cit.*, p. 6.

earth would not admit his testimony? But if a philosopher offers his head to demonstrate the truth of his opinions and alleged proofs, what sensible man would be willing to trust such evidence?"[12] Those, he said, who had died rather than abjure their faith in Mohammed, or in Luther or Calvin, had died only for their religious opinions. They were therefore not martyrs but fanatics, and their death could prove nothing, because on matters of opinion they might have been deceived. But men are not deceived by their own senses; and the true Catholic martyrs, when they died, only meant to testify to what they had touched with their hands and seen with their bodily eyes, namely Christ risen from the tomb. Catholic martyrs were thus not fanatics; they were witnesses, and their death had a positive value as evidence. And Catholics who had died for their faith since apostolic times had also died for facts, not for opinions, for even if they had never themselves seen a miracle or a martyr, they could trust in tradition, which, joining the first century with the eighteenth in the unchanging Church Universal, brought it about that "the facts of the Gospel are as certain with respect to us as with respect to the apostles who saw them." By the mystical unity of the church, Catholics of all ages were witnesses to the facts that had happened in Galilee, and if necessary they might seal these facts with their death.[13]

It is evident that something was assumed here that was not purely factual. Even as Bergier states the case, it appears that later martyrs died less for facts than for the validity of tradition, which, as has been seen in the preceding chapter, was nothing other than the authority of the church itself. The Catholic martyr proved the authority of the church by dying for facts, but he knew the facts through the authority of the church. His death was therefore not likely to prove much to infidels, although he may be the more admired for having died for his faith instead of for historical particulars. Nor could the eyewitnesses of apostolic times, who themselves saw the miracles, be said to have died for their knowledge of visible facts alone, since even if these facts were as reported, they added to them the faith that God existed and was speaking to them in this extraordinary way. To meet this difficulty

[12] N. Bergier, *Certitude des preuves du christianisme* (Paris, 1773), Vol. II, pp. 48-9.
[13] *ibid.*, pp. 44-52.

the apologists usually proved the existence of God by other arguments.

The theory of martyrs remained factual enough, however, to raise serious questions about the religious thinking of the time. The martyrs, according to the theory, were pure empiricists. They died for mere phenomena. A true martyr was one who, with little interest in doctrine, testified to the occurrence of certain facts. A man who died for a doctrine, for a moral conviction, a sense of justice or an idea of life, was, by the theory, a false martyr and a fanatic. The business of the martyrs was to certify the miracles. It was to establish the fact of revelation. The meaning and content of the revelation it was not for them to understand. However wild, improbable, or unintelligible they might think the revealed doctrine to be, they were to accept it because the man who revealed it had baffled them with prodigies.

Some apologists seemed even to maintain that the improbability of Christianity was strong evidence of its truth. When the infidels dismissed Jesus as an impostor, these defenders of the faith replied that if he had really expected to impose on men he would have made his teaching more plausible.[14] Let us turn to the Abbé Chaudon, who was felicitated by two popes for his great work in writing the *Dictionnaire anti-philosophique*.

Chaudon was of the opinion that the usual works of apologetics were too ponderous to be read by the worldlings who most needed them. He composed, therefore, a popular work, *L'homme du monde éclairé*, in which he set out to meet the infidels with their own weapons, joking and trifling with the subject in order to win attention.[15] One of his arguments, which he certainly meant to be taken seriously, was, to put it plainly, that Christianity was so absurd that it could have been fastened on men only by the supernatural. "If the omnipotence of the Supreme Being had not shown itself in the birth of Christianity, by evident and indisputable wonders, would the world have believed in mysteries which at first glance seem so incredible? Would it have submitted to practices so rude and harsh? Would it have put its heart and mind to such vexations because a few fishermen of the lake of Galilee, simple men without

[14] Denyse, *op. cit.*, pp. 16-17.
[15] A. Monod, *De Pascal à Chateaubriand* (Paris, 1916), p. 431; *Journal ecclésiastique* (1774), p. 90.

influence or culture, had come to impose chains upon them? Is such a change in the nature of man? Is it conceivable, without recourse to the supernatural?"[16]

Chaudon, it will be noted, had his idea of the "nature of man." It was human nature as seen in the people of eighteenth century Paris, civilized and sophisticated, urban and sensible, little inclined to ecstasies or intuitions, and still less to ascetic rigors. The Christian religion was thus not one that men would be likely to have embraced naturally. This was precisely the opinion of the infidels. The difference was that the unnaturalness of Christianity was explained by one party as a result of human cunning, and by the other as a sign of supernatural will.

There was consequently a tendency to regard Christianity as a burden, a discipline imposed from without. The less it seemed to spring from the nature of man, the more it seemed to be a system of positive law dictated by authority. Such a tendency was especially to be observed among the Jesuits, who both took what rationalists would call an enlightened view of human nature, and at the same time were the most insistent upholders of the principle of absolute authority. Hence some modern and unfriendly critics of Catholicism have thought that the further the church departed from the theology of St. Augustine the more it passed into legalism and became a system of police.[17] And the more acutely the dogmas were felt to be incomprehensible and at variance with what was known or assumed about the physical world, the more did belief in them come to be emphasized as a merit, and submission to the unintelligible eulogized as a virtue. The effect seems to have been to make the unbelievers more narrowly rationalistic in Catholic countries than in Protestant, and the faithful more resolute in insisting both on inconceivable doctrines and on the empirical occurrence of miracles.

Apologists often spoke of the "sacrifice of the mind" as necessary to Christian piety. To worship God in spirit and in truth, said Gauchat, meant humbly to accept the dogmas. "Yes, my brethren," cried Torné, a leading preacher of the day, "it is a proof of a noble nature and an elevated mind to believe in the mysteries of religion. There is a certain pettiness of spirit in rejecting them because we

[16] L. Chaudon, *L'homme du monde éclairé* (Paris, 1774), pp. 34-5.
[17] cf. F. Heiler, *Der Katholizismus* (München, 1923), pp. 106-7, 149-57.

do not understand them. In repressing the unjust revolts of reason we lift ourselves above humanity; we move toward the divine intelligence; we soar, where we were made to crawl."

And the alternative to reason, the means of soaring, for Torné as for others, was not unregulated intuition or imagination or any mystical or romantic sense; it was belief in "the oracles of supreme authority," founded on such empirical phenomena as miracles. The Catholic Church, according to an official statement of the French clergy, by transmitting these oracles to its members, relieved them from the need of examining doctrine. It was necessary that the mysteries should remain inaccessible to the human mind. "Would a man wish that God, by lowering the barriers, should deprive him wholly or partly of the merit of his obedience and of his faith?"[18]

The view of religion as a system for conferring merit was expressed frankly by a certain Father Gamaches. "Since we are destined to win merit, we necessarily have duties to fulfil and even sacrifices to make." Ordinary duties like benevolence and truthfulness, he says, are natural to us; hence in performing them we make no sacrifice and can deserve no supernatural reward. To win merit we must do what we do not wish to; we must feel the burden of a positive law. The Christian revelation provides such a law. "It requires of a man that by the practice of the virtues that it consecrates he sacrifice his tastes, the tenderest inclinations of his heart, his dearest affections; it demands that to this painful sacrifice he add that of his mind and his intelligence [*lumières*], and prefer to them the mysterious obscurities of a quantity of dogmas capable of astonishing his reason; and finally, since there should remain for the Christian no faculty that does not furnish material for sacrifice, religion offers to the eyes of his faith an august object which specious appearances conceal, and of whose reality he can assure himself only by the sacrifice of his senses." This august object, needless to say, is the consecrated host. It is difficult to find, in the rest of the book, any evidence that the author saw much independent significance in either the mass or the in-

[18] Gauchat, *Lettres critiques,* Vol. XVII, pp. 18, 146; A. Bernard, *Le sermon au dix-huitième siècle* (Paris, 1901), p. 424; *Avertissement de l'Assemblée Générale du Clergé de France sur les effets pernicieux de l'incrédulité* (Paris, 1775), p. 10. This *Avertissement* was written by Le Franc de Pompignan, in whose *Oeuvres* it is included.

carnation of Christ. The value of the mass, for him, seems to have lain in the opportunity it gave the believer for winning merit by disregarding the evidence of his eyes.[19]

In all the great enterprise of proving the invisible by the visible, of resting religion upon a basis of fact, there was an embarrassing difficulty to overcome, namely the circumstance that similar facts were reported from erroneous religions. The infidels raised the objection with much glee: heretics and Mohammedans, they pointed out, had their miracles, which they believed in as firmly as orthodox Catholics in theirs. And there were the Jansenists, declaring that God had vouchsafed them miracles within five minutes' walk of the Sorbonne, at the tomb of their Abbé Pâris, in the years following 1730. If, then, miracles proved a doctrine, heresy and heathenism seemed to be proved.

Clearly, from the orthodox point of view, these outlandish prodigies could not be true miracles. But could they be shown to be false purely by arguments of fact? If not, then the whole attempt to prove the true religion by facts alone was brought into question. If the facts had to be selected before they proved anything, then it was the principle of selection that was the real proof. The apologists could hardly escape arguing in a circle: they wished to prove Catholicism by miracles, but their only means of telling which miracles were genuine was to ask which of them proved Catholicism. The principle of selection was precisely that truth of doctrine which the facts selected were supposed to establish.

The resulting confusion was well illustrated in the *Journal Ecclésiastique*. In one place, in a review of a book by the Abbé Hooke of the Sorbonne, the writer maintains, with Hooke, that the doctrine cannot be made the test of the miracles. To argue so, they agree, is hopelessly to embroil the whole question. The miracles must prove the doctrine, not the doctrine the miracles.[20] But in another place, in a "Dissertation sur la force probante des miracles," a more ambiguous position is taken. The author of this article admits that the prodigies of false teachers may often be, to all appearances, genuinely miraculous. These false teachers, he holds,

<hr />

[19] E. Gamaches, *Système du philosophe chrétien* (Paris, 1746), pp. 1-33. On the idea of earning reward by free sacrifice cf. P. Antoine, *Theologia moralis* (1783), p. 11: ". . . ut actio sit meritoria debet esse nostra, sic ut illam dare possimus velut pretium pro praemio."

[20] *Journal ecclésiastique* (1774), February, p. 178, March, pp. 273-4.

are impostors working in collusion with the devil. Purity of the doctrine distinguishes the true miracle, which then in turn confirms and fortifies the doctrine.

The author is torn between his desire to show that prodigies really prove something and his fear that they may prove too much. He quotes from the Bible: "If a prophet arises among you who prophesies some prodigy, and even if that prodigy comes to pass, should he say, Let us follow strange gods, and serve them; you shall not listen to him." No miracles then, we are to believe, may justify a religious innovation. But had not Christianity once been an innovation? No, the author stoutly maintains; for the God whom Jesus invoked was the God in whom the Jews already believed. The miracles of Jesus, like those of Moses, were true miracles with a positive value as evidence, because the doctrine of Jesus and Moses was true. For the same reason the Catholic miracles performed since apostolic times are known to be genuine, and when Calvinists dispute them they are mistaken. "I say to the Calvinist . . . you assert that our doctrine is false; that is your error." Having this view of the matter, the author is never able to explain why the miracles are not superfluous, since the true doctrine is known without them. All that he shows is that by the miracles the doctrine is confirmed, signalized, and, as he says, given a certain *éclat*.[21]

The enlightened *Journal de Trévoux,* edited by the Jesuits, was particularly concerned to find means by which such prodigies as those of the Jansenists could be disposed of. The question was discussed in a review of François's *Preuves de la religion de Jésus-Christ*. The reviewer commended François for relying chiefly on the argument from miracles, which he agreed was the safest, but he found that François had not set up sufficient tests for distinguishing true miracles. "It seems that it would be well also that the doctrine to be established by miracles should be recognized in advance as good, that is, such in itself that there be seen in it no opposition either to the natural law or to the positive divine law, if any be already revealed. This requirement has the advantage of shutting at one stroke the mouths of heretics who claim to establish by miracles a doctrine contrary to the Gospel and to the teaching of the church."

---

[21] *ibid.* (1768), April, pp. 1-19. The quotation from the Bible is from Deut. xiii.

Thus in effect it was to be tradition and natural law, rather than prodigies, that supplied the authority for belief. "If any pretended thaumaturge came to announce a doctrine contrary to the principles of that primordial law engraved on our hearts and destined to bring light on our actions, we should have to reject him, and consider his prodigies as fables and lies. . . ."[22] Clearly the reviewer was talking much like a *philosophe.* The Jansenist miracles, so untimely and embarrassing in the eighteenth century, gave the orthodox a taste of the skepticism felt by the unbelievers.

The Jansenists maintained that if their miracles were false, then those reported in the New Testament were false also. The orthodox were shocked at the idea, which if true would seem to make all Christianity as dubious as Jansenism, and hence they held it impossible for the supernatural power that had founded the church to be now working against it. Like the *philosophes,* and in the same terms, they denounced the Jansenists as convulsionaries and their miracles as hocus-pocus. They might have said, by changing one word, *roi* to *foi,* in the famous epigram which someone coined when the king's officers suppressed the manifestations at the grave of the Abbé Pâris:

> De par la foi, défense à Dieu
> De faire miracle en ce lieu.

Churchmen argued that the Jansenist miracles were known to be false because Jansenist doctrine was known to be heretical.[23] It is not clear whether they realized that they thus implicitly denied the possibility of proving anything by miracles alone. It seems impossible to say of France, as Leslie Stephen said of England, that by the middle of the century the argument from miracles had

[22] *Journal de Trévoux* (1751), pp. 2393, 2395. On the Jansenist miracles see P. Mathieu, *Histoire des miraculés et convulsionnaires de Saint-Médard* (Paris, 1864); A. Gazier, *Histoire du mouvement janséniste* (Paris, 1922), Vol. I, pp. 276-96; E. Préclin, *Les jansénistes du dix-huitième siècle* (Paris, 1929), pp. 133 *ff.*, 173 *ff.* Some of the cases of faith healing and stigmatization seem to be as well authenticated as any in history.

[23] J. Fumel, bishop of Lodève, *Instruction pastorale sur les sources de l'incrédulité* (Paris, 1765), pp. 261-2. "N'êtes-vous pas scandalisés, M. T. C. F., d'entendre dire que la voix dont les Prophètes, le Messie, les Apôtres et leurs disciples ont été les organes, s'explique aujourd'hui par le ministère de ces Prophètes ou Prophétesses convulsionnaires qui n'ouvrent la bouche que pour blasphémer contre les successeurs de Jésus-Christ et contre tous les fidèles soumis à leur enseignement?"

sunk to a place of secondary importance. The Catholic Church had
to stand by its miracles, because the authority that it claimed was
so absolute as to require palpable evidence of the supernatural.
In pure logic, however, the attempt to prove religion empirically,
by the testimony of eyewitnesses to sense phenomena, became exceedingly difficult to sustain. Like the rationalists with their reason,
the apologists had, in the tradition of the church, a higher test
by which they could reject as impossible the phenomena that told
against them.

The peculiarity of this eighteenth century apologetic was that it
made revelation an historical event. It took pride in believing on
testimony, that is, on the experience of others. It sought its strongest evidence in the past. If religion thus seemed to degenerate into
a question of history, it was not entirely the fault of the religious;
they were forced into such a course by the necessities of debate,
and some of the apologists, when not troubled with infidels, were
men of genuine personal devotion. Nevertheless, one retains an
impression that the prevailing religious atmosphere was rather cool.
Believers were content to regard revelation as a purely factual
question that had been settled long in the past. They thought of
the first converts as level-headed sensible men, who had carefully
examined the evidence set before them, because the believers themselves, as men of the eighteenth century, knew that that was what
they would do before accepting a new religion. It seemed to them
that if the first Christians had been convinced, later comers would
do well to accept the findings of those who might be presumed to
know best; that if the revelation had been false it would have
been disproved long ago by philosophers; that since many ancient
philosophers, instead of disproving it, had been converted to it
despite their earlier persuasions, philosophers of the eighteenth
century should know that their objections were feeble and ill-
advised.

The Abbé Nonotte wrote a whole book on this last point. He
represented Origen, Tertullian, and other ancient thinkers who
had voluntarily embraced Christianity as men of vast learning and
deep understanding, and contrasted them with the vain, noisy,
superficial, self-styled *philosophes* who in the eighteenth century
wilfully rejected it. There was a general feeling that the modern
unbelievers only raised objections that had long ago been answered,

and the Assembly of the Clergy, as a part of its program for refuting the infidels, arranged for the publication of new editions of the Fathers. The idea that the *philosophes* would read the Fathers with any patience may be accounted one of the pious illusions of the time.[24]

We may summarize the defense of revelation, and form a picture of one of the defenders as an individual, by giving some attention to Nicolas-Sylvestre Bergier, who was then the most respected of the apologists. Bergier, though of obscure family and no connections, managed to rise by his abilities to a position of moderate distinction. He was born in 1718 in a small village in the Vosges. He attended the neighboring college of Besançon, and after being ordained went in 1745 to study at Paris. Then for sixteen years he served as parish priest at Flangebouche in the diocese of Besançon. Besides attending to his parish duties, and apparently greatly endearing himself to his flock, he entered into such intellectual life as provincial society afforded, and regularly took part in various contests held by the Academy of Besançon.

While still at Flangebouche, Bergier wrote his *Déisme réfuté par lui-même,* first published in 1765. It was a criticism of Rousseau, and was in effect the answer of a real curé to the Savoyard Vicar of Rousseau's imagination. In 1766 Bergier was made a member of the Academy of Besançon, and about this time became also director of the college. In 1767 he produced his *Certitude des preuves du Christianisme,* a reply to the now forgotten infidel Fréret. Two popes sent him letters of congratulation, and various rulers of Europe (which ones or how many we are not told) presented him with their portraits in miniature as tokens of esteem.

In 1769 he became a canon of Notre-Dame in Paris, and soon afterward moved to Versailles, to serve as confessor to "Mes-

---

[24] Bergier, *Certitude des preuves,* Vol. I, pp. 76, 222; I. Berruyer, *Histoire du peuple de Dieu,* Second Part, Vol. I, pp. 10-11; P. Sennemaud, *Pensées philosophiques d'un citoyen de Montmartre* (La Haye, 1756), 93; C. Nonotte, *Philosophes des trois premiers siècles de l'église, qui, ayant embrassé le Christianisme, en sont devenus les défenseurs par leurs écrits* (Paris, 1789); L. Troya d'Assigny (a Jansenist), *Saint-Augustin contre l'incrédulité* (Paris, 1754), and *Saint-Augustin en contraste avec les philosophes du siècle* (Paris, 1770); B. Rivière, Abbé Pelvert (another Jansenist), *Exposition succincte et comparaison de la doctrine des anciens et des nouveaux philosophes* (Paris, 1787); *Procès-verbal de l'Assemblée Générale du Clergé . . . tenue à Paris en l'année 1770* (Paris, 1776), pp. 116, 591.

dames de France," the daughters of Louis XV. In 1770 the Assembly of the Clergy granted him a pension of 2,000 livres a year, to give him leisure to write against the unbelievers. He composed a critical examination of Holbach and a great many less important writings, and took charge of the theological section of the *Encyclopédie Méthodique,* a venture even vaster, if less revolutionary, than Diderot's *Encyclopédie* of twenty years before. Bergier's articles on theology, filling twelve volumes when published independently, were reprinted as late as 1873. The last twenty years of his life he spent at Versailles, living quietly and industriously until his death in 1790.[25]

Fundamentally Bergier's argument was the same as Houteville's. It proceeded from the visible to the invisible, from the tangible facts of miracles to the intangible and inconceivable doctrines of religion. In minor ways Bergier showed the effects of the eighteenth century criticism. He declared, for example, to the great scandal of the Jansenists, that the Jews of the Old Testament had been a barbarous people with many primitive institutions, and that the language of the Bible was that of oriental metaphor, which often had to be understood in a figurative sense.[26] Since Houteville's time critics had found new grounds for believing that many books of the Bible had not been written by the authors whose name they bore. Bergier, who was concerned almost entirely with the New Testament, accepted the fact as possible, but replied that the Gospels did not for this reason necessarily become spurious. He suggested, like more modern critics, though the suggestion probably seemed sophistical to contemporary infidels, that early Christians with some knowledge of their own might have written down what they had experienced, and then named their story after one of the apostles without intention to deceive. He thought also that some of the apocryphal gospels, such as those to the Hebrews and the Egyptians, instead of throwing doubt on the canonical books as the infidels usually maintained, might be useful in giving corroborative evidence.[27]

[25] "Notice historique sur l'Abbé Bergier," in Bergier's *Dictionnaire de Théologie* (ed. 1831), Vol. I, pp. 1-21; *Procès-verbal de l'Assemblée Générale du Clergé . . . tenue à Paris en l'année 1770* (Paris, 1776), pp. 630-1. On Bergier see also below, pp. 215-18.

[26] *Nouvelles ecclésiastiques* (1771), pp. 5-6, 11.

[27] *Certitude des preuves,* Vol. I, pp. 1-80.

To the searching queries of Rousseau, who was often more a Protestant than a rationalist in spirit, Bergier gave an answer that was distinctively Catholic. Rousseau had complained, time and again, that too many men stood between him and his God, and declared that if God had spoken then he, Jean-Jacques Rousseau, ought to have heard. This was the protest of religious individualism. Bergier questioned the individualist premises on which it was based. Religion, he said, was not merely a private and personal experience; it was an alliance between God and man; and God had revealed himself, not to individuals, but to the human race as a unit. The revelation was mediated to mankind through a "corps of ambassadors," whose sovereign had provided them with unmistakable credentials. By this "corps of ambassadors" Bergier meant the first apostles and the Catholic clergy who succeeded them; and by their credentials he meant the miracles, martyrdoms and other evidences of God's favor. To reject this embassy was for Bergier to cease to be Christian. Rousseau, he thought, in the warm praises of Jesus put into the "Profession of Faith of the Savoyard Vicar," spoke not as a Christian but as a "sectary of Christian morality."[28]

Rousseau had also demanded that religious truth be intelligible, and here again he was more the Protestant than the infidel, since his object was not to discredit religion so much as to find it. He thought that revealed knowledge should throw light upon natural, and he affirmed the belief that God neither would nor could propose to men mysteries which they were unable to conceive and which had no bearing on their natural existence. He therefore held that the objects of faith should be open to critical examination. "Faith," he said, "becomes surer and firmer through the understanding."

Bergier denied these assertions, which, whether made from Protestant or from infidel motives, were obviously rationalistic. He explained that a communication from an infinite to a finite being must necessarily surpass the comprehension of the latter. He denied the rationalist assumption that if men used their reason they would all agree on a few simple truths. Unregulated reasoning meant for him intellectual anarchy. He thought that if the test of belief were to be the private judgment of individuals there

---

[28] *Le déisme réfuté par lui-même* (Paris, 1771), Vol. I, pp. 127-35. This work was reprinted as late as 1838.

could be no possibility of arguing against the atheists and materialists whom Rousseau himself so heartily detested. He added
that only belief in the unintelligible could confer any merit, and
that God wished a free and willing sacrifice of the mind. Rousseau's distaste for ritual seemed to him as perverse as his dislike
of dogmas. Since religion, for Bergier and for Catholics generally, was not so much a system of morals as an alliance between
God and man, it followed that ceremony and ritual were a necessary part of it, and that God would have revealed the form of
worship that he was most pleased to receive. There was, moreover,
the practical argument that "without an external, public, and uniform cult, religion could not long subsist among men."[29]

It was not enough for Bergier to show that God could have made
a revelation, or that men in any case were obliged to accept much
that they could not understand. It was necessary to show that God
had entrusted a specific revelation to the Catholic Church. Bergier
argued this point in the same way as the other apologists. Revelation, he said, was a free act of God, arising only from his will; it
might or might not have taken place, and the only way to decide
the question was by appeal to empirical facts.[30] Bergier thus rested
his case heavily on the miracles.

When Rousseau raised the common objection, arguing that
miracles had been performed by the unorthodox, and that therefore
we can tell the genuineness of the miracle only by the purity of
the doctrine, Bergier, more bold than most contemporaries, stoutly
insisted that false miracles could always be exposed by empirical
tests, that the prodigies of impostors were never as wonderful as
those of true believers, and that the magicians of Pharaoh, for
example, had been able to imitate only a few of the true miracles of
Moses.[31] He announced that the miracles certified the doctrine,
never the doctrine the miracles. He understood the implications
too well ever to depart willingly from this principle. To make concessions, he was aware, would be to allow the very criticism of
doctrine that Rousseau demanded. Hence to strengthen his argument he was logically obliged, as in any case he was tempera-

---

[29] ibid., passim, but especially Vol. I, pp. 16 ff., 46, 66-7, 82-4, 95-105, Vol. II,
pp. 167-8; Rousseau, Oeuvres, Vol. VII, pp. 25-37.

[30] Le déisme réfuté par lui-même, Vol. I, pp. 119-28.

[31] ibid., Vol. I, pp. 151-3, Vol. II, pp. 170-4, 180-259. Certitude des preuves,
passim.

mentally inclined, to represent the early Christians as cool judges of evidence, and the martyrs as disinterested witnesses to sensory phenomena.[32]

But Bergier was no more able than others to maintain this position unshaken. The Jansenists offered the miraculous cures of their Abbé Pâris as proof that they possessed God's true revelation. Fréret and other infidels lost no time in seizing their advantage and explaining all miracles as products of human credulity. The orthodox had to concede the credulity of the Jansenists, but they drew distinctions. "The people," said Bergier, "may sometimes let themselves be seduced when they have nothing to risk or an advantage to gain; but when life and fortune are concerned it is neither prudent to try them nor easy to succeed." Offering an example that would seem to endanger his whole position, he asserted that a Turk who performed miracles in Paris would convert no one to Mohammedanism. The Jansenist miracles he attributed merely to the enthusiasm of a fanatical sect. "Prejudiced persons obstinate in certain opinions wanted miracles in order to give themselves authority; they were resolved to have them at any price, and it is not surprising that they should boast of having succeeded. But it is not Christianity that gave birth to the miracles of Christ and the apostles; it was the miracles that gave birth to Christianity. Those who saw them were not prejudiced in favor of Christ and the apostles nor had they any interest in seeing miracles; they were Jews and Pagans when they saw them; and it was by the miracles that they were converted, and it was against their prejudices, at the cost of their peace, their fortunes and their lives that they saw and attested them."[33] That is to say, men had followed Christ against their will, because they were persuaded by miracles that, whatever his teaching was, it must be true and binding. In contrast to these men, the Jansenists were stubborn in their convictions; their primary interest was in doctrine. The real objection

[32] *Examen du matérialisme* (Paris, 1771), Vol. II, p. 32, where it is argued that the Christian revelation is the more certain for having been "née dans un siècle très-éclairé, établie sur des faits publics et éclatants, non point sur des visions ou des révélations particulières, prêchée d'abord à des peuples qui avaient une religion différente, et naturellement prévenus contre les faits et contre des dogmes qu'on leur annonçait." See also *Certitude des preuves*, Vol. I, pp. 136, 214-15.

[33] *Certitude des preuves*, Vol. I, pp. 228-31.

to them, in the minds of the orthodox, was that they raised doc-
trinal questions that were supposed to have been put to rest once
and for all. "You who are Christians," said Bergier, addressing
them, "believe that God performed manifest miracles to found
his church, with which he promised to remain until the consummation of the ages; then God could not, without contradicting
himself and failing in his word, today perform miracles to author-
ize a doctrine contrary to that of his church."[34]

This line of reasoning unfortunately begged the question that
the Jansenists raised, namely, what the true doctrine of the church
was. Bergier was denying his own principle, and using correctness
of doctrine to determine the validity of miracles. To that extent
he was no longer arguing from empirical fact, and it was one of
his virtues that he intermittently admitted it. He declared, like
others, that the authority of the church rested not on Scripture
but on the apostolic succession and continuity of tradition. Christianity was thus not supported by the mere evidence of books.
"As for the miracles, it is false that they have no guarantees
*except books whose truth can be proved only by recourse to his-
tory.*" The miracles are not known simply by written testimony;
they are "sufficiently attested by the whole world, by the monuments they have left, and by the astonishing revolution that they
produced."[35] What he means is that the subsequent existence of
the church, continuing into the present, was evidence of the facts
upon which Christianity was thought to be founded. The Christian
religion, he said, could have existed without any written scriptures, and the Catholic Church would not for that reason be the
less authentic.

In arguing thus, Bergier in effect shifted his position from
history to tradition, in the sense given to these words in the preceding chapter. He founded his belief in the true miracles and

---

[34] *Le déisme réfuté*, Vol. I, p. 158.

[35] *Certitude des preuves*, Vol. II, pp. 165-9. The words in italics were so written by Bergier, as a means of showing that he quoted them from Fréret. cf.
ibid., Vol. I, p. 233: "Les miracles de Jésus-Christ ont pour garant le monde
entier converti, l'aveu de ses propres ennemis, le témoignage sanglant de ceux
qui les ont vus, la Religion Chrétienne toujours subsistante, malgré dix-sept
siècles de combats . . ."; and *ibid.*, Vol. II, p. 169: "Il est vrai qu'en examinant
ces miracles selon toutes les règles de l'histoire les savants peuvent en acquérir
un nouveau degré de certitude, et affermir par leur témoignage la foi des simples
déjà suffisament fondée."

supernatural mission of Christ on his faith in the living existence of the supernatural church. In deciding which of many reported "facts" to consider valid, he was guided, not purely by the evidence of historical documents, and in the last analysis not at all by such evidence, but by his belief that the church possessed in its tradition a means of validating facts independent of evidence. He applied in practice the arguments that Hardouin and Berruyer had accepted in principle. Strictly speaking, however, if Bergier and other apologists were ultimately forced into this position, they were perhaps in a logical difficulty no worse than that of their opponents. Catholics could not prove, nor unbelievers disprove, the occurrence of miracles on empirical or historical grounds. Both had to set limits to the uses of testimony. Faced with any quantity of such testimony or with any number of witnesses, Catholics would not believe that true miracles could be performed by the unorthodox, nor *philosophes* that they could be performed at all.

Both parties used historical evidence within the framework of a larger faith, which for the one party was belief in the tradition of the church, and for the other the conviction that nature conformed to general laws uniformly through the ages. We begin to suspect that the German was right who said that man is saved not by history but by metaphysics.

CHAPTER V

SOME MODERNIZERS

THE apologists of what may be called the official school, such men as Houteville and Bergier, as we have just seen, sought chiefly to prove revelation as an historical event, on which the authority of the church was founded. They argued from what they supposed the infidels would find most convincing, the empirical data of sense, perceived by the eyes and hands of witnesses. It was in the physical world of sensory phenomena that they saw most clearly the workings of the supernatural; these workings they called miracles, and they proposed to deal with them, as most thinkers of the time proposed to deal with all phenomena, by the method of observation and experience. They eschewed reasoning about the content or meaning of the dogmas. Even the Abbé Lignac, probably the most considerable metaphysician among defenders of the church, deplored the attempt to reconcile faith and reason, arguing that the truths of faith would be compromised if associated with the ephemeral productions of the human mind.[1]

Faith itself drove believers into a kind of skepticism. In the fear that reason might endanger their religion they sometimes took a position familiar to us today, holding that reason was only a mental faculty, and that systems built by reason were mere fashions of the times.

In pure apologetic, directed against unbelievers, this separation of faith from reason had the great advantage of making most objections to Christian doctrine formally irrelevant. But apologetic is a strained and artificial form of religious thinking; the rules, the field, and the weapons must all be chosen with an eye to the enemy. The separation of faith from reason, limiting religious thinking to a study of evidence, and turning attention away from

[1] J. Le Large de Lignac, *Le témoignage du sens intime et de l'expérience opposé à la foi profane et ridicule des fatalistes modernes* (Auxerre, 1760), Vol. III, p. 224.

the content of doctrine, although it might be useful in dealing with infidels and might even be recommended to the faithful by the authorities in the church, could not be wholly satisfying to men serious in their religion. Such men could not shut off religion from the rest of their mental life. They continued to think and to reason about Christianity. When, instead of arguing about revelation, they could either assume it or drop it from consciousness, it was possible for them to give up discussions of historical testimony, and to enter into questions of moral or metaphysical significance. Some Christian thinkers, by throwing doubt on the sensationalist psychology, attacked the vast structure of Enlightenment at its base. The *philosophes* ridiculed them for their belief in "innate ideas," but did not entirely answer their arguments. Others carried the offensive into other quarters, criticizing the accepted ideas of the infidels on nature, pleasure, progress, time, and the creation of the world.

In the present chapter, however, a somewhat different group of theorists calls for examination. They hardly constitute a group at all, except by an act of arbitrary classification. They had in common a passion for explanations. They usually set out to understand certain mysteries which more cautious thinkers held to be unintelligible. Most of them passed beyond the bounds of orthodoxy, and some of them were officially condemned. Against the objections of infidels they set up their own views of the meaning and content of Christian doctrines, sometimes inventing whole cosmologies to suit their needs. They thus differed from the official apologists in not limiting the defense of religion to the question of historical fact. They differed from the more searching critics mentioned above in having no keen sense of their adversaries' assumptions. They thought of themselves as standing in the full course of the modern Enlightenment. Among them may be recognized various types that have since been familiar in Christendom: the person who wants desperately to keep up to date; the somewhat befuddled progressive who hopes to embrace new ideas without losing anything of value in the old; the matter-of-fact toiler who reconciles science and theology, usually by turning theology into a celestial physics; the enthusiast who seizes upon every new natural wonder as further evidence of the invisible world; the outright madman, who brings together religion and science by reducing both to a cabalistic symbolism.

A mild kind of unconscious modernization, which had nothing to do with doctrine or ideas, became apparent simply through the habits of speech and literary manner of the time. Something of this influence would make itself felt almost universally. A particular example is furnished in the *Christiade* of the Abbé La Baume-Desdossat. The author wished to write a work of Christian piety in the form of an heroic poem. Choosing the life of Christ as his subject, he hoped to produce a sequel to Milton's *Paradise Lost*. He followed the conventions of epic poetry, introduced lists of high-sounding names, and put stiff speeches into the mouths of the characters. It was in prose, however, that he really wrote, though in a style which he elevated as much as he could. Long prose-poems were not uncommon in that age, when men found it easier to be stately than poetic.

The Abbé La Baume was perfectly matter-of-fact. Leaving nothing to imagination, he inserted long footnotes, more copious than the text itself, to explain in plain language at the bottom of his pages what he meant to say in the more exalted diction at the top. In the life of Jesus he saw a career of common sense punctuated by miracles. The temptation in the wilderness he presented as a kind of conversational duel, in which Jesus debated with Satan, remonstrated with him, analyzed his errors, and then stated his own views, only to be whisked off into the air by the evil spirit in the end. Prosy though the poem may have been, it satisfied some readers; Fréron, always a religious man and often a discerning critic, pronounced it to be as far above Milton's *Paradise Regained* as *Paradise Lost* was above any epic in the French language. Others found it dangerous and unseemly. The Parlement of Paris formally condemned it. It is likely that they took alarm at its superficial resemblance to the second part of Berruyer's *Peuple de Dieu,* which appeared in the same year. The *Christiade,* like the *Peuple de Dieu,* gave offense because it seemed to turn the Gospel into a fashionable romance.[2]

[2] Abbé J. F. de La Baume-Desdossat, *La Christiade, ou le Paradis reconquis, pour servir de suite au Paradis Perdu de Milton* (Bruxelles, 1753) ; Fréron, *Année littéraire* (1754), Vol. I, pp. 171-2; *Nouvelles ecclésiastiques* (1753), pp. 45-8.

Among modernizers who consciously sought to reconcile science and religion the most numerous and the most orthodox were the people who demonstrated God's Providence through the newly discovered intricacies of nature. They enjoyed their greatest popularity during the first half of the century, and produced a large number of books, among them a series by the German Lesser, available in French, called the *Theology of Stones, The Theology of Insects,* etc. There was a general belief, among both deists and Christians, that materialism had been discredited by certain discoveries associated with the difficult names of Malpighi, Muschembroek, Hartzoeker, and Nieuwentyt, "the heralds of Providence." These men, among the early microscopists, had made notable discoveries on the structure of living bodies. Their work led to the framing of the germ theory, which held, in its eighteenth century form, that every organism developed from a germ which had probably existed since the creation of the world, and which contained within itself the full organism in miniature. Hence men of all kinds, from orthodox apologists to Diderot himself, argued that life had not arisen from a concourse of material atoms, and that the process of growth showed the existence of plan and purpose in the world.[3]

The best known French representative of the teleological school was the Abbé Pluche. His *Spectacle de la Nature,* in eight volumes, was first published in 1732 and many times reprinted. It was partly a work of popular science, partly a general survey of civilization, and partly a compendium of arguments for the truth of Christianity, graded to meet the intellectual needs of various kinds of readers. Pluche was one of the great popularizers of the age, and quite possibly was the most widely influential, since many people could read him with confidence who would distrust every statement made by a known infidel.

Of five hundred private libraries of that time whose catalogues have been examined by Professor Daniel Mornet, the *Spectacle de la Nature* was in 206—the most frequently found of all works written in the eighteenth century, except only Buffon's *Histoire naturelle.* In these same five hundred libraries the works of mili-

---

[3] *Journal de Trévoux* (1753), pp. 1423, 1431; N. Pluche, *Le spectacle de la nature* (Paris, 1732); Diderot, *Oeuvres* (Paris, 1875-77), Vol. I, p. 133; B. Nieuwentyt, *L'existence de Dieu démontrée par les merveilles de la nature* (Paris, 1725); F. Lesser, *La lithothéologie, ou La théologie des pierres* (1735), and *La théologie des insectes* (1738).

tant enlightenment were much more rare: the *Encyclopédie* was to be found in 82, Rousseau's spectacular *Discours sur l'origine de l'inégalité* in 76, and the *Contrat social* in only one.[4] Pluche was competent and informed, and understood the art in which the French excel, that of making difficult matters clear to laymen; but he probably owed much of his success to the air of piety which he diffused over all the miscellaneous knowledge that he presented. He thus made it possible for the religious to keep abreast of new ideas in science and history. At the same time, and quite unintentionally, he prepared their minds for some far-reaching shifts of emphasis.

For example, except in the final volume where he turned to the proofs of revelation, he set most clearly before his readers a conception of a general providence, or of God as Contriver rather than as Father. His idea of man's place and destiny in the world was not very different from that of the rationalists, and even contained the germ from which a sentimental humanitarianism might be developed. With entire orthodoxy, he argued that the whole creation had been made expressly for man, since man was the image of God. But in explaining the high mystery of the image of God, he showed himself to be a child of the prevailing Enlightenment. Man was the image of his Maker, according to Pluche, because he was destined to control nature and to use the world as a source of enjoyment.

Pluche argued this proposition at great length, proving it from the ingenuity of man's anatomy, from "the certitude of animal functions," from capacity for pleasure, and from the possession of intelligence, memory, free will and conscience, which thus became, in his view, accessory to the higher end of control and enjoyment. He put great emphasis on the existence of pleasure as a sign of man's destiny. "The tender goodness of God toward man," he wrote, "shows itself openly in the quality and number of pleasures with which he has endowed him"; and he added that God wished pleasure to be lively and stimulating, to guide men more surely through their earthly life.[5]

[4] D. Mornet, "Les enseignements des bibliothèques privées, 1750-1780," in *Revue d'histoire littéraire de la France*, Vol. XVII (1910), pp. 449-96.
[5] Pluche, *op. cit.* (ed. Paris, 1771), Vol. V, pp. 20 *ff.*, 114-15, 167 *ff.*

Man's destiny was further elucidated by an obscure Dom Louis, who, toward the end of the century, undertook to bring up to date the mysteries of heaven. His views would not have been endorsed by the church, but may well have been shared by many members of the clergy. He called his book *Le ciel ouvert à tout l'univers*. He hoped to make everybody Christian by representing Christianity as pleasant, easy, and seductive. "How different is God from what we have thought! How great he is, how kind, how good, how merciful! How he scatters his blessings on the earth! How extensive are the rights of man!" The author declares that hell exists only in men's imagination, and he is inclined to attribute the invention of it to scheming priests. He maintains that everyone will go to heaven, and that men will differ there only in the amount of eternal happiness that they enjoy.[6]

Such ideas of eternity usually arise from a kind-heartedness that cannot look upon the irreducible ghastliness of evil, and it is not surprising that the author regarded the good as something that men could hardly avoid possessing. After defining virtue as the sentiment of a man who takes his proper part in "the admirably organized whole" of nature, and after commenting on the varied delights of the four seasons, he went on: "O fair Iris, how happy is man, how lovable woman! . . . To see what we love, what is most charming in Nature! two sensitive eyes, a fresh complexion, vermilion lips, *a mouth that calls for kisses, a tender look that tells us we may dare*—what enticements, what attractions, what joys! To embrace virtue, to die of pleasure in its arms, to be born again, to reproduce ourselves, to see our own image, a thing we have created, to caress our children. . . ."[7]

This is strange language to come from a Benedictine monk, and we hardly know whether to smile at such heated fancies, in which embracing virtue seems to be identical with falling on vermilion lips, or to take pity on a man who had shut himself off,

[6] Dom Louis, *Le ciel ouvert à tout l'univers* (1782), pp. 145 ff.

[7] *ibid.*, p. 154. Italics are Louis's. Louis may well have known Pierre Cuppé's *Le ciel ouvert à tous les hommes*, written in 1716, published in 1768, reprinted in 1783. I. O. Wade, in his *Clandestine Organization and Diffusion of Philosophic Ideas in France from 1700 to 1750* (Princeton, 1938), pp. 33-44, has noted thirty manuscript copies of Cuppé's work, more than of any other of the 102 surreptitious manuscript works that he has traced. The work circulated in manuscript as late as 1790. Dom Louis adds to the idea of universal salvation an erotic and sentimental note more characteristic of his time than of Cuppé's.

by religious vows, from the licit enjoyment of the things he most valued. The author, however, felt that he was a good Christian and Catholic, for he proceeded on the same page, by a sudden transition that would have been difficult to make in any century but the eighteenth, to exhort infidels to read the Bible, and he concluded sternly: "Outside the Church, the Truth and the Gospel there is no salvation."

Dom Louis's ideas, if somewhat irregular in a monk, were at least those of a normal and natural man. In a few scattered individuals the attempt to give a natural meaning to mysteries that had not been intended as descriptions of nature resulted in, or was induced by, a state of mind that can only be called deranged. One such unfortunate was Pierquin, who wrote a *Dissertation physico-théologique* on the virgin birth. Another was Bebescourt, who set out to show that the Christian mysteries were "physically true."

According to Bebescourt, the idea that the dogmas were unintelligible was embarrassing to believers and gave comfort to the infidels. He thought that the medieval philosophers had obscured the truth in a barbarous jargon. His own system, however, was extremely esoteric. He treated the Bible as a kind of cryptogram, arguing, for example, that Noah represented water, Ham earth, Shem fire and Japheth air. His reason for this last interpretation was that the Greek Ἰαφετης meant Sagittarius, and that it was in the form of *arrows* that the sun's rays were perceived in the air. He traced back the Trinity to emblematic triangles of ancient Egypt, and maintained that the three Persons expressed God perfectly, because the word "person" came from the Latin *perfecte sonans*. Such speculations were no doubt wild enough, but the author was in accord with the advanced thinkers of his time in his irritation at the scholastics, his feeling of personal enlightenment, his eagerness to give explanations, and his tendency to turn religion into a theory of phenomena.[8]

[8] J. Pierquin, *Dissertation physico-théologique* (Amsterdam, 1742); Bebescourt, *Les mystères du christianisme approfondis radicalement et reconnus physiquement vrais* (Londres, 1771), Vol. I, pp. 303-5, Vol. II, p. 5; see also the work of a man known to have lost his reason in youth, J. Chassaignan, *Cataractes de l'imagination, déluge de scribomanie, vomissement littéraire, hémorrhagie encyclopédique, monstre des monstres, par Epiménide inspiré. De l'antre de Trophonius, au pays des visions* (1779); *Biographie universelle,* "Chassaignan"; and a work of eccentric Bibliolatry by P. Dutoit-Mambrini, *La*

Some of the gravest difficulties for the traditional religion were presented by the new cosmology. The Copernican view of the world had come into the general thinking of the educated at the close of the seventeenth century, through the labors of such men as Newton and Fontenelle. In this view the universe was thought of as consisting mostly of open space, through which moving spheres were everywhere distributed. The earth became a tiny and lonely body following its sun through the cold wastes of infinity, ceaselessly moving but going nowhere, since neither center, boundary, nor direction was to be found. For men to whom this cosmic picture was particularly vivid, it became difficult to believe that the earth received any special attention from the Almighty. Some, called deists, argued that God was most purely conceived of as the designer of so intricate a machine, who made known his will to men not by special revelation but through natural laws that prevailed uniformly through his work. Those who kept their faith in special revelation no longer opposed the Copernican astronomy in the eighteenth century, but they were content not to follow its implications too far, and they would argue that, whatever might seem abstractly reasonable, a revelation was in fact known to have taken place on earth. A few, however, felt the full weight of the difficulties. Like the deists, they sought to preserve the uniformity of the universe by showing that the earth was not unique and that men were not specially favored. They constructed strange cosmologies, and lost themselves on dizzy heights of imaginative speculation; but their purpose was the matter-of-fact one of reconciling science and theology.

One such person wrote a short work famous in its day, called the *Traité de l'infini créé,* which circulated secretly in manuscript for more than twenty years, and was published anonymously in 1769.[9] The author is thought to have been the Abbé Terrasson, and was at any rate a disciple of Descartes, from whom he took his

philosophie divine (n.p., 1793), diffuse, enthusiastic and unintelligible, belonging to the illuminist school of the end of the century.

[9] *Traité de l'infini créé, avec explication de la possibilité de la transubstantiation et un petit traité de la confession et de la communion* (Amsterdam, 1769). The appended treatises are of no importance. Some editions bear the name of Malebranche, but he was certainly not the author. F. C. Bouillier, *Histoire de la philosophie cartésienne* (Paris, 1868), Vol. II, pp. 608-16, feels that there is enough reason to attribute it to Terrasson.

astronomy. He disclaimed, "what would be a crime," any desire to introduce anything new into Catholic faith; but, on the plea of merely renovating philosophy, he advanced some extremely heterodox opinions. With Bruno's passionate sense of unending worlds, and Descartes's philosophic belief that the objective universe was fundamentally pure extension, he maintained that space and matter were infinite, in the sense that they could be endlessly prolonged in straight lines—and eternal, in the sense that they existed through an endless series of moments in time. His conceptions of infinity and eternity, based on the idea of quantity rather than the absence or irrelevancy of quantity, were thus those of eighteenth century physics rather than of the more mystical forms of religion. He maintained, however, that this extended world, though it had no beginning and no bounds, was nevertheless created, since it was sustained and kept in being by a power not its own.

According to Terrasson (if he was the author), God created this infinite cosmos only to glorify himself, and could be glorified only by spiritual beings. There were therefore countless planetary systems inhabited by creatures comparable to men. And since, though matter was eternal, particular configurations came and went, there were at every moment many planets in all stages of Christian progress: some in the state of innocence, others in the state of sin, still others in process of redemption. In all, sooner or later, the Word became flesh and the inhabitants found union with God. There were thus an infinite number of Saviours, all different so far as they were human, all the same being so far as they were divine. Each planetary system was eventually dissolved into the unformed matter from which it came; the Last Judgment then took place, and the damned became devils, who henceforth roamed the universe doing evil in other planets, while the saved became troops of angels who wandered through infinity led by their man-God, glorifying their Creator, and watching over the worlds in which his purpose was not yet complete. Perhaps, the author suggested, it was these men-Gods who appeared to Abraham in the difficult passage in Genesis where the visitors are referred to sometimes as men, sometimes as God.[10]

Earthly Scripture was to be believed when it spoke of the creation of the world in time, but it was to be understood to mean only

[10] *Traité de l'infini créé*, pp. 43 ff., 95 ff., 126-9.

the assembling of the solar system from preexisting matter. The author explained that the Holy Spirit had dictated only what was necessary for salvation, and had purposely refrained from mentioning other worlds. He thought it likely that every planet had its own Scripture suited to its own needs. He never openly raised the question, which would have caused consternation in ecclesiastical circles, whether every planet had also its own Catholic Church and its own pope. He concluded his book with a hope that the church would approve his ideas, offering to change them rather than deviate from the faith, and declaring that they glorified God in a way never known before. The story is told of the Abbé Terrasson that, seeing no sense in poetry, he once dumbfounded a company in which Homer was being read aloud by asking bluntly "what that proved." If Terrasson wrote the *Infini Créé,* it may be said that he had more poetic imagination than most of his contemporaries to whom reading Homer was an elegant diversion, and that his weakness was in not knowing enough about poetry to recognize it when it took possession of him. He had a conception as magnificent as that of *Paradise Lost*; but, living in the age of prose and reason, he treated it as an hypothesis in physics, and became argumentative rather than poetical.

Another religious cosmologist was the Swiss Protestant, Charles Bonnet of Geneva. He had gained an international reputation as a biologist and microscopist, when weakened eyesight turned him to philosophy. A friend of the German Platonist Moses Mendelssohn, and of Lavater, the inventor of the supposed science of physiognomy, he was himself something between a sober scientist and a dreamer. In a superficial classification he might be set down as a belated thinker, a *philosophe attardé,* still troubled by outmoded superstitions; but it was precisely his religious beliefs that led him to anticipate certain nineteenth century ideas, by outlining a plan of organic and cosmic evolution. Bonnet, departing from the Christian idea of the perfectibility of the individual soul, arrived not at the idea of social progress so common among his contemporaries but at a theory of gradual development of the physical universe. There are historians who think that evolutionary ideas became possible in Europe because Christianity, unlike the religions of Asia, had implanted in the minds of its believers a strong sense of the reality of time and of temporal process. In Bonnet this transition is particularly evident.

Although he repeated the past and foreshadowed the future, Bonnet was very much a man of his time. He thought most easily in terms of matter and mechanism. Religion, he once said, was "a wheel in a machine," a cog which joined man to God and this life to the next. Like other followers of Locke, he thought that human personality could exist only with conscious memory, memory only with sensations, and sensations only with organized matter. In this conscious personality he saw the essence of the soul. It followed, therefore, that the soul must have a physical or at least a physiological basis. Since Bonnet firmly believed the soul to be immortal and destined to perfection in a future state, his problem was to find a material substance to which it should be attached both in this world and the next. He postulated a "subtle matter" or "small ethereal machine." Like Descartes, he thought this subtle matter to be enclosed in the pineal gland, which had no discoverable anatomical function, though strategically placed between the two halves of the brain; but he doubted whether anatomists would ever be able actually to see it.[11]

The subtle matter, or ethereal machine, was for Bonnet practically identical with the soul itself. The antithesis in his mind was not between body and spirit, but between gross matter and subtle matter, both of which he regarded as physical. The survival after death of the subtle matter was necessary to bring about the resurrection of the body promised by revelation, which Bonnet considered a deeply philosophical doctrine, and to give continuous personality to the individual on earth and in heaven. Granted this theory, said Bonnet, "the small ethereal machine would be the germ of that spiritual and glorious body which revelation distinguishes from the base animal body. The more or less durable impressions produced by the nerves and ['vital'] spirits on the small machine . . . become the foundation of personality and connect the present to the future state. The Resurrection would then be only the prodigiously accelerated development of this germ now hidden in the pineal gland."[12] Or again: "It is the germ

[11] C. Bonnet, *La Palingénésie philosophique, ou Idées sur l'état passé et sur l'état futur des êtres vivants* (Genève, 1770), Vol. II, pp. 145 *ff*., 403 *ff*.
[12] *La contemplation de la nature* (Amsterdam, 1764), pp. 86-90.

enclosed in perishable integuments that would be the true seat of
the soul, and would properly constitute what may be called the
personality of man. The gross and terrestrial body that we see and
touch would be only the casing, the envelope or the husk."[13]

This identification of the soul with the germ was the keystone
of Bonnet's system. It joined the doctrines of revelation with
the recent hypotheses of experimental biologists. It made religion
scientific, by providing a physical machinery for immortality; and
at the same time it introduced into science, or at least into Bonnet's
scientific speculations, the old religious faith in a cosmic tendency
toward improvement. The Christian destiny of the human soul
became the destiny of a "subtle matter" active throughout the universe. With his idea that the soul was in a sense physical and that
it took form through sensations, Bonnet was willing to believe
that something like a soul existed in all animals.

Many infidel philosophers of the time also believed in the *âme
des bêtes;* the idea followed naturally from the philosophy of
Locke, and was useful in throwing doubt on revealed religion.
With Bonnet, however, religious beliefs gave the idea an unusual
significance. In conferring souls upon the animals he conferred
on them also the faculty of perfectibility, which most infidels held
to be the distinguishing attribute of man. Bonnet, putting angels,
men, and animals into one comprehensive physical system, passed
from eschatology to evolution.

"Will a philosopher," he asked, "deny that the animal is a perfectible being, and perfectible in an unlimited degree? Give the
oyster the sense of sight which it apparently lacks, and how greatly
will you improve its being! How much more would you not improve it in giving it, lowly as it is, a greater number of senses
and corresponding members!"[14] Thus far he only repeated what
some others, among them Diderot, had already said. He proceeded
to add his own explanations, a strange mixture of the religious
idea of immortality and the scientific idea of the continuity of
life. "What philosophic reasons require us to believe that death is
the end of this animal's existence? Why should so perfectible a
being be forever annihilated, when it possesses a principle of per-

[13] *Recherches philosophiques sur les preuves du christianisme* (Genève, 1770),
p. 20. This work is a reprint of part of the author's *Palingénésie.*
[14] *Palingénésie,* Vol. I, p. 182.

fectibility to which we can assign no limits? . . . It will be understood, of course . . . that the animals must not be thought of
as having in their future state the same form and structure, the
same parts, the same consistency, and the same size as we see in
them in their present state. They will differ as much from what
they are today as the state of our globe will differ from its present
state."[15]

Bonnet did not mean that the animals were to go to heaven.
He did mean (and it was his whole message) that by the same
process as that by which men became heavenly beings the animals
would be raised into higher organic forms. The reasons he gave
for their evolution were exactly the same as those he gave to explain the resurrection of man. "I have shown fully enough . . .
how probable it is that the animals are called to put on some day
another state, which will improve and ennoble their faculties. I
have made it evident that the physical means of this improvement
may exist in the animal now, and may have existed since the
beginning of things. I speak of that imperishable germ to which
I conceive the soul to be united and which it cannot abandon. It is
this soul forever united to this invisible body [the subtle matter]
which constitutes, in my hypothesis, the true personality of the
animal. All else is but the covering, the envelope or the mask."[16]

In this system not only was the disparity of men and animals
done away with, but the distinction between natural and supernatural, between earth and heaven, was abolished. Worlds themselves were arranged in a rising order, in which some globes were
as far above the earth as man was above the monkey; and beyond
these worlds, as highest members of the same series, were the
hierarchies of the angels.[17] The whole creation was moving up-
ward with a single impulse, by which man would eventually reach
the angelic spheres, and the apes and elephants would succeed to
man's supremacy on earth, producing their Newtons and their
Leibnizes, and able in turn to know and glorify God.[18] Bonnet
never reached the point of saying that the human form had de-

[15] *ibid.*, Vol. I, p. 184.
[16] *ibid.*, Vol. II, pp. 4-5.
[17] *Contemplation de la nature,* Vol. I, pp. 84-6. On the idea of the "scale of
being," see also the author's *Essai de psychologie* (Londres, 1755), pp. 364-5,
371.
[18] *Palingénésie,* Vol. I, pp. 200-4.

veloped from the animal, or that animals would one day get to heaven; but he clearly believed that all living things, in heaven and on earth, differed only in the outer forms in which they clothed their inner substance, the subtle matter.[19] This subtle matter, identified as it was with the germ and with the soul, turns out, on close examination, to be much the same as what we today call simply "life." It was the substance underneath the forms, the subject of which evolution was the biography.

It cannot be emphasized too strongly that Bonnet was prompted to cosmic dreaming by the intense fervor of his religion. He used his theories to uphold the truth of the Bible: Moses, he said, had only described in Genesis the most recent of the geological cataclysms, but had taught the highest theological truth in referring the world to its Creator.[20]

But Bonnet was not one of the plodding host who set out to make the Bible seem reasonable. He was a troubled spirit, like Pascal—an accomplished experimental scientist, and an earnest Christian, who, when he looked at the heavens, could not share the cheery admiration of the philosophers for a universal blank. A seeming materialist, he filled the universe with a "subtle matter" to assert the principle of life; a seeming mechanist, he arrived at a thoroughgoing vitalism; a believer both in the uniformity of nature and in the moral destiny of man, he brought all living things into the same stream of progression toward God. He could not believe that man's was the highest created intelligence, and so he put at the summit of his "scale of being" the choirs of angels, whom he could imagine smiling with benign amusement on the

[19] "Remarquons enfin que nous lions une espèce de société avec les grands animaux." *Contemplation de la nature,* Vol. I, p. 74. It is to be noted that Bonnet, in his desire to order all living beings along a progressive scale, implicitly gives up the Christian idea of the equal worth of all men, arguing that the difference between the cannibal and the *Français humain,* or between the dull Huron and the *profond Anglais,* is so large as to show that men are not separated by any sharp break from the animals. *ibid.,* Vol. I, p. 82. Bonnet uses the word "evolution" in the following passage, and at the same time shows how he thought of it as a movement *away* from an initially created state: "Abuserais-je de la liberté de conjecturer, si je disais que les plantes et les animaux qui existent aujourd'hui sont provenus par une sorte d'*Évolution* naturelle [italics Bonnet's] des êtres organisés qui peuplaient ce premier monde sorti des mains du Créateur?" *Palingénésie,* Vol. I, p. 250.
[20] *ibid.,* Vol. I, pp. 241-57.

feeble reasoning of men. For himself, he looked forward to the time when, joining these hierarchies, he should soar from planet to planet and move from perfection to perfection in pure contemplation of the eternal. The last thirty pages of his greatest book, the *Palingénésie,* were an outpouring of religious ecstasy.

Bonnet, however, besides being a Protestant, was most eccentric in his theology, and stood quite outside the usual course of contemporary argument. Like Terrasson and some others, he is interesting for his very peculiarities, and so is not of great significance in the general trend of events. Lonely sallies decide no battles in the warfare of ideas. In this warfare, in the critical years after 1750, the two chief organized hosts, encamped in the narrow ground of the Latin Quarter, were the Faculty of Theology of Paris and the collaborators in the *Encyclopédie.* They came to grips for the first time over a purely academic incident, the presentation of a thesis for the licentiate in theology by the Abbé de Prades. Prades, who belonged to both sides, rose to fame by their struggles. He was looked upon by the *philosophes* as one of their most notable martyrs, and was regarded by the orthodox as an apostate, to be mentioned in the same breath with Bayle, Spinoza, and Voltaire. Thirty-five years later he was not forgotten, and the memory of his name was enough to cause trouble for a man supposed to have been his accomplice, the Abbé Yvon.[21]

No satisfying study of Prades has ever been made, although his case constituted one of those sensational *affaires* by which, at least in the opinion of foreigners, the French public is periodically convulsed.[22] He was born probably in 1720, and in 1752, when his doom fell, he had already been living in Paris for several years. He met Marmontel in 1746 or 1747, when the two had rooms in the same house in the Latin Quarter. Prades, according to Marmontel,

[21] Bachaumont, *Mémoires secrets,* Vol. XXXIII, p. 87.

[22] There is a thirty-two page study by C. Daux, *Une réhabilitation: l'Abbé Jean-Martin de Prades* (Arras, 1902), reprinted from *La Science Catholique,* October 1902. Daux is very sketchy on the critical year 1751, and gives most of his attention to Prades's later life in Germany. The most informative contemporary work is *Le Tombeau de la Sorbonne* (1752), printed in Voltaire, *Oeuvres* (1883-85), Vol. XXIV, pp. 17-28. The editors are doubtful of Voltaire's authorship. Bouillier, *op. cit.,* Vol. II, pp. 632-7, gives an account of the Prades affair. See also Feret, *La Faculté de Théologie de Paris et ses docteurs les plus célèbres,* Vol. VI, pp. 183-94.

was a studious young man of regular habits, and was working at a translation of the theology of Huet.[23] Marmontel at that time was already a protégé of Voltaire. He had recently come from Gascony to seek his fortune as a man of letters and *bel esprit* in the *salons*. It does not appear that Marmontel and Prades were ever very friendly; but it is safe to conjecture that a certain amount of fraternizing went on among the various kinds of intellectuals in that congested area, where students of theology and devotees of the new learning rubbed elbows every day, and drank their coffee over the same tables.

Diderot, who lived in the same neighborhood and earned a precarious living by writing short tracts calculated to astonish the conservative, had just undertaken the task of directing a new encyclopedia, which a combination of publishers had decided to issue as a commercial venture. The project was widely supported, even among men of the church, many of whom, like the laity, felt that they lived in an age of peculiar enlightenment, and thought it an advantage to have the new knowledge brought together in one place. It was not generally foreseen that Diderot and a few colleagues would capture the new encyclopedia, and turn into an engine of opinion a work that was expected to be a vehicle of information. The opposition developed after the publication of the first volume in July 1751, and was greatly stirred up by the Prades affair, which came early in 1752. The Prades affair was for many people the first revelation that the *Encyclopédie* was in the hands of religious unbelievers. For some years, however, there continued to be persons who seemed not to realize that fact, persons who wished to be on the side of enlightenment but could not see to what end enlightenment was leading. Billardon de Sauvigny, for example, a minor poet, published in 1758 his *Religion révélée*, which he concluded with an exhortation "to the deist,"

> *Puissent mes faibles vers allumer dans ton âme*
> *Le flambeau de la foi qui m'inspire et m'enflamme;*

but he included in the same small volume a second poem defending the Encyclopedists against the "cabal" that was attempting to suppress them:

[23] Marmontel, *Mémoires d'un père* (Paris, 1827), Vol. I, p. 160.

Diderot et d'Alembert, aux autels prosternés,
Des mains de la vertu se trouvent couronnés;
L'univers applaudit, et l'obscure cabale
Se replonge en tremblant dans la nuit infernale.[24]

Men who had such sentiments as Billardon, it is clear, could admire the *Encyclopédie,* or even associate themselves personally
with Diderot, without dreaming of questioning the Christian religion.

Diderot for his part needed a few theologians on his staff,
if only to make his enterprise presentable to the censors and to
the redoubtable Faculty. He therefore entrusted certain articles
to the Abbés Prades and Yvon. Yvon was the more important to
him; he was put in charge of the metaphysical section, and wrote
the articles "Âme," "Athée," "Dieu" and a few others. It is doubtful whether any of the leading contributors ever took their col-
league Yvon very seriously. Diderot, who in his prospectus called
him a profound metaphysician, later described him as a plagiarist.[25]
Yvon was, in fact, a man who had great respect for orthodoxy,
but wished also to keep up intellectually with the times, and who
therefore was regarded by true *philosophes* as an outsider, and
suspected by the religious authorities as unsound. His *Histoire
philosophique de la religion,* written in later life, was, as plain
history, better than anything written by the infidels on the subject;
but it revealed a state of mind almost pathetically confused; for
on the one hand he approved of systematic doubt, inveighed against
prejudice, and gave a categorical statement of the idea of progress,
and on the other hand declared man to have been created perfect,
argued indignantly against deists, and showed himself horrified
by the ideas of Holbach, seeing no connection between unbelief
and "philosophy."[26]

[24] L. Billardon de Sauvigny, *La religion révélée, poème en réponse à celui de
la Religion naturelle* (Genève, 1758), pp. 48, 64.
[25] *Encyclopédie,* Vol. I, p. xli, and *Oeuvres* (Paris, 1875-77), Vol. XX, p. 132.
cf. Grimm, "un autre théologien, ennuyeux comme il convient à sa profession,"
Correspondance littéraire, Vol. V, p. 392; Voltaire, "loin d'être un philosophe,
est un docteur en théologie," *Oeuvres,* Vol. XLI, p. 116.
[26] *Histoire philosophique de la religion* (Liége, 1779), Vol. I, pp. 3, 55, 264,
Vol. II, pp. 450, 453, 477-8. Yvon, who fled from France during the Prades
affair, returned in 1762. Bachaumont, *op. cit.,* Vol. I, pp. 41, 156, says that "tous
les matérialistes applaudissent au retour de cet illustre apôtre," but that he is on
good terms with the archbishop. During his exile Yvon wrote a book called *La*

From Prades Diderot accepted at least one article, a very important one, "Certitude." According to Diderot, who introduced the article in the *Encyclopédie* with some remarks of his own, this essay on certitude formed part of a general defense of Christianity which Prades was then preparing. The article aimed at showing that moral certainty might be equal to mathematical, and that historical evidence might give positive knowledge of past events. It thus served to strengthen the orthodox apologetic of the time. The second volume of the *Encyclopédie,* containing Prades's article, was published at the end of the year 1751.

Meanwhile, on November 18 of the same year, Prades came up for examination at the Sorbonne. His thesis, called *Jerusalem caelesti* and noteworthy for the elegance of its Latinity, was offered as a summary of arguments by which the Christian revelation might be proved. Prades defended it in Latin and French with great dash and assurance, and was passed unanimously by every one of the assembled doctors.

A few days later complaints began to be heard. Where they originated is not known—perhaps from students jealous of such a brilliant success, perhaps from Jansenists who wished to discredit the University, perhaps from Jesuits who wished to strike at the Encyclopedists. From whatever source, it was commonly reported by the end of the year that a collaborator in the Encyclopedia had managed to get monstrous impieties accepted at the Sorbonne. Critics looked back to an earlier thesis, successfully defended by the Abbé Brienne in October, which they said contained the same poison of materialism.[27]

Since an approved thesis became part of the official doctrine of the University, and since not a single voice had been raised against Prades at his examination, it seemed that the trusted upholders of orthodoxy were themselves tainted with the forbidden ideas. All Paris took alarm. Men spoke in frightened tones of an infidel plot against the faith.[28]

liberté de conscience reserrée dans des bornes légitimes (Londres, 1754), which was put on the papal index. F. Reusch, *Index der verbotenen Bücher* (Bonn, 1883-85), Vol. II, p. 939.

[27] C. Mey, *Remarques sur une thèse soutenue le samedi 30 octobre, 1751* (n.p.n.d.) ; *Nouvelles ecclésiastiques* (1752), p. 46.

[28] d'Argenson, *Mémoires* (Paris, 1859-67), Vol. VII, pp. 30, 47, 56-8, 63, 95, 97 ; Barbier, *Journal* (Paris, 1847-56), Vol. V, pp. 146-53.

Unfortunately it is at this point that everything becomes doubtful. It was alleged at the time that Prades's thesis had been written by Diderot. Modern scholars deny Diderot's authorship, but give no positive evidence. It is certain that the thesis was wholly in the tone of the Encyclopedist philosophy. It was, in fact, a masterpiece of compact expression of that philosophy, beginning with a concise statement of the sensationalist theory of the human mind, deducing society from the atomistic behavior of primitive individuals, proceeding to establish natural religion, exposing the conflicting chronologies of the Old Testament, reducing the miracles of Jesus to the same level as those of Esculapius, and arguing that the miracles of Jesus were of value as evidence only because prophets had foretold them. Prades's thesis thus differed from ordinary infidel writings only in its treatment of prophecies. Had Diderot wished to undermine revelation while seeming to defend it, he might well have chosen just such a course of argument as this.

Evidence that Prades could not have been the author was offered by the Abbé Bonhomme in 1754. Bonhomme printed what he asserted to be the three short preliminary theses which Prades, as a candidate for the licentiate, had offered in 1748, 1750, and July 1751. These three documents, all written in barbarous Latin, propounded commonplace theological problems in the clumsiest possible manner. All three, according to Bonhomme, were in the usual style of bachelors of theology.[29] The difference between them and the famous *thèse majeure* is immense. The hand of a practised writer is immediately evident in the latter, and the ideas expressed in it come from a different world. If Prades actually wrote the three theses published by Bonhomme, it may be considered as proved that he could not have written the *Jerusalem caelesti*. On the other hand it seems improbable that the studious young translator of Huet described by Marmontel, or the candidate who impressed his examiners by his showing in oral dispute, or the author of the article "Certitude" and of the *Apologie* issued two years later, could have penned the infantile jargon attributed to him by Bonhomme.

[29] Abbé Bonhomme, *Réflexions d'un franciscain sur les trois premiers volumes de l'Encyclopédie* (Berlin, 1754), pp. 179-88.

The *Jerusalem caelesti,* in fact, was written with a directness, a closeness of texture and an air of easy competency that suggest the style of d'Alembert rather than the ungoverned rambling of Diderot or the diffuse mediocrity of Prades's known writings. It was charged at the time, and with truth, that the thesis repeated in summary large parts of d'Alembert's *Discours préliminaire de l'Encyclopédie.* D'Alembert's *Discours,* however, was itself only a formal statement of ideas that the *philosophes* very generally entertained.

All we are warranted in concluding is that Prades, who is known to have been on good terms with Diderot for at least several months, may have received help and encouragement from his philosopher friends of the summer of 1751. In view of the style and content of the thesis, and considering that Prades was certainly a man of receptive rather than critical mind, it is quite possible that this help and encouragement went very far, and that, while Prades fancied himself to be the author, the thesis was practically manufactured in the editorial workshop of the *Encyclopédie.* If this be true, then Prades, when he came to take his examination, was in his own mind a volunteer in the Encyclopedist cause, and in the minds of the Encyclopedists a pawn whom they purposely advanced into an extremely hazardous position. The *philosophes* kept a discreet silence on the origin of the thesis, but one of them, Helvétius, is reported to have called the thesis "a dove sent out from the ark to see whether the sea of prejudice had not yet subsided."[30] It was commonly thought at the time that the *philosophes* hoped through Prades to have some of their principles accepted by the Faculty, so as to be able later on to defend the views expressed in the *Encyclopédie* by appealing to doctrines officially endorsed by the University.[31]

The second and greater question, more delicate than the question of authorship, is how the examining theologians came to give Prades their unanimous approval. The fact that they had done so became highly embarrassing when the outcry arose a few weeks later. The professors responsible for the thesis then declared that they had not read it, explaining that the print was too fine for their eyesight—an excuse matched in fatuity only by the assertion of

[30] E. Regnault, *Christophe de Beaumont* (Paris, 1882), Vol. I, pp. 346-7.
[31] Barbier, *op. cit.,* Vol. V, p. 150.

Prades that the elegance of his metaphors was such that the learned doctors had misunderstood his meaning.

There were in reality no misleading metaphors in the thesis, nor did the size of the print have much to do with the matter, since the real difficulty was to explain how Prades had slipped through the oral examination. The oral examination, in the educational system then in use, was purely a defense of the written thesis. Conceivably Prades, to get the thesis passed, may have fooled the examiners by debating irrelevant questions. This is highly improbable; for such a procedure would imply, first, that Prades was extraordinarily ingenious, when all the evidence goes to show that he was unsophisticated in such matters, and, second, that the professors were unbelievably negligent, and not only had not read the thesis, but also failed to learn what it was about even at the oral examination. It is impossible to say whether any of the examiners knew at the time that Prades was associated with the *Encyclopédie*. It seems unlikely that Prades should have concealed a fact of which he had every reason to boast, namely that he was about to publish, in the great new dictionary of the sciences, an article confirming the evidences of Christianity. Unless the professors lived in an aloofness difficult to imagine in Paris, some of them should have got wind of the honor befallen one of their students; and if any of them did, it is unlikely that Prades's examination would have been purely perfunctory.

The most reasonable explanation seems to be the obvious one: that the examiners passed Prades because they took his thesis for what it was offered as being, a defense of the Christian revelation; and that, whether or not they agreed with his opinions, they considered these opinions to be tenable by a Catholic. That they did so becomes more probable when we learn that the examination was presided over by the Abbé Hooke, whose susceptibility to certain modern ideas has already been noted. Hooke, incidentally, fell into disgrace by the Prades affair. He was dismissed from his chair of theology, then recalled a year later, in 1753; but he had lost the confidence of the authorities, and in 1762 the archbishop, Beaumont, forbade students to attend his courses.[32]

[32] On Hooke see above, pp. 40-1, 51; *Biographie universelle,* "Hooke"; J. Flammermont, *Rémontrances du Parlement de Paris* (Paris, 1888-98), Vol. II, p. 465, n. 2.

What the Prades affair seems to show, although both Catholic and non-Catholic historians may find reason to question it, is that in 1751 the line that separated the orthodox from the philosophical was indistinct. There were educated men in the church who were willing to give a hearing to the new ideas. They were favorably inclined to the sensationalist metaphysics formulated by Locke and Condillac, and were prepared to tolerate, in men who professed their belief in revelation, some pretty free inquiry into the miracles of the New Testament or the chronology of the Old. They were interested in modern ideas, and had faith in the enlightenment of their day. Like modernists and progressives generally, they may be praised for their open-mindedness, or blamed for not seeing the consequences of their own ideas, or regarded with sympathy for their attempt to keep their hold on two different schemes of thought. They required that a man preserve his faith in revelation; yet they made no serious objection to the principles and methods of thought by which certain thinkers were led to dispense with revelation altogether. So long as the *Encyclopédie* was not definitely known to be at war with the Christian revelation and the Catholic tradition (and that fact was not common knowledge in 1751), they could consider its philosophy without suspicion, and look forward to its publication in the coming years without alarm.

But the populace of Paris soon buzzed with the rumor that the miracles of Jesus were questioned in high academic circles. Serious thinkers found it disquieting, in addition, that so categorical a statement of the sensationalist psychology, with its implications of materialism and doubt, should be officially sanctioned by the University. The heretic Jansenists rushed forward to accuse the Faculty of heterodoxy. The Jesuits, usually tolerant of much of the enlightened philosophy, also found an advantage in the commotion. According to the *philosophes,* they feared that their *Dictionnaire de Trévoux* would suffer by competition with the *Encyclopédie*; and it is quite possible that they were afraid of losing their intellectual leadership and took this opportunity to reassert it. Pressure was thus brought from all sides upon the University to reverse its decision and cast out the Encyclopedist Prades from its ranks. The Faculty hesitated; it could not reverse its decision without convicting itself of an inexcusable blunder; and there were moreover, as was shown later, some forty doctors who thought either that Prades's thesis was a good one, or that Prades, as a member of the University, should be protected against clamor from outside.

The Jesuits urged the minister Mirepoix, a bishop, to use the authority of the government. The Abbé Le Gros, one of the most capable of the doctors of the Sorbonne, tried in vain to dissuade Mirepoix from acting. The University finally yielded—according to Voltaire, because the opponents of Prades had packed its assembly with a hundred "alumni" monks who had never read the thesis. If true, Voltaire's statement is highly significant, for roughly a hundred votes were cast against Prades. Late in January 1752, it was decided by a majority of 82 to 54 that Prades should be condemned unheard, and, by 105 to 41, that he should be censured and disowned, his thesis expunged from the records of the University, and he himself deprived of his academic standing and degrees.[33]

Ecclesiastical thunders immediately began to roar. The archbishop of Paris, advised by a special council of five theologians, condemned the thesis on January 27. The bishops of Auxerre and Montauban soon followed. The Parlement of Paris did the same, and on March 22 came the sentence of the pope. "Hitherto," said the bishop of Montauban, "hell has vomited its poison drop by drop; today torrents of error and impiety tend toward nothing less than the submergence of Faith, Religion, Virtue, the Church, Subordination, Law and Reason."[34] On February 7 the government revoked its license to print the *Encyclopédie*. About a year later legal publication was resumed, only to be definitely denied in 1759, when the appearance of later volumes, and the scandal caused by Helvétius's *De l'Esprit,* made it evident that Christianity and the doctrines of the *philosophes* were irreconcilably opposed.

Prades, outlawed and penniless, took refuge with the king of Prussia. He was invited by Voltaire, who, thinking he saw a philosopher in distress, wrote him a letter admirable for its delicacy

[33] d'Argenson, *op. cit.,* Vol. VII, p. 80; M. Picot, *Mémoires pour servir à l'histoire ecclésiastique pendant le dix-huitième siècle* (Paris, 1816), Vol. II, pp. 244-8.

[34] *Recueil de pièces concernant l'Abbé de Prades* (Paris, 1753), pp. 36-7. The other condemnations, and the thesis itself, are printed here.

and kindliness.[35] Prades had hardly reached Potsdam when he issued his *Apologie,* in two parts, which must have been disappointing to his new protectors, for Prades showed himself to be at bottom a believer.

The *Apologie* is our chief source for a knowledge of Prades's character; and what it shows is a man who, though thirty-two, seems very youthful, dazed by the sudden fate that had struck him, and unable to understand the magnitude of the controversy in which he had entangled himself. Protesting with pathetic sincerity that he was a faithful son of the church, he insisted that the views expressed in his thesis were purely academic, and that he had never supposed them to be anything but Christian. He felt that he had nothing to retract, and innocently repeated all the strong talk he had heard among the philosophers back in Paris, outdoing himself in wordy explanations, adding social to religious questions, and maintaining, for example, that society was anarchical in origin and that all men were at all times equal, without seeming to realize that his opinions might have something more than an academic sense, and if acted on would destroy the things in which he believed.[36]

After two years, having reflected further, and finding Frederick's favor cooled, Prades made his peace with the church, recanted his thesis, and was restored to his honors in the University

[35] A. Gazier, *Mélanges de littérature et d'histoire: Voltaire et l'Abbé de Prades* (Paris, 1904), where a letter from Voltaire to Prades and one from d'Argens are published.

[36] It was not necessary for Prades to go to the philosophers to hear equalitarian theory. He might have heard it in the classroom at the Sorbonne. See the book published by his teacher Hooke a few months after his examination, *Religionis naturalis et moralis philosophiae principia, methodo scholastica digesta* (Paris, 1752-54), Vol. I, pp. 623-4: "Status est hominis conditio permanens, varia jura et longam obligationum seriem includens. Estque vel *naturalis,* quem constituit ipsa natura, vel *adventitius* ab aliquo hominum facto vel instituto ortus. . . . Per *statum naturae* eum intellegimus in quo essent positi homines qui nulli imperio subjicerentur, sed sola naturae similitudine aut pactis privatis adunarentur. . . . In statu naturae omnes homines aequales sunt et paribus gaudent juribus. Nam in illo statu discriminant homines solummodo dotes vel mentis vel corporis, quibus praestant alii aliis." The italics are Hooke's. Note that Hooke regards the state of nature as a *conditio permanens,* not merely a historical situation; and observe the shift from subjunctive to indicative mood, i.e. from hypothetical to affirmative statement.

of Paris. He died in 1782 as a canon of the cathedral of Glogau in Silesia.[37]

Meanwhile in Paris the mighty struggle continued. Diderot, apparently with Prades's knowledge, wrote a "third part" to Prades's apology. Since it was not known that Diderot was the author, this third part put poor Prades into still more difficulties. It had none of the air of naïve honesty and injured protestation of the first two parts. Diderot, as a veteran *philosophe,* understood the art of saying more than he seemed to. He averred, what no Christian of that time was prepared to deny, that the proofs of religion could not be too rigorously sifted, and that it would be "a blasphemy to suppose them incapable of sustaining human criticism"; adding that "not to devote a considerable part of one's life to this study is to be a Christian in the same way as one might be a Mohammedan."[38] He managed to represent himself as a defender of the Faculty by expressing special indignation at the Jansenist bishop of Auxerre, who in condemning Prades had severely blamed the Faculty for its carelessness and had hinted broadly at the unsoundness of its doctrine. Caylus, bishop of Auxerre, replied; and Diderot seized the opportunity to prolong a controversy so unfortunate for the church, by issuing a *Suite de l'apologie de M. l'Abbé de Prades.*

Other champions entered the lists. Voltaire seems to have taken a hand; the anonymous *Tombeau de la Sorbonne* is thought to have come from him. On the side of orthodoxy various collections of documents were published, which, in printing both the thesis and the official condemnations, brought Prades's errors to the attention of persons who might otherwise not have known them.

The Abbé Bonhomme "reflected" in three volumes on Prades and the *Encyclopédie;* a theologian issued a large work in Latin; and the ubiquitous Gourlin, his pen always ready to flow in Jansenist causes, devoted half his book on Prades to an attack on the Jesuits, who, he said, with their ideas of the state of nature and their habit of reasoning on moral obligations, had opened the floodgates to

[37] *Apologie de l'Abbé de Prades* (3 vols., Amsterdam, 1753). The second and third volumes are by Diderot; see his *Oeuvres,* Vol. I, pp. 431 ff. On Prades's later life in Berlin see Daux, *op. cit.*; W. Grundlach, *Friedrich der Grosse und sein Verleser Jean-Martin de Prades* (Hamburg, 1892); D. Thiébault, *Souvenirs de vingt ans à Berlin* (Paris, 1860), Vol. II, pp. 423-5.

[38] *Apologie de l'Abbé de Prades,* Vol. III, pp. 18-19.

religious incredulity. The Prades affair thus turned into a general brawl between Jesuits and Jansenists, philosophers and priests; and it remained as a symbol of that strife long after Prades himself had quietly slipped back into the fold.[39]

The decade that followed the Prades affair saw the turning-point of the century. In 1750 men of many shades of belief could feel confidence in the enlightenment of their age. In 1760 they were divided into two camps, more clearly defined than ever before. Those claiming to be enlightened were more openly irreligious; those claiming to be religious took alarm at the enlightened ideas. In the intervening years Voltaire turned from poet to crusader; Rousseau became known as a propounder of paradoxes; Helvétius antagonized all Christians, and some philosophers, by reducing life to physiology and good and evil to pleasure and pain. Almost every year, with industrious regularity, Diderot dispatched another volume of the *Encyclopédie* to his four thousand subscribers. The philosophers won friends in high places: Malesherbes favored them at the censor's office, and Mme. de Pompadour in the royal apartments at Versailles. The Academy, which had received d'Alembert in 1754, was on the point of coming over to their side.

The church undertook to stiffen its opposition. In 1755, for the first time, the Assembly of the Clergy seriously deliberated on the problem of infidelity. Apologists became more numerous and more bitter, and more given to personal attacks on individual unbelievers. But the church was distracted by worldly preoccupations. Church and state, at odds over financial questions, could not cooperate to resist an intellectual movement which seemed increasingly to threaten both. The church, moreover, was torn by the discontents that went under the name of Jansenism. The state and

---

[39] For this controversial literature see, besides works mentioned in the preceding notes: G. Brotier (S. J.), *Examen de l'Apologie de l'Abbé de Prades* (n.p., 1753); anon., *Pièces nouvelles et curieuses sur l'affaire de l'Abbé de Prades* (Paris, 1754); Abbé Paris, ed., *La religion vengée des impiétés de la thèse de M. l'Abbé de Prades* (Montauban, 1754); anon., *Thesis Joannis-Martini de Prades theologice discussa et impugnata* (Paris, 1753), with a long review of this work and examination of the whole question in the *Journal de Trévoux* (1753), pp. 1415-37, 1597-692; *Nouvelles ecclésiastiques* (1752), pp. 33 *ff.*; Gourlin, *Observations importantes au sujet de la thèse* (n.p., 1752); L. Chaudon, *Dictionnaire anti-philosophique* (Avignon, 1767), art. "Prades"; A. Paulian, *Dictionnaire philosophico-théologique portatif* (Nimes, 1770), art. "Philosophes"; J. Duhamel, *Lettres flamandes* (Lille, 1752), letters xv to xxviii.

the Jansenists joined forces long enough to destroy the Jesuits in 1763, although practically every bishop in France had declared the Jesuits necessary to the maintenance of religion. The loss was a major calamity. Some of the best trained and ablest men in the church were thus exiled or reduced to silence. The Jesuits, perhaps, constituted the one group which might have found some means of reconciling traditional authority with eighteenth century belief.

In the University, after the Prades affair, any inchoate modernism that may have existed was seriously checked. The professors were committed to a philosophy which the enlightened regarded as antiquated. By condemning the sensationalist metaphysics of Prades, the Faculty abandoned the principle which it had held since the Middle Ages, *nihil in intellectu nisi prius in sensu,* and embraced the Cartesian philosophy of innate ideas which it had previously opposed.

The philosophers, who when they changed their own minds called the change progress, could see only stark inconsistency in the reversal of the theologians. In reality, however, the sensationalist philosophy meant something very different in 1750 from what it had meant in the Middle Ages. The theologians, in opposing it, furnished a criticism that might have been salutary had it been listened to. But the philosophers rarely listened to the objections raised by priests; they could not distinguish criticism that had intellectual value, because they were convinced that all criticism was prompted by a superstitious attachment to an intolerant authority. Much though they insisted on the value of free speech, they had the weaknesses of men not in the habit of respecting those who disagree with them—they were undoubtedly hasty, self-assured, irritable and doctrinaire. The theologians who opposed them fell into the oblivion that receives most thinkers whose views happen to be out of fashion. Their opinions, however, are worth disinterring, for something like their doctrine of "innate ideas" came to life in the mind of Immanuel Kant, and has been raising questions ever since.

CHAPTER VI

SOUL AND MIND

QUIS est ille cuius in faciem Deus inspiravit spiraculum vitae? "Who is he in whose face God breathed the breath of life?" This question, taken from Genesis, stood as the general heading to Prades's famous thesis. It is the grand question of all philosophy in all ages, and the final importance of human thinking lies in the answer that it gives or assumes.

In the eighteenth century the question was particularly urgent. Religious and secular ideas of man's nature were struggling for dominance. The issue was not always sharply drawn or clearly perceived, but it was fundamentally a dispute between those who wished to believe that man is somehow endowed with faculties independent of the world into which he is born, and those who preferred to think that he is wholly shaped by the physical world, and has no resources, powers, or purposes not conferred on him by his environment.

This divergence of opinion showed itself in various ways, sometimes in the controversy over innate ideas and sense impressions; sometimes in the question whether man had been created perfect in the garden of Eden, or whether, as many were coming to suspect, he had at first been a kind of brute; sometimes in the tendency to see the most effective moral sanctions not in supernatural rewards but in the opinion of contemporaries and the ultimate judgment of posterity. On the whole, the religious took the former of these alternatives, the philosophical the latter. There was, indeed, much confusion of issues. The Abbé Bergier, though he later criticized a similar opinion expressed by Holbach, at one time looked to a kind of immortality in the judgment of posterity.[1] Palissot, a writer of comedies, who thought the infidels both dan-

[1] R. R. Palmer, "Posterity and the Hereafter in Eighteenth Century French Thought," in the *Journal of Modern History*, Vol. IX (1937), pp. 145-68. An unpublished manuscript of Bergier's is mentioned in this article.

gerous and absurd, accepted without reservation their sensationalist philosophy.[2] But the ablest of the Christian thinkers, when they considered the subject with care, rejected this philosophy as unsound.

The importance of the sensationalist philosophy to men of that time cannot be exaggerated. The Abbé de Prades asserted it as Proposition One, in answer to the Biblical question: "Man [is he] whose ideas, still rude and unformed, are produced by sensations; hence from sensations, as branches from a trunk, all his cognitions take their rise." All progressive thinkers would have concurred in this statement. It was Proposition One of the whole philosophy of enlightenment. By expounding it clearly, John Locke had ushered in the enlightened age, thus at last writing, as Voltaire said, the history of the human mind where earlier thinkers had but written the romance. It was with this Proposition One, much expanded, that d'Alembert, at the climax of the age, opened his *Discours préliminaire de l'Encyclopédie,* and that Condorcet, at the close, began his *Tableau des progrès de l'esprit humain.* The assent of Diderot, Condillac, Helvétius, and Raynal was entire. The fact, or supposed fact, that knowledge is produced by experience received through sensations was the guarantee by which the scientific method of the *Encyclopédie* was thought to be valid, and by which the future progress of mankind was thought to be assured. Sensationalism was not only a psychology but a metaphysics, and not only a theory of knowledge but a theory of human nature. Quite properly, therefore, it was, after revelation, the point on which religious and irreligious thinkers were most consistently divided.

It is unfortunate, in the light of pure philosophy, that the intellectual foundations on which the *philosophes* claimed to be standing had been seriously undermined by one of their own number. David Hume, as early as 1739, had pushed the sensationalist doctrine to its last extreme. Berkeley had shown that a consistent adherent of the doctrine could not believe in the existence of matter; Hume now added that it was impossible for him to believe in good and evil, cause and effect, or even in himself as a being with any personal identity. Nothing was left but an ebb and flow of

[2] C. Palissot de Montenoy, "Lettre sur l'âme," *Oeuvres* (Paris, 1788), Vol. IV, pp. 251-9.

sensations, and of images that were only sensations in decay; a phantasmagoria that could not even be called subjective, since no perceiving or conscious subject could be found; a flux of impressions in which no real time could be known, since the past was perceived only by impressions fainter than those of sense, conventionally called memories; a whirl of experience in which an "association of ideas" seemed to take place, but in which no experiencing or organizing mind, living through time, could be assumed. Unable to deny his own existence, or to embrace any system of thought by which that existence became philosophically probable, Hume naturally lost faith in philosophy, and became the one genuine skeptic in an age of vehement unbelief. In France, as elsewhere, his philosophical works made little impression. That the human mind could prove nothing important was the last doctrine that enlightened thinkers wished to hear.

In a document that he refrained from publishing in his lifetime, Hume suggested a conclusion in which apologists of religion might have taken comfort could they have read it. "To be a philosophical skeptic," he said, "is, in a man of letters, the first and most essential step towards being a sound, believing Christian."[3] No doubt he wrote the words with the wry irony of a man who in a world of partisans finds himself on neither side of the question, and has lost the hope of making himself understood. Certainly he was not himself a believing Christian, nor is any believing Christian of that time known to have been a philosophical skeptic. Yet between Hume and the Catholic apologists of France there was an affinity, which both would have preferred to disown but which nevertheless was real. It has already been noted, in connection with belief in miracles and supernatural intervention, how the orthodox apologists were in some respects skeptical. They denied the absolute validity of human reason, the invariable uniformity of nature, the necessary sequence of physical cause and effect. Hume also doubted these things; it was only because he doubted in addition the trustworthiness of testimony that he differed with the apologists on the probability of miracles. Hume, perhaps inadvertently, exposed the weaknesses of the reigning philosophy. That was, of

[3] Hume, *Dialogues Concerning Natural Religion* (London, 1779), pp. 263-4; see also Carl Becker, *The Heavenly City of the Eighteenth Century Philosophers* (New Haven, 1932), pp. 68-78.

course, precisely what religious critics were constantly trying to do. But where Hume saw reasons for believing all philosophy futile, the apologists saw reasons for believing the particular philosophy of the *philosophes* to be false. In the sensationalist doctrine there was an element missing. This element the skeptical Hume could not supply, but the religious thinkers could. It was not necessary for them to appeal to revelation. They could, and did, supply the missing element from a mixture of Christianity, Cartesianism and common experience.

The missing element in the sensationalist philosophy, as the conclusions of Hume should have shown, was nothing less than the human mind itself. Originally an empty void, a *tabula rasa,* the mind remained, in this theory, nothing but a receptacle for experience. It was purely passive; its perception was simple reception; it contributed nothing to the raw data of sense. Except for such peculiarities of sensation as those by which some phenomena appeared as color, others as sound, the mind in no way modified the world in the process of looking at it. An individual mind derived its whole character from the surroundings in which it lived. It was identical with the contingent experience that befell it. It had no absolute being apart from its store of sensations and impressions. Personality was only the recollection of continuous experience in the past. The active and outreaching elements in human nature, all that philosophers and psychologists have called the will, played no part in either the forming of experience or the development of the self. All opinions and attitudes, all knowledge and critical judgments, all purposes and ends and values, were implanted in each man by an experience received through sensation and differentiated by pleasure and pain.

Paradoxically, the men who trusted so highly in the powers of intelligence regarded the mind as essentially vacant and inert; the idea of the passive mind was indispensable to their system. It was the guarantee that the truths of nature might be perceived without distortion. It was the basis for the distinction, then so important and so clear, between enlightenment and prejudice. It was the metaphysical groundwork for the belief that men were equal, and that they possessed the quality of *perfectibilité,* that is, susceptibility to progress. Minimizing the effects of will, denying original predisposition, refusing to see any inevitability in human nature, the doctrine was flatly contrary to the Christian idea of sin; and by representing man as a passive child of circumstances, easily abused by his environment, it slipped sometimes into a notion that human nature, when crude, is good; that polish and civilization are bad; and that order, restraint, discipline, and suppression are affronts to man's dignity and freedom.

How heavily the influence of religion weighed against this philosophy is shown by no one more clearly than by Rousseau. Rousseau certainly believed that men were by nature good. He is generally thought to have believed, more than his contemporaries, that all men were originally equal. His *Emile* is usually taken to imply that inequalities arise from environment. The truth is, however, that he had many misgivings on this point. The reason is not hard to find. The idea that men possess equal mental powers came directly from the sensationalist psychology. Rousseau, with his religious or at least introspective nature, could not tolerate the thought that his mind and soul were only a heap of sense impressions produced by an external world.

The issue became clear for him when he read Helvétius's *De l'Esprit*. This book, which caused a great stir in 1758, was really noteworthy for its very want of originality, being only a full and open exposition of ideas shared by most of the leading Encyclopedists. Helvétius set out by declaring that the mind possesses "two faculties, or, if I may so put it, two passive powers," physical sensibility and memory; and he concluded by asserting that, except for the effects of education, all minds were equal and identical.[4]

Rousseau says that he planned a thorough refutation, but gave up the idea when Helvétius got into trouble with the authorities. In his "Profession of faith of the Savoyard Vicar" he stated his own position, criticized pure sensationalist theory, and affirmed, as a first principle of his religion, the existence of himself as an active, positive, judging, willing individual person. For these opinions he says that the *philosophes* detested him. He was more explicit in certain marginal notes which he wrote in his copy of

[4] Helvétius, *De l'Esprit*, in *Helvétius: Collection des plus belles pages* (Paris, 1909), pp. 16-25. ". . . worth your reading, not for its philosophy, which I do not highly value, but for its agreeable composition." David Hume to Adam Smith, *Letters of David Hume* (Greig ed., Oxford, 1932), Vol. I, p. 304.

Helvétius's book. These notes he took pains to keep secret, stipulating, when he sold his library in London, that this volume should not be made public before his death.[5]

What was the doctrine that Rousseau wished to hide from the caustic notice of the enlightened? It was, in substance, the doctrine that Catholic writers had been asserting for years, namely, that the ability to compare, combine, unify, and judge the data of sense does not itself arise from pure sensation. *Juger, c'est sentir*, Helvétius kept repeating; judgment is only a property of the senses. Rousseau, for all his sensibility, saw here the fundamental fallacy. "To perceive objects," he wrote, "is to have sensation; to perceive relationships is to judge."[6]

The final comment is worth quoting at length. It shows Jean-Jacques in an unfamiliar and not discreditable light: "The principle from which the author deduces in the following chapters the natural equality of minds, and which he attempts to establish at the beginning of this work, is that human judgments are purely passive. This principle has been affirmed and discussed with much depth and philosophy in the Encyclopedia, article 'Evidence.' I do not know the author of this article; but he is certainly a great metaphysician; I suspect the Abbé de Condillac or M. de Buffon. However that may be, I have tried to combat this principle and to establish the activity of our judgments in the notes written at the beginning of this book, and above all in the first part of the 'Profession of faith of the Savoyard Vicar.' If I am right, and if the principle of M. Helvétius and the above mentioned author is false, the reasoning in the following chapters falls to the ground, being only a consequence of this principle, and it is not true that the inequality among minds is the effect of education alone, though education may be of great influence."[7]

What the true cause of this inequality might be Rousseau does not say. Presumably, whatever it was, it was transmitted by heredity. That question is not important here. The significant point is that Rousseau, by denying that judgments were purely passive, denied that sensation was sufficient to produce an intelligent crea-

[5] Rousseau, *Oeuvres* (Bruxelles, 1827-28), Vol. VI, pp. 230 *ff.*; *Correspondance* (ed. Dufour, Paris, 1924-34), Vol. VIII, p. 109, Vol. XVI, p. 277.
[6] *Oeuvres*, Vol. XIX, p. 195.
[7] *ibid.*, pp. 203-4.

ture, and opened wide the doors to those bugbears of the enlightened thinkers, innate ideas.

The dispute was more than a technical discussion of epistemology. The soul itself was at stake, the *âme,* a word which meant soul, mind, and consciousness without connotation of piety, and which must be translated by various English terms. It was to vindicate their belief in immortality that religious people usually entered the argument. This prepossession had its value; it compelled them to recognize psychological facts which the infidels, with their different prepossessions, found it useful to ignore. Christianity conditioned the whole course of eighteenth century philosophy. If it provoked a somewhat excessive empiricism among its critics, it kept alive also the ideas by which a dialectical balance might be restored. The critical student, remembering the strong Protestant bias of Kant, will not dismiss the Catholic speculation of the time as philosophically negligible. What he finds in common in the German idealists and the French Catholic apologists he may, with some plausibility, set down to the influence of the Christian religion.

It was an influence mediated through Descartes. The importance of Descartes in religious apologetic has been demonstrated by Lanson, chiefly however for the seventeenth century.[8] In the eighteenth century the bedrock of Catholic philosophy was the Cartesian dualism, categorically affirmed and endlessly reiterated. It was a strong line of argument to take, for the infidels themselves, despite attempts to overcome it, really accepted many of the implications that this dualism produced. Never was the difference between mind and matter more clear-cut or more absolute. Never was matter conceived of more distinctly. Matter, it was agreed, was extended quantitative substance, inert in itself but characterized by motion, and divisible into homogeneous and mutually external parts, which affected each other by impact. It followed that whatever was not quantitative, not inert, not divisible, and not activated by impact must be spirit, and that this spirit, not being subject to the laws of matter, could well be imperishable, as it was in fact known to be by revelation.

One doctrine of Malebranche was also much in favor, the doctrine of "occasional causes." Occasionalism, like Leibniz's pre-

[8] G. Lanson, "De l'influence de la philosophie cartésienne sur la littérature française," in *Revue de Métaphysique et de Morale,* Vol. IV (1896), pp. 517-50.

established harmony, was a theory in which, by an elaborate metaphysics, two irreducible and primordial substances were brought together in the same universe. Mind and matter, soul and body, it was held, occupied different planes of being; neither could reach the other; neither could produce changes in the other by direct interposition of causes. Motion, the form of action in matter, could never produce thought, feeling, will, or consciousness, the forms of action peculiar to the soul. What really happened, therefore, when changes in the body seemed to affect the mind, was simply that these changes gave occasion to changes in mental experience, which in reality arose from an active power in the soul itself.

Mind and body thus accompanied each other through life, hand in hand although eternally parted; and their mutual responsiveness was a supreme mystery, a sure evidence of God's existence, and a continuing expression of his power. It followed that the soul, which had never needed the body, lost nothing by the body's death. This belief, which in one form or another was an inevitable supplement to the Cartesian dualism, by the middle of the eighteenth century had almost reached the level of popular thinking.[9]

Descartes, when he formulated his conception of matter, made possible mathematical science, but he also greatly lightened the task of apologists for religion. It was often argued that we may be assured of the existence of God and the soul, precisely because we have an exact idea of matter. It was agreed that matter was quantitative and mathematically measurable. How then could thought be material? "What is a round or square thought?" asked Ilhahart de La Chambre, and he voiced only a common query of the religious writers, whose books are full of requests to be shown a square thought, a convex pain, a quarter of an idea, or a cubic foot of reasoning.[10] The absurdity was supposed to clinch

[9] Occasionalism appears in a great number of the eighteenth century religious writers, of all shades of ability, sometimes in direct exposition, sometimes by way of allusion. See Cardinal Polignac, *L'Anti-Lucrèce* (Paris, 1751), Vol. II, pp. 34-41; Denesle, *Examen du matérialisme* (Paris, 1754), Vol. I, p. 180; L. François, *Examen des faits qui servent de fondement de la religion chrétienne* (Paris, 1767), Vol. I, p. 33; É. Fréron, *Année littéraire* (1754), Vol. VII, p. 302. In F. Pluquet, *Examen du fatalisme* (Paris, 1757), Vol. III, pp. 141-4, as in many of the more capable thinkers, the same idea takes the form of Leibniz's preestablished harmony. The idea is of less importance in such writers as Lignac and Monestier who incline toward a kind of idealistic monism.

[10] Ilhahart de La Chambre, *Abrégé de philosophie* (Paris, 1754), Vol. I, pp.

the argument, and indeed in the eighteenth century it was a formidable objection.

Again, matter was known to be dead and ponderous stuff, which could not be moved without a directing intelligence. The same argument that proved the existence of God as a Prime Mover proved also the existence of the soul. A leading surgeon and anatomist, A. Louis, who later contributed to the Encyclopedia, in 1747 wrote a short *Essai sur la nature de l'âme*. He began by clearly defining the body as "a prodigious assemblage of pipes, hydraulic and pneumatic machines, and levers of all kinds." The body was "an assemblage of infinitely small and infinitely solid particles," the soul "all sensibility and activity."[11] In these few words we may discern in passing, at this early date and in a practical man, the way in which the Cartesian dualism led to the fatal disharmony of modern times, the split between controlled scientific thinking and free expansive romanticism.

Notions of this kind easily produced some extremely commonplace philosophy. There was danger of falling into the crude theory of a human being as a "ghost in a corpse." A book called *La dignité de la nature humaine,* by one Villiers, in effect reduces human dignity to this cadaverous status. It is argued that the soul must be a kind of god in order to move such an unwieldy structure as the body, which it operates, so to speak, by pressing buttons and pulling levers, using the bulky apparatus as a means of ruling the material world. The arts and sciences, libraries and cities are evidences of this ghostly intelligence; but apparently for Villiers the evidence was highly inferential, for he concluded that without special revelation we should never know that man is a spirit.[12]

299-304. See also N. Bergier, *Examen du matérialisme* (Paris, 1771), Vol. I, p. 156; H. Hayer, *La spiritualité et l'immortalité de l'âme* (Paris, 1757), Vol. I, p. 6; C. Richard, *La nature en contraste avec la religion et la raison* (Paris, 1773), pp. 62-3; anon., *L'âme, Pensées philosophiques* (1757); Roussel, *La loi naturelle* (Paris, 1769), pp. 16-17; B. Sinsart, *Pensées sur l'immatérialité de l'âme* (Colmar, 1756). The argument about "square thoughts," etc., was not new, having been used by Malebranche. See J. Laird, *Hume's Philosophy of Human Nature* (London, 1932), p. 165.

[11] A. Louis, *Essai sur la nature de l'âme* (Paris, 1747), pp. 11, 17.

[12] M. Villiers, *La dignité de la nature humaine* (Paris, 1778); see also Denesle, *op. cit.*, Vol. I, p. 6: "Que l'on coupe un cadavre par pièces; on dit qu'il ne sent plus rien: ce qui n'est qu'un préjugé fondé sur les apparences; car ce corps, mort ou vivant, n'a jamais rien senti; mais en donnant à l'âme l'occasion de sentir, il a paru lui-même sentir."

There were, however, a number of competent Cartesians. There can be no agreement in selecting the most important, but any list should include the names of Lignac, Cochet, Hayer, Boullier, Roche, and Monestier. Of these, all but Monestier wrote during the critical years of the 1750's. Hayer was the most definitely a religious apologist, Cochet a professor of philosophy at the Collège Mazarin, Roche a man of great piety who lived in seclusion for many years at Saint-Germain l'Auxerrois. Lignac was the most successful in constructing a philosophic system. Boullier was a Protestant living in Holland, Monestier a Jesuit who in some ways anticipated the German idealism.

It is difficult to say precisely what they had in common beyond their rejection of the sensationalist metaphysics. All surely would have agreed with Boullier's *Apologie de la métaphysique à l'occasion du Discours préliminaire de l'Encyclopédie*. Boullier, while praising the plan of the Encyclopedia and calling d'Alembert's discourse a work of high merit, put in a few telling critical strokes. "Let me be allowed a slight reproach : that for a philosopher so hostile to prejudices he gives himself up a bit too much to the taste of his nation and his century." Metaphysics, he observed, was not "the experimental physics of the soul," nor did Locke create it, as d'Alembert alleged. Boullier suspected that the Encyclopedist philosophy, like the Cartesian, would some day seem antiquated to the progressive. "And does that not come from the fact that men are no less obstinate in modern prejudices than in old ones, and that the love of novelty seduces at least as many minds as respect for antiquity?"[13]

These Cartesians affirmed at the outset the independent existence of the mind. Hayer, on the first page of his book, contrasted his views with those of the *philosophes*. "I am a body, and I think ; I know no more, says a modern philosopher [Voltaire]. I am a soul, and have a body, says Plato with the wisest of antiquity. The question, then, is to examine whether my body is my whole being, or only a thing belonging to me, my possession ; whether this Body is Me, or simply Mine."[14] This was the problem exactly : to deter-

[13] D. Boullier, "Apologie de la métaphysique à l'occasion du Discours préliminaire de l'Encyclopédie," in *Pièces philosophiques et littéraires* (n.p., 1759), pp. 80, 90, 102-3.
[14] Hayer, *op. cit.*, Vol. I, pp. 1-2. "Bonne lecture pour ennuyer les moines," says Grimm, *Correspondance littéraire* (Paris, 1877-82), Vol. III, p. 367. Fréron,

mine the process by which, in human speech, it is possible to have pronouns in the first person singular, and to objectify the most intimate parts of experience, such as the body, into things detached from, but somehow belonging to, a thinking subject.

In the age of the "mechanico-corpuscular" philosophy, as Coleridge called it, when the body was regarded as an inert assemblage of mutually external particles, the strongest argument for the existence of the soul was to stress the unity of the self, the ability to perceive diverse sensations simultaneously, and to combine and judge the heterogeneous objects of experience. The self, said Hayer, "is unique, simple, indivisible, spiritual." Its immateriality is proved by the fact that the changes in the matter forming the body, and in the ideas filling the mind, do not cause substantial changes in the self, and do not impair its individual identity. No one, he observed, who tried to explain the mind by particular bits of sensitive matter could explain why there was only one self and not several. "For in reality this comparing self, this judging self, could not be matter; and the reason is evident. We have said it a hundred times: matter has no unity, a material self would necessarily be the product of various parts which would have no relation to one another, no community of feelings and operations. One part of this material self would see, while another heard; one would be aware of odors, another of tastes."

Hayer elaborated his case with some highly formal arguments, such as that sensation cannot arise from matter because "the effect cannot be more perfect than the cause" (which alone would draw snorts of impatience from the enlightened); but his major objection, based on the atomistic conception of matter made popular by the Newtonian physics, offered a real conundrum to the sensationalist philosophy.[15]

Lignac gave the same argument in stronger form. It is possible that he had read Hume, some of whose philosophical essays had been translated into French two years before the publication of his *Témoignage du sens intime*. "What are sensations in the mind?" asked Lignac. . . . "I hear a sound, I see a picture, I feel

op. cit. (1757), Vol. V, p. 20, calls Hayer's book "l'ouvrage le plus philosophique, le plus profond, le mieux détaillé, le plus complet et le mieux écrit que nous ayons sur cette matière."

[15] Hayer, *op. cit.*, Vol. II, pp. 7-8, 27, Vol. I, p. 31.

sorrow; which of these three impressions informs me of my individual existence? How does the sensation of sound, which I cannot confuse with the two others that I experience at the same time, inform me that I am the same person as sees and sorrows? . . . The unity of my person, if I do not know it otherwise, cannot be announced to me by three such disparate modifications."

Hume might have written these words, except that he would not have called the three impressions "modifications." Impressions for him were not modifications of any underlying substance, but were themselves substances, the only substances known to men. Having assigned substantiality exclusively to separate impressions of sense, he could only proceed, logically, to deny it to the joining and combining faculties of the mind, and to disbelieve, philosophically, in the unitary existence of his own person. For Lignac such a conclusion was the most positive evidence of faulty assumptions. Those who professed to doubt their own existence, he thought, were simply not telling the truth; they were philosophic *poseurs*. We do not demonstrate our existence, we feel it; we make it not the end of philosophic inquiry, but the beginning. Accordingly, he based his philosophy on the "testimony of the intimate sense" of his own being.[16]

The Cartesian thinkers, as they turned away from pure sensation, turned away also from the idea of the passive mind. Stressing the faculties of comparison and judgment, they had the rudiments, developed by some more than by others, of a theory in which the mind should be represented as essentially active, a positive energy which itself contributed to the making of its ex-

[16] Le Large de Lignac, *Le témoignage du sens intime et de l'expérience opposé à la foi profane et ridicule des fatalistes modernes* (Auxerre, 1760), Vol. I, pp. 40-4. For further examples of this common assertion that the self is a unit, and that feeling, judging, etc., are indivisible acts not to be explained by collocations of atoms, see also: Bergier, *Examen du matérialisme*, Vol. I, pp. 131-2, 156-7, 345; P. Dufour, *L'âme* (Avignon, 1759), pp. 153-4; P. La Croix, *Traité de la morale* (Carcassonne, 1767), p. 3; C. Richard, *op. cit.*, p. 63; Fangouse, *Réflexions importantes sur la religion* (n.p., 1785), 11-13. "Il est donc vrai," says Fangouse, "que la pensée ne saurait se diviser; il est donc vrai que son principe est indivisible comme elle. A raison de son indivisibilité je l'appelle spirituelle, pour la distinguer du sujet de la division que j'appelle matière." Fangouse thanks Charles Bonnet for this idea, but it is clearly only a corollary to the Cartesian dualism. The same argument for the immateriality of the soul is given by Bayle, *Dictionnaire*, art. "Leucippe," note E, and probably is as old as the atomist theories which it opposes.

perience. It is their belief on this point, fundamentally, that explains why they identified sensationalism with materialism and fatalism, to the confusion of later students and the great indignation of contemporary *philosophes*. The exponents of the sensationalist metaphysics often maintained that, far from being materialists, they really made no pretense of understanding matter, and dealt only with appearances as known to the human mind. These sensationalists, however, made the mind purely a tablet for the registering of experience. Their doctrine that the mind received all its ideas from environment alone was the source of one of their most embarrassing dilemmas (how, namely, to improve the environment); the doctrine also explains why their critics called them materialists and fatalists—fatalism in those days meaning nothing more than determinism.

To call the mind an active force was in effect to assert the freedom of human will. The controversy over free will was an ancient and intricate one, kept alive in the eighteenth century on the one hand by the Jansenists and on the other by the philosophers of universal mechanism. Of the latter the most eminent was Holbach, whose *Système de la Nature* was, in effect, a system which disposed of God and the soul on the ground that motion was essential to matter and that therefore no spiritual substance was necessary to move it. All nature, according to Holbach, was a spontaneously active whole. But, he argued, the particular objects in nature were all passive and inert; they could move only when they received motion from other objects. A human being, therefore, could act only so far as he was impelled from without. He was "a passive instrument in the hands of necessity." The Abbé Bergier, in his *Examen du matérialisme,* replied to Holbach by appealing to the usual dualism, which he upheld with much critical skill. He asserted that the concept of motion had no place in dealing with mental phenomena. It was erroneous, he said, to believe that a mind can give out only as much motion as it receives, that sensations are agitations of minute particles striking on one another, or that ideas and perceptions impinge upon the brain by disturbances in space. "The mind can move such and such a part at its choice by a simple act of its will. It need not move or be moved; *to be moved* applies only to matter. The mind does not impart

[17] Bergier, *Examen du matérialisme,* Vol. I, pp. 16-24, 132, 164-5.

movement to the body by communication or shock, but by *action*."
Bergier concluded that human behavior could never be reduced
to mechanics, and that man was free at least in the sense of not
being a mere passive object for the operation of physical causes.

Lignac made active will the basis of a positive system, which
the *Journal de Trévoux* declared to be so convincing that the materialists would be afraid to read his books. He started, as we have
seen, with the *sens intime* of his own being. We know ourselves,
he said, not by inference from the flux of impressions, but by
an immediate feeling of our own activity. We are forces, not mere
sensitized and passive tablets. We have—by some other means than
sensation, since sensation alone would never give us such knowledge—"the notions of our will and liberty, and the power to affirm, to deny and to doubt." This persistent sense of our ability
to act and choose is the substantial part of ourselves. Along with
it we distinguish a part that is more contingent and accidental,
the various sense impressions to which we are subjected, and which
cannot be essential to our nature, since without hearing the particular sounds we hear or seeing the particular objects we see, we
should unquestionably be the same person. We have therefore an
idea of power, drawn from our own will, and an idea of almighty
power, drawn from our sense of being constantly modified by
something not ourselves. We thus form the idea of God. This idea
is not innate; no idea is innate in the common or vulgar sense; it
is simply that some ideas are implicit in the nature and condition
of man.

"Even the idea of God is not innate, though any sensible man
can find it in himself when he wishes. To possess this idea, we
must have the intimate sense of our own liberty, without which
we cannot see the relation between a free cause and contingent
effects. For without this liberty we sense only our own existence
and its cause, God and ourselves, two separate and individual
terms. The idea of God is then obscure and imperfect. The term
necessary for grasping the idea of omnipotence, that free activity
that realizes what it wills, is lacking; this necessary term is the
sense of our own activity, without which we can form ideas neither
of possibility nor of omnipotence."[18]

[18] Le Large de Lignac, *Élements de la métaphysique* (Paris, 1753), p. 80. C.
Buffier, a prolific Jesuit writer of the 1720's whom even Voltaire mildly praised,

It is by means of this idea of God, according to Lignac, that men arrive at all universal and abstract ideas. Such ideas are notions of omnipotent power applied to objects of our experience. An idea is a notion of the possible—not, as the followers of Locke maintained, a "decayed sensation." The universal idea of a thing is the notion that the thing can be reproduced infinitely by infinite power. Thus every idea has its empirical base in our experience, but becomes a true idea only through our belief in God. For example, we form notions of matter, space, and motion from the feeling of our own bodies, which we perceive immediately by the *sens intime,* not by sensations of sight and touch. We cannot honestly believe the body to be only a mental image; hence the notion of matter. We cannot imagine it two-dimensional; hence the notion of space. We cannot deny that it walks from place to place; hence the notion of movement. But these notions become general ideas only when we universalize them through the belief that God can prolong space infinitely, produce matter indefinitely, and apply to all things any conceivable degree of motion and velocity.

Similarly the idea of man arises from our sense of ourselves together with the idea of God, by which we recognize ourselves as types that may be infinitely multiplied. The idea of a circle is our perception of an actual circle, generalized by the belief that omnipotence may infinitely reproduce the same circle with the same properties.[19]

Lignac's philosophy has been praised by students qualified to judge it, and not much criticism can be ventured here. One observation, however, may be made. The system seems to offer slight support for any distinction between the individual and the universal, the actual and the ideal. The idea of man, according to Lignac, is the idea of oneself indefinitely repeated; but it cannot be all the qualities of oneself that go to make up the idea of man; and Lignac

declares, much like Lignac, that the idea of God is not strictly innate but is an easy and natural one, and that ideas more immediately evident are (1) that I am not the only existing being (2) that I am not a necessary being (3) that bodies exist (4) that the order in matter indicates an intelligence. *Traité des premières vérités* (Paris, 1724), pp. 32-4.

[19] On Lignac's theory of ideas, see his *Élements de la métaphysique,* pp. 63-5, 77, 80-1, 132, 137, 241, etc., and *Témoignage du sens intime,* Vol. II, pp. 25 *ff.* For a technical analysis of his philosophy see F. Le Goff, *De la philosophie de l'Abbé Lignac* (Paris, 1863), and F. Bouillier, *Histoire de la philosophie cartésienne* (Paris, 1868), Vol. II, pp. 621-31.

seems to have no means of determining which shall be left out as peculiar and merely individual. The idea is not a norm by which the actual can be judged; it is a possibility that the actual may be indefinitely copied. Lignac's philosophy of will, like the philosophy of pure sensation, is thus heavily weighted towards empiricism, and provides small comfort to those who wish a metaphysical foundation for values. The reason, no doubt, is that God is regarded chiefly as power.

How far Lignac deviated from normal Cartesianism may be seen when he is compared with his contemporary Cochet. Where Lignac derives the idea of God from the sense of human free will as modified by a non-human force, Cochet, more close to the Cartesian and Catholic tradition, derives it from the sense of human imperfection. According to this argument, which was denied by the empiricists, the sense of imperfection could not exist without the idea of perfection, nor knowledge of the finite without the idea of the infinite; and the human feelings of sorrow, error, evil, ignorance, and limitation arose from native ideas of bliss, truth, good, omniscience and omnipotence, perfections which were the attributes of God. The idea of God was thus innate, and if not innate could never have been formed. No amount of looking at nature and marvelling at its wonders, said Cochet in answer to the deists, would ever in itself produce the idea of God, "for that idea represents something that has no similarity with the things represented by impressions made on our organs."[20] On this matter Cochet was probably right. It is doubtful whether mere contemplation of nature would arouse the idea of God in anyone who had not already formed the idea from some other source.

Of all the Cartesians of the time, perhaps the one who most definitely saw in the mind an active and working force was Monestier, a Jesuit who taught philosophy at Toulouse. His purpose was to defend religion by showing that infidelity stressed the baseness in man, religious truth the grandeur. By innate ideas he meant "ideas in the mind independent of the senses, of education, and of reason itself." Some of these ideas were moral, such as that benevolence is better than cruelty, or that keeping one's word is a virtue—ideas which even the *philosophes* usually held to

[20] J. Cochet, *La métaphysique, qui contient l'ontologie, la théologie naturelle et la pneumatologie* (Paris, 1753), pp. 116 ff., 133.

be "natural" if not innate. Some were metaphysical, such as the ideas of the self, unity, time, space, being, the whole, the part, yes and no—ideas which the *philosophes* believed were acquired through sensation. These ideas, according to Monestier, were impacted in the human mind at birth, and were to be regarded as the gifts of God. Without them to serve him no man would ever learn anything. Any man born a real *tabula rasa* would forever remain one.[21]

Writing with the enthusiasm of a prophet, delighting in the expansive powers of the mind, seeing in the whole universe a reflection of human nature, Monestier was unmistakably a philosopher of romanticism. The world was for him, as for Wordsworth, a thing that he half perceived and half created. There was a transcendent harmony in it, "a sovereign action which gives the most perfect unity to so many forms of being, and brings it about that the whole world . . . so joins with the mind to make one whole, that the mind, once made sensible of impressions of the material order gravitating about it as toward its center, gives in its turn to the world, by a kind of reaction, its beauty and magnificence and grandeur, and lends it a part of its reality."

Monestier did not go the whole way into idealism. He declared that distance and magnitude were relative to human nature and produced by human perception, but he seems to have thought space itself an actual medium in which men moved. He was willing to concede that without the mind this spatial world was a bleak and barren place. "If the universe seems empty when deprived of the qualities we lend it, it seems so, perhaps, only to those who have too great an idea of matter and too slight a one of mind. . . . Who can understand them, these riches that an almighty hand has poured into man's being? His treasures are so immense that the mind [or soul, *âme*] lavishes them on the whole material order and is not itself made poor. Yes, it is from the mind, as from an inexhaustible source, that come the splendor of light, the brilliance of the stars, the azure vastness of the skies, the crystal of the waters, the verdure of the plains and forests, the varied painting of the flowers. What is man doing when he admires this innumerable host of beauties that art and nature display in profusion before his eyes? New Narcissus! It is himself he admires without know-

[21] B. Monestier, *La vraie philosophie* (Paris, 1773), pp. 295, 303, 309

ing it. O greatness, O loftiness of man! How far superior to the whole world is his soul!"[22]

This Jesuit professor at Toulouse, unlike most of his contemporaries, would have understood what Shelley meant, when he called life a dome of glass staining the radiance of eternity.

These same questions that kept busy the metaphysicians were vigorously agitated on more familiar levels, particularly in the quarrel that raged over the *âme des bêtes.*[23] Descartes had pronounced animals to be automata, which, despite appearances, felt no sensations. The school of Locke held that the more complex animals, having organs analogous to man's, must also have sensations similar to his. In proportion as they explained the human mind by sensation alone, the followers of Locke, therefore, found themselves arguing that the mental life of men and animals was fundamentally the same.

Now, by a peculiarity of the French language which in this instance may or may not add to clarity, the word for mental life is *âme,* which also means what is vaguely spoken of in English as the soul. This word, it appears, is fast becoming archaic, being seriously used only in moments of high solemnity, or by persons who wish to adumbrate their meaning rather than express it. The word, however, is worth analyzing, for the controversy over the *âme des bêtes* was perhaps largely a dispute between those who understood *âme* as mind and those who understood it as soul.

The opinion may be hazarded that the conception of the soul can have vital importance only when joined with the ideas of God and eternity. The soul seems to differ from the mind or personality in being regarded as a destiny, a thing whose experience is irrevocable, whose life, once lived, cannot be lived again. Where the personality is thought of as a character formed in the individual, the soul is rather the capacity for receiving a character, with the fact, in addition, that this character, when once acquired, is the only one that the individual will ever have.

[22] *ibid.,* pp. 289, 31-7.

[23] Belief in the *âme des bêtes* was one of the commonest affirmations in the surreptitious literature of the earlier part of the century, and probably has been characteristic of irreligion since the time of the Greeks. See I. O. Wade, *The Clandestine Organization and Diffusion of Philosophic Ideas in France from 1700 to 1750* (Princeton, 1938).

It is thus of the essence of the soul to be able to win or lose for all eternity, i.e., in theological terms, to be saved or damned. Its fate is significant because there are absolute values which to miss is to miss the object of living, and an everlasting truth which not to have seen is to remain forever blind. The soul is the individual considered as pointed toward ends, not as arising from causes; it is thus not developed during life, but exists entire from the moment of conception, and is never called either young or old, mature or immature. These ends toward which it is pointed are held to exist outside of time, subject to no fluctuation, and outside of life, being goals to which life is subjected, not aims that life itself creates.

The empirical philosophy, of course, knew nothing of destiny or eternity, absolute values or goals not created by life itself. The sensationalist philosophers were too much interested in the formation of the mind to think much about its metaphysical ends; and too preoccupied with making psychology a science, and explaining the mind by sequences of observable incidents in time, to have need for the conception of the soul. Explaining the mind by sensation and experience, they wound up by identifying the soul with personality or consciousness. Personality, according to Locke, was the conscious feeling of continuous and coherent experience. Religious writers objected that, under this definition, very young children and the insane would have no personalities, though they were recognized as persons by common sense, the law, and the church.

Suppose, said the Abbé Roche, that a man knowingly commits all manner of wickedness, then forgets his past and imagines himself to have been someone of great virtue. He would then, according to Locke, possess an unblemished personality, and it would be unjust for God to punish or man to censure him. Or again, asked Roche, what advantage could Locke see in baptizing a newborn infant? "Could he regard as a Temple of the Holy Spirit a being that has not a trace of personal existence?"[24] Dogma apart, it appears that Locke was arguing for a subjective theory of the self, Roche for a theory in which the self had an objective existence independently of its own self-consciousness, and stood in

[24] A. Roche, *Traité de la nature de l'âme* (Paris, 1759), Vol. I, pp. 360 ff., Vol. II, p. 512. See Hayer, *op. cit.*, Vol. II, pp. 49 ff.

an inevitable relation to certain ends and values, whether it knew it or not.

The empiricist theory of the self was criticized also by Le Guay de Prémontval, a convert to Protestantism and member of the French colony in Berlin. Perhaps because he lived under a régime of toleration, Prémontval, more than most French philosophers of the time, could be a disinterested critic of ideas. His critical essays were written without sarcasm or acrimony, and he could discuss difficult questions without being constantly reminded of his own enlightenment. One of these essays dealt with the difference between the soul and the personality. He found that most contemporary philosophers made no distinction, and that they identified both with the conscious self. These philosophers, he thought, saw only the moral self, not the metaphysical. They allowed for no substratum of being, no deeper self to which the fate of the personality was a matter of concern.

The true reason, in his opinion, why men rightly take an interest in their own personalities was that they possessed a soul, a substance in the depths of themselves that stood to lose or gain by the direction that the personality took. The personality he thought largely contingent, adventitious. On any day of childhood something might have happened to make it different. Was it of no consequence what the actual personality turned out to be? How could it be of consequence to the man concerned, if he was himself nothing but this contingent and actual personality? To a child, said Prémontval, it certainly mattered whether he grew up to be a happy man, even though the man should have forgotten the experience of the child; and similarly to the adult man it certainly mattered whether he should enjoy bliss in another life, even though he should then have no recollection of life on earth; for child, man, and immortal spirit were all phases of the same self, were all one substance whose destiny was to assume successive forms.[25]

It is not necessary to go further into these discussions of the "real" and the "empirical" self; indeed, it is hardly possible, for the dispute was rarely conducted in those terms. What alarmed the religious was the belief in the *âme des bêtes,* which, in removing the difference between men and animals, denied some of the

[25] A. Le Guay de Prémontval, *Vues philosophiques* (Berlin, 1761), Vol. II, pp. 162 ff.

most important teachings of Christianity. The Catholic thinkers perhaps charged their opponents with more belief on this point than they actually entertained. Few philosophers meant wholly to identify the human mind with the animal, and most of them therefore regarded the accusation as a calumny.

The Catholic critics, however, were less interested in what the *philosophes* meant to say than in the assumptions and consequences which their doctrine implied. In view of the later triumph of the idea of organic evolution, with its corollary that men and animals are of one piece, it is hard to deny that these religious thinkers, as often happens with parties in opposition, foresaw the future with considerable accuracy.

It was thus clearer to Roche than to Locke himself that Locke's identification of the soul with the empirical self must end by making the mind essentially animal. This assertion was the first in Roche's list of objections to Locke's philosophy.[26] The two men differed perhaps even more fundamentally than they could know. Roche, thinking in terms of teleology, defined human nature by the ends for which he supposed it to exist: to know truth and do good, to find God and win salvation, to escape from time and come to rest in eternity. Locke, thinking in terms of causation, understood human nature by the process by which he supposed it to be formed. Problems of creation and final ends became irrelevant, because the mind, a *tabula rasa,* was endowed with nothing at birth, and the whole human being could be explained by the experience which it underwent in the temporal world. Roche took the religious and moral view, Locke the scientific and the secular. For Roche the *âme* was a soul, for Locke simply a mind, which was formed by sensation, and which, by the premises of his method, had nothing to distinguish it from other creatures whose sensations might be similar.

In the eighteenth century almost everybody conceded that the animals had true feeling and sensation. Men of scientific and secular outlook thus emphasized the similarity between human and animal nature. Men of religious and moral outlook, when they conceded sensation to animals, were only confirmed in their opinion that human nature was more than mere sensation. The theological and the classical argument, at this point, would urge man's ability

[26] Roche, *op. cit.,* Vol. I, pp. 350 *ff.*

to perceive truth and to know the difference between right and wrong. But in the eighteenth century all thought was affected by a deep subjectivism, and those who turned to this argument sometimes tended to stress, not so much these high and inaccessible abstractions themselves, as human sentiments toward them. The pleasures of truth and the delights of virtue, for many people, were more immediately real than truth and virtue themselves. The throbs and quivers of romantic sensibility arose from a metaphysical uncertainty, from a vague uneasiness in which men not accustomed to doubt hoped to assert their values by the very heat and intensity with which they felt them.

The point may be illustrated from the *Lettres Helviennes* of the Jesuit Barruel, a man who later became famous for his theory that the French Revolution was produced by a conspiracy of Freemasons and philosophers. Religion, he said, does not prevent our attributing some kind of *âme* to the beasts, but it does not follow that this *âme* is of the same kind as the human. From this mild beginning he proceeded in a few words to make sentiment divine. "Is man then man because the sun warms him, and winter benumbs his limbs, because toil fatigues him, or because the different parts of his body cannot be mangled without his feeling pain? No, these are not the pleasures and pains of man; these he can share with the brute. But by the single quality of being sensitive [*sensible*] he leaves the brute far behind. He feels joy in truth, and sorrow in falsehood. Vice he dislikes; he is revolted at the sight of crime, and his soul is torn when he is himself the author of it. He is transported by virtue; sobs of pain shake him when he sees it oppressed; he pours tears of joy upon it when he sees it triumphant. These are the pleasures and pains of man; this is the man of feeling, the image of God even in his pains and pleasures."[27] The vagaries of interpretation through which the phrase "image of God" has passed would form a curious chapter in intellectual history.

On the whole, however, it was not the orthodox who were most inclined to turn sentimental. The most acute of the orthodox thinkers had other ideas in mind, when they rejected the sensationalist philosophy and its corollary of the *âme des bêtes*. These ideas, in sum, were that the mind was an active force, that it contributed to

[27] A. Barruel, *Lettres helviennes* (7th ed., Paris, 1830), Vol. II, p. 365.

the making of its experience, that its perceptions were not only agitations of the sense organs but acts of its whole being, that the whole gave life and function to the parts, and that the living creature was to be understood, not as an accumulation of pieces, but as an indivisible unit in itself.

We are familiar with these ideas in biology and psychology today. By the theory of evolution a place has been found for the *âme des bêtes,* at some cost to the *âme des hommes,* but it is doubtful whether, in sharing his life with the animals, man has fallen to a less desirable position than that assigned him by the eighteenth century mechanists. It is at least possible, today, to regard the mind, life and soul, the *âme* or *anima,* as something more significant than a mass of sensations and impressions, and to see in the body something more valuable than a collection of pipes, levers, and hydraulic machinery.[28]

Yet even on these questions of the mind and soul the religious thinkers did not all stand together, nor were they all on their guard against subtle influences of the prevailing philosophy. The church was too large for the opinions of its members to be uniform; and the clergy included, among its scholars, many men of temperament not primarily religious. In 1751 there were certainly

[28] On the *âme des bêtes,* see further: Gauchat, *Lettres critiques, ou Analyse et réfutation de divers écrits modernes contre la religion* (Paris, 1755-63), Vol. V, pp. 78 *ff.*; Le Large de Lignac, *Lettres à un américain sur l'Histoire Naturelle de M. Buffon* (Hamburg, 1751), Vol. III, pp. 1-9, 27; L. Chaudon, *Dictionnaire anti-philosophique* (1767), art. "Bêtes"; A. Chaumeix, *Petite Encyclopédie* (Anvers, n.d.), *passim,* and *Préjugés légitimes contre l'Encyclopédie* (Paris, 1758), Vol. I, p. 241; F. Para du Phanjas, *Principes de la saine philosophie* (Paris, 1774), Vol. I, p. 164, where the *âme des bêtes* is made a third irreducible substance, equally removed from mind and from matter; P. Dufour, *op. cit.*; L. Troya d'Assigny, *Saint-Augustin contre l'incrédulité* (Paris, 1754), pp. xi *ff.*; Cardinal Polignac, *op. cit.,* Book VI; Ilhahart de La Chambre, *op. cit.,* Vol. I, p. 314; Gauchat, *op. cit.,* Vol. II, letter xxii; D. Boullier, *Essai philosophique sur l'âme des bêtes* (Amsterdam, 1728); Sinsart, *op. cit.*; Pichon, *Cartel aux philosophes à quatre pieds* (n.p.n.d.); *Indiculus propositionum extractarum a libro cui titulus De l'Esprit* (Paris, 1758), in which the Paris Faculty of Theology condemns, among many others, the propositions that the human and animal minds are alike, and that if men had hooves instead of hands they would still be wandering in the forest. Fréron, *Année littéraire* (1760), Vol. I, pp. 83 *ff.,* with his usual moderation and good sense, says he sees nothing wrong with the idea of the *âme des bêtes,* reasonably understood, and takes Dufour to task for distorting the idea in criticizing it.

men at the University of Paris willing to accept the Abbé de Prades, whose view of the world was a naïve sensationalism, remotely supplemented by the admittedly unintelligible doctrines of revelation. By the 1770's there were teachers in schools and universities throughout France who favored the system of Locke and Condillac, and expressed themselves as openly as local conditions or their own discretion would allow. They were fairly numerous as the Revolution approached; and their existence may be taken to show either that the education of the time was not so utterly stultified as the *philosophes* pretended or that in the schools themselves dangerous philosophy was being taught.[29]

At the Collège Royal of Metz an incident occurred in 1765 which was a provincial equivalent of the Prades affair in Paris. A student was defending his thesis before an assembly made up of ecclesiastics and four or five laymen. He argued "that the souls of animals, *les âmes des bêtes,* in essence and in substance, are the same as those of men, and that there are some animals more intelligent than some men." Asked what became of the soul of a horse after death, he declined to give a definite answer, but supposed that it might pass into another animal.

A layman then arose and pointed out several heretical propositions in the thesis: that light is improductible and so presumably eternal, that fire and matter may also be uncreated, that other worlds may be inhabited, and that there is no perpetual or daily creation, though the creation of new souls is the faith of the church. The layman then concluded: *"The formation of man* (you do not say of man's *body,* but of *man,* whom you define a few lines above as a being composed of body and soul) *the formation of man does not appear to differ in origin from that of animals.* I cannot, sir, convey to you my amazement at seeing a thesis in which the language is so similar to that of the materialism of our time." The student then offered to explain, but the clergy present, uneasy at seeing one of their number discomfited by a layman, changed the subject, and the matter was dropped. It soon produced a general controversy. The older people agreed with the layman. One of the

[29] C. Jourdain, *Histoire de l'Université de Paris* (Paris, 1888), Vol. II, pp. 424-6.

professors of philosophy formally endorsed his objections. To the younger people, both lay and ecclesiastic, this professor seemed excessively zealous, unnecessarily *dévot*. The younger generation at Metz in 1765 seems to have countenanced ideas that were to shock Victorian England a hundred years later.[30]

[30] This whole story is drawn only from the Jansenist *Nouvelles ecclésiastiques* (1765), p. 158. The italics in the quotation are so printed in the *Nouvelles*.

CHAPTER VII

CREATION AND CAUSALITY

I T has been seen in the preceding chapters how the religious
thinkers of France, so far as they escaped the influence of their
opponents, believed in tradition and revelation as valid sources
of factual knowledge, and in innate ideas as elements of the human
mind. In the conception of the world which these beliefs reflected,
matters of ultimate importance were held to be independent of
time and change. Tradition was immutable, and as old as the world
itself. Revelation was absolute, and to be imparted by the church to
all peoples and all generations. The individual himself was an immortal spirit, to be understood not as essentially a mind that had
grown in time but as a soul directed toward timeless ends, existing
entire from the moment of conception, and already a person before
setting out in the world of experience. Man stood in an immediate
relation to God, who watched over him by his Providence, enlightened him by revelation, endowed him with innate ideas, and
was present to him perpetually through the tradition and the sacraments of the church.

Very different was the kind of thinking that had spread widely
in the seventeenth century. Time in it was fundamental. Events
were seen against the background of the clock or the calendar. A
matter was thought to be more fully understood when, instead
of being referred directly to God, it was referred back to a series
of other observed events that had preceded it. From this new habit
of mind, which the civilization and daily life of Europe had somehow made very general, science and history as we know them both
arose. Attention shifted from final to efficient causes, from general
reasons for existence to the particulars of what actually happened.
The new thinkers conceived of nature more easily than of God,
of time more easily than of eternity, of chains of cause and effect
more easily than of a single act of universal creation. Natural

knowledge contended with revealed, history with tradition; and the sensationalist psychology offered to explain the human mind as a product of temporal process.

It remains now to see how the same conflict of ideas took place in the disputes over human origins. Here again, as in the psychological questions dealt with in the last chapter, it was human nature itself that was on trial. Where man came from obviously had much to do with what he was; and the reasons, if any, for his first appearance on earth might be reckoned as intimations of his ultimate destiny.

The theologians put a value and meaning into the world by their doctrine of the creation. Creation was different from causality, and the idea of a Creator was not the same as that of a First Cause. David Hume had no trouble in dismissing the usual arguments for the necessity of a First Cause, but it is doubtful whether his criticism quite reached the heart of the question of creation. The common arguments for a First Cause were based on an analogy. From the connection between the objects of the natural world of everyday phenomena conclusions were drawn as to the relation of the whole natural order to a power which, by definition, existed outside it. The idea of creation, on the other hand, though no doubt it also rested on analogy, had little to do with empirical phenomena or the normal sequence of physical cause and effect. It was an idea most at home in a realm of Platonic abstraction. It denied that time, as normally perceived, was of primary importance; and it therefore taught that the relation of cause and effect, of antecedent and consequent, was not ultimately significant. It held change to be a sign of imperfection, and maintained that the actual world, subject to variation and decay, had only a contingent existence, and was dependent on an unseen world of constant and universal truths.

The doctrine of creation thus referred the visible to an invisible order. It asserted the immediacy of God and the world, teaching that a divine power was intimately present everywhere, and that the universe owed its existence to plan and purpose and ideal values, which were more real than the empirical phenomena of the senses.

This metaphysical theory had been identified with the story recorded in Genesis, and as a result, although the idea of creation was best suited to a kind of thinking to which chronology was hardly relevant, the world was supposed to have come into existence about four thousand years before the birth of Christ. In the eighteenth century many persons were coming to feel that four thousand years were relatively brief. With a new sense of the importance of temporal sequence, they could not imagine a state of affairs in which no time existed. Unable to conceive of the absence of time, they thought of eternity not as timelessness but as an infinitely long series of moments. They were therefore moved to inquire what God had done before 4004 B.C., and why he had waited so long before creating the world.

To this query the religious thinkers had various answers. It was possible to reply that, while the whole matter was mysterious and incomprehensible, it was known by revelation and so must be accepted. More able thinkers gave more philosophical explanations. They denied the conception of absolute time on which the argument of the infidels rested. Thus Bergier answered Holbach's contention that God, though presumably changeless, at one time wished the universe not to exist, and then later wished that it should exist. Any competent theologian would have dismissed as anthropomorphic this supposition that God willed or acted in time. Holbach's idea, said Bergier, was absurd and false. "It is absurd to suppose a time, a duration, a succession before the creation. Time, being only the duration of the universe, was only created with it, and before time there was only eternity without succession."[1]

Bergier, representing the Christian and Platonic tradition, conceived of eternity by removing time and the natural world from his mind. Holbach, like other unbelievers, thought of eternity as temporal succession infinitely prolonged. The difference was between a man who could imagine something apart from the natural order, and one for whom the natural order included everything real.

There were many others who pointed out the metaphysical assumptions of those who asked why God had "waited" before the creation. One of these was Pierre Changeux, who in early youth wrote a treatise on certain principles of reality. Changeux never

---

[1] Bergier, *Examen du matérialisme* (Paris, 1771), Vol. II, p. 143. Bergier quotes Holbach.

fulfilled the promise of his first book, perhaps because, although not especially a religious writer, he advanced a metaphysics favorable to religious doctrines. He never won the sympathy or even the attention of the intellectual leaders of his day, and seems himself to have lost interest in purely philosophical questions, and to have turned to speculations on the origin of language. He saw no difficulty in believing the world to be, as he thought, only eight thousand years old. Time, he said, like space, was an "abstract idea" which had meaning only for beings living in the physical world. Apart from this physical world there was no time, no early and late, no before and after. To think of anything "before" the creation was thus a misapprehension, for the possibility of priority came into being with the world itself. Apart from the world there was eternal changelessness; as apart from natural life there was the immortality of the soul, in which an eternity spent in pain would be as a moment, since without time there was no summation of experience, no memory, and no hope of improvement.[2]

With similar ideas Gaspard de Forbin, who spent his life as a soldier and mathematician, undertook to reconcile reason and faith. He gave little attention to the unbelievers, and perhaps wrote chiefly to satisfy his own mind. He maintained that men existed in both time and eternity, either of which they could perceive at will. "If I think that my father really produced me and is the sole cause of me, and my grandfather the sole cause of him, and so successively back to the first man, I see myself as existing only by a series of causes and effects that follow each other in time. I then see a relative time and a relative existence, but if I reach at once to the true cause, which is God, I no longer know in what time I am produced, for in God I see nothing older or younger than myself."

The perception of serial time and of cause and effect, according to Forbin, gave knowledge only of nature; and if this were the only mode of perception there would be no knowledge except of the natural world. Skeptics and infidels might have agreed with him here, but they would have added that, this being the only trustworthy mode of perception, scientific knowledge was alone certain. Forbin, however, maintained that men possessed another

[2] P. Changeux, *Traité des extrèmes* (Amsterdam, 1767), Vol. I, pp. 168-203, Vol. II, pp. 548-9.

mode of perception by which they saw the limitations of relative time and of natural cause and effect, knew themselves to exist on another plane than the natural, and so entered into the absolute realms described by religion. He thus managed to assure himself of the rationality of the Catholic mysteries, and to accept the story in Genesis as a true, if somewhat allegorical, history of the creation.[3]

The Abbé Pluquet was more aggressive in purpose than Changeux or Forbin. He meant to criticize and refute the ideas of the infidels. Professor at the Sorbonne and at what is now the Collège de France, he was a man of philosophical accomplishment. Even Voltaire, after reading his *Examen du fatalisme,* said nothing against it. Pluquet found that the "fatalists," a term by which he meant those thinkers who held the world to be uncreated, attributed to the material universe the qualities of necessary being, infinite size, and eternal duration. He argued, in reply, that infinite space, an infinite succession of moments in time, and an infinite series of numbers were all phantoms of the imagination, which arose from the fact that in the limited experience of men all objects were presented in a serial order. The stars and sands, he said, however numerous, were numbered; everything actual, however old, had once begun. The infinity of the true "necessary being" was not the sum of actual objects but the total of all possible realities. The eternity of this being was not an endless series of moments, but the absence of change and of beginning. The true necessary and uncreated being was therefore not the actual world of nature, but a reality apart from and presiding over the natural world.[4]

[3] G. de Forbin, *Accord de la foi et de la raison* (Cologne, 1757), pp. 12-13, 34-5, 51, 293-4.

[4] F. Pluquet, *Examen du fatalisme* (Paris, 1757), Vol. II, pp. 296-326. The alleged *éternité du monde* was one of the ideas most frequently attacked by the apologists. For further examples see: N. Bergier, *Le déisme réfuté par lui-même* (Paris, 1771), Vol. II, pp. 8-9; Gauchat, *Lettres critiques, ou Analyse et réfutation de divers écrits modernes contre la religion* (Paris, 1755-63), Vol. II, p. 63, Vol. XV, pp. 190-1; N. Jamin, *Pensées théologiques* (Paris, 1769), pp. 1-24; H. Fabry de Moncault, comte d'Autrey, *Le pyrrhonien raisonnable, ou Méthode nouvelle proposée aux incrédules* (La Haye, 1765), pp. 52 ff., 102-3; C. Nonotte, *Les erreurs de Voltaire* (Avignon, 1762), Vol. II, pp. 236-8; C. Yvon, *Histoire philosophique de la religion* (Liége, 1779), Vol. I, pp. 115-16; P. Boudier de Villemert, *Pensées philosophiques* (Paris, 1784-86), Vol. I, pp. 1 ff.; Le Large de Lignac, *Le témoignage du sens intime opposé à la foi profane et ridicule des fatalistes modernes* (Auxerre, 1760), Vol. II, pp. 258 ff., where belief in the

Philosophy of this kind was what the *philosophes* meant by metaphysics when they used the word as a term of opprobrium. Such philosophy might incline a man to skepticism, as with Changeux, or to acceptance of revealed doctrines, as with Forbin and Pluquet; but in either event it implied that natural and empirical knowledge was insufficient, an unwelcome thought to the leading thinkers of the time. The *philosophes,* finding that such ideas led into an invisible world, were sure that those who held them could not possibly understand what they were talking about. Such philosophy, therefore, they dismissed as a juggling with words. Men like Diderot, Holbach, and Helvétius were not patient of criticism of their assumptions.

Unable to imagine the absence of time, and seeking always to push further back the chain of discoverable causes, the new thinkers kept enlarging and elaborating their picture of the past. The more acutely they felt the past as time requiring explanation, rather than as a reflection of eternity already explained by tradition, the more they were impelled to find facts or propose theories to fill the void; and the more facts and theories they assembled, the more past time they needed in which to deploy them. As a result, the eighteenth century saw the rise not only of a new kind of history but of historical geology and cosmology as well.

Men who had lost religious faith, and who could not see in the world a closed temporal system whose significance lay in its relation to an eternity outside it, were drawn to the idea that the universe itself was without beginning or end. The eternity of the world had been a doctrine of ancient pagan philosophers. These ancient philosophers, to fill infinite time, had advanced the theory of perpetual recurrence, by which cycles of exactly the same events were repeated forever. Two circumstances, it appears, enabled Europeans to escape this solution. First, the religious tradition, in which time contained an unfolding drama directed toward absolute ends, left in the minds of modern unbelievers an otherwise inexplicable horror for an endless and meaningless repetition of cycles. Second, the rise of empirical science, the impulse to search interminably for new facts and new data, seems to have induced a

eternity of matter is called "un acte de foi profane"; *Journal ecclésiastique,* March 1774, p. 237, where the biologist Needham disavows the inferences drawn by some thinkers from his scientific discoveries.

sense of infinite variety in the world; and with an infinite variation
even an infinite time may be filled without perpetual recurrence.
When an unlimited variety is distributed over a time scale and
thought of in terms of cause and effect, the ideas of progress and
of evolution very easily follow. Both ideas did in fact arise in the
eighteenth century.

For the idea of evolution, perhaps the best statement of the
metaphysical groundwork was made by the philosopher Robinet.
Robinet, like Changeux, had the misfortune of not being wholly
acceptable to either party in the great controversies of the time,
and it is probably for that reason that he is little known today.
Though compared to Diderot for the audacity of his opinions, he
differed greatly from Diderot and the deists, for he made God a
vital part of his philosophic system. At the same time, and with
good reason, he was held in horror by the religious. There was,
however, an abstract and philosophic piety in much that he wrote,
and he died in 1820 in the bosom of the Catholic Church.

Robinet held that the only absolute, necessary, uncreated, and
eternal being was God. The world of nature he thought derivative
and contingent, but without beginning or end. It had always existed
and would always exist, but it was not to be thought of as eternal.
Distinguishing between eternity and time, Robinet saw in eternity
the changeless existence of a being not of this world, to whom all
reality was present as in one instant, and in time a succession of
moments in an infinitely flowing stream. Eternity and time, he
thought, so far as they were comparable at all, were coextensive,
existing respectively in the absolute and in the contingent order.
They were kept together by the creation, which was not an event in
the past, but a perpetual act by which the world was held eternally
in existence. But if this creative act was sustained forever, would
there not reappear, from time to time, the same patterns that had
already been produced? To think so, said Robinet, was the fallacy
of the ancients, who, because they had no adequate conception of
God, had failed to realize the infinite possibility of variation in
created things.[5]

[5] J. Robinet, *De la nature* (Amsterdam, 1761-68), Vol. III, pp. 202-11. See also
Robinet's *Considérations philosophiques sur la gradation naturelle des formes de
l'être, ou les essais de la nature qui apprend à faire l'homme* (Paris, 1768).

All this was no doubt highly abstract. Fortunately there was a more picturesque work on the subject, the *Telliamed* of de Maillet, written a generation before Robinet's *De la nature*. De Maillet had no discoverable religious interests and his metaphysics were all taken for granted. But his work illustrates, on a more concrete and common-sense level than Robinet's, exactly the same point: how the belief that the world could have had no beginning, together with a sense of endless variety, led to a theory of evolutionary change. The *Telliamed* was extremely well known in its day. Read at first only in manuscript in select circles, it was published in 1748, and its name soon became a byword, sufficiently understood when barely alluded to, standing for the most horrendous doctrines of the materialists. The book was made up of close observations, shrewd guesses and fantastic theories, and was dedicated to the memory of Cyrano de Bergerac.

"If I were to consult my reason, the sole guide of a philosopher," said de Maillet guardedly, "I should say that my inability to understand how matter and motion could have begun would be enough for me to believe them eternal." He then raised the usual question, why God had waited until only six thousand years ago to create the world. The orthodox answer to this question he turned to his own use: God, being changeless, wills eternally what he wills; hence the world has always existed. But, says de Maillet, it may be objected that if the world were eternal it could no longer be what it is—the mountains, for example, would all be flattened down. To this objection his answer is that change is perpetual and the number of possible forms inexhaustible. ". . . I shall presently establish that the globe we inhabit, like all the others contained in the vast extent of matter, is in truth subject to such vicissitudes that, even supposing it eternal, it would appear to us today no otherwise than as we see it."

So de Maillet, believing in advance in these vicissitudes, set out to find them empirically. The earth, he held, had once been covered with water. Currents in this primeval ocean laid down lines of sediment, which, as the water evaporated, emerged from the sea, and are today the highest ranges of mountains. Near these early shores many marine species lived, the ancestors of later species on land. Birds, most probably, had developed from flying fish tossed up by accident on the shore, walking animals from the heavier creatures that crawled on the ocean bed.

To explain how man came directly from the sea de Maillet made use of a questionable method, abandoning the natural evidence of fossils, stratified rock, and comparative anatomy on which his other theories, however mistaken, were built, and resorting to human testimony, legends, rumors, travellers' tales and sea captains' reports. In the existing state of knowledge he could hardly do otherwise, granted the theory that he wished to prove; but the results were unfortunate, for he was much less skilful in criticizing human opinions than in interpreting natural phenomena. Mermen and mermaids were for him the link that joined men to the sea. He thought that migration from water to land went on continually in the polar regions, and that the men of northern Europe and Asia were more hardy than others because they were the most recently emerged.[6]

There was little enough evidence at that time for most of de Maillet's conjectures, but many people who had lost faith in revelation and needed a new explanation of the origin of the world were ready to receive them with considerable respect. Buffon knew the *Telliamed* and adopted some of de Maillet's ideas, though as a responsible scientist he rejected those which rested on supposed facts that no one had ever observed. Diderot, in such hidden corners of the *Encyclopédie* as the article on the "Philosophy of the Ethiopians," suggested that life had begun from a fermentation in matter, and that men were descended from animals. Holbach, arguing that the world was eternal, was forced to consider whether each living species was eternal, specially created, or subject to variation and part of an unending flux; and it was the third theory that he favored. Carra, a prophet of revolution and later a Girondist, took over most of the *Telliamed* entire, and read into it a social significance of which de Maillet had never dreamed. "Thus millions of generations," he said, "heaped upon one another in the bosom of their mother [Nature] are unsuccessful and preparatory attempts condemned by Nature in advance, and whose frightful history shows us the annals of stupidity, ignorance and

---

[6] B. de Maillet, *Le Telliamed* (Amsterdam, 1748), *passim,* but especially Vol. I, pp. 62-71, 108 *ff.*, Vol. II, pp. 61-3, 101 *ff*. A life of de Maillet is prefaced to the edition of 1755. The name Telliamed is de Maillet's name spelled backwards.

barbarism of past races, and the means . . . of amendment for races to come."[7]

To such speculations the religious writers usually answered briefly that they were absurd. So far as the marine origin of life was concerned, this was also the opinion of those unbelievers, like Voltaire, who were most averse to theorizing. The Jesuit *Journal de Trévoux,* as often happened, expressed the general view of the judicious and the educated, when it set down de Maillet as a victim of his own credulity, and observed of Buffon's *Théorie de la Terre* that a man with Buffon's known dislike for general systems should avoid embarking on such hazardous hypotheses. The Abbé Gauchat noted with confident irony that de Maillet's ideas rested less on evidence than on the hope of finding evidence in the future and the belief that evidence now destroyed had existed in the past. In the then existing state of empirical information such criticisms were only reasonable.[8]

[7] Buffon, *Théorie de la terre* and *Époques de la nature*; *Encyclopédie,* art. "Éthiopiens, Philosophie des"; Holbach, *Système de la nature* (Londres, 1770), Vol. I, pp. 81-2; Diderot, *Oeuvres,* Vol. II, pp. 15-16; Carra, *Système de la raison* (Londres, 1782), p. 31.

[8] Gauchat, *Lettres critiques,* Vol. XV, p. 164; *Journal de Trévoux* (1749), pp. 631 ff., 2226 ff. Later, after Buffon's "recantation," a writer in the *Journal de Trévoux* (1754), pp. 153-5, gives a fair statement of Buffon's idea of the gradation of species, and notes of this system that Buffon "le combat par la révélation." Satisfied with Buffon's ostensible deference to revelation, the writer calls him a man "du mérite le plus rare." This is only one example of the way in which the *Journal de Trévoux* sought to reach an accommodation with the new philosophy. T. M. Royou, *Analyse et réfutation des Époques de la nature* (Paris, 1780), finds Buffon's work "un tissu de suppositions gratuites, de faits imaginaires, de contradictions palpables," equally repugnant to reason and to scripture. Bougainville, translator of Polignac's *Anti-Lucrèce,* mentions having seen a manuscript of the *Telliamed,* which he regards as scandalous and extravagant: *Anti-Lucrèce* (Paris, 1749), Vol. I, p. xl. Lignac, *Lettres à un américain* (Hamburg, 1751), Vol. III, p. 27, thinks that certain philosophers, from Buffon's hypothesis of the gradation of species, draw materialistic conclusions which Buffon never intended. Linguet, *Annales civiles,* Vol. XIV, pp. 57-8, by no means a religious apologist, thinks Buffon's theories too far fetched to endure. Bergier, against Holbach's supposition that species may change, pronounces it to be more incredible than the idea of creation: *Examen du matérialisme,* Vol. I, pp. 143-8. See also Sennemaud, *Pensées philosophiques d'un citoyen de Montmartre* (La Haye, 1756), pp. 14 ff.; Chaumeix, *Préjugés légitimes contre l'Encyclopédie,* Vol. I, pp. 56 ff.; M. Villiers, *Dignité de la nature humaine* (Paris, 1778); *Nouvelles ecclésiastiques* (1750), p. 25; H. Fabry, comte d'Autrey, *Pyrrhonien raisonnable,* pp. 82-3; Palissot, *Mémoires* (Paris, 1803), Vol. II, pp. 122-4; Raynal in Grimm, *Correspondance littéraire,* Vol. I, pp. 337-8; Yvon,

But the primary issue was not whether natural evidence was sufficient in amount, but whether in any amount it was the proper kind of evidence to use. As the Jansenists made clear, the question was whether the learned world was going to trust modern naturalists or the sacred writers—"the admirable M. de Buffon or Moses inspired by God." Gauchat, neither a Jesuit nor a Jansenist, conceded that the Bible was not a work of physics, but insisted that it must be retained as an authentic history. The world, he thought, must be of the age indicated in the New Testament. Otherwise Moses would have deceived us; we could not believe his account of God's dealings with mankind. De Maillet's theories were furthermore impious in implying belief in the *âme des bêtes*. "For in brief," said Gauchat, "if men have been fish, and if there are still fish in the sea destined to be men, of two things one must follow: either men have no spiritual and immortal soul, or fish have."[9]

Gauchat had many other arguments, and his long dissertation on the new cosmogonies summed up about all that the religious writers had to say. He declared that the function of science was only to discover truths useful to men. It was hopeless and useless, he thought, for human reason to try to penetrate to the origin of the world. How could a man, after looking at a few layers of rock and a few petrified bones, soberly conclude that the world was 100,000 years old? From such methods, he said, only mythologies as extravagant as those of the ancients could result. He held that the only reason why the earth with its strata of rock existed as it did was that God created it so, but added that in ordinary phenomena such as the discharge of a cannon, for which natural laws could be known, it would be absurd to appeal directly to God's will.

Gauchat thus distinguished between creation and causality, hoping to safeguard the former. The distinction was a compromise, and a precarious one. Removing the element of creation from such facts as the discharge of a cannon, it reserved it for

Histoire philosophique de la religion, Vol. I, pp. 22-8; F. Feller, *Examen impartial des Époques de la nature* (Luxembourg, 1780).

[9] *Nouvelles ecclésiastiques* (1767), p. 65. The editors note with alarm that the *Journal des savants*, in its issue for December 1766, praises the theories of Buffon, de Maillet, Mairan and others who argue for an immense antiquity of the world. Gauchat, *op. cit.*, Vol. XV, pp. 67, 224.

the history of the earth only as a special exception. Gauchat might have been on stronger ground philosophically, though his position in controversy would have been weaker, had he asserted that both the discharge of the cannon and the history of the earth might be referred, according to the purpose in hand, either to God's will or to anterior causes. So the Catholic Forbin or the free-thinking Robinet might have argued, but their views seem to have been little understood.[10]

Some of the objections that seemed strongest to Gauchat must have seemed to his adversaries beside the point, for he thought in terms of creation and of the immediacy of man and God, where his adversaries thought in terms of natural causes. He believed that the universe existed for a purpose, and that this purpose was to serve as the habitation of man. Not only could he not sympathize with a contrary view, he could not even comprehend it. Nor could he imagine why the sun and other physical bodies should have existed long before the appearance of the earth, as Buffon held. "What was the object of the sun? What did it do, idle in its vortex [*tourbillon,* the Cartesian word]? Has not its destination always been to light and fructify the earth?" All such cosmology seemed to him needlessly complicated, and held together by trivial causes. To attribute to a mere comet, casually striking on the sun, so momentous a fact as the origin of the earth seemed to him plainly absurd; and to spin elaborate theories over inconceivable reaches of time was only to raise difficulties where none before had existed. "Supposing the earth was arranged ages after its emergence from the sun, how can the animals have peopled it? How can man have possessed it? A new creation would be necessary. But why not recognize the creation of the earth? Could not God create man and his habitation by one decree?" It is to be noted how this objection, designed to make philosophers accept Moses, would be more likely to incline them toward ideas of evolution.[11]

The idea of progress also, it was suggested some pages back, arose partly from the new habit of looking to causality rather than to creation. That this idea was not the fruit of a gratuitous opti-

[10] Gauchat, *op. cit.,* Vol. XV, pp. 130 *ff.,* 171-85.
[11] *ibid.,* pp. 285-7.

mism, but a logical consequence of the infidel beliefs, becomes evident when we see how religious writers sometimes hoped to overthrow their opponents by arguing, in effect, that progress was impossible. The important question here was the origin of human intelligence.

Was the human mind the product of generations of experience in time, or was it placed purposely in the world at the beginning, created with man himself? Religious people took the latter view. Infidel opinion was confused. When the infidels thought of nature as a standard of correct values and wished to show faults in existing society, they usually had a high opinion of primitive man's intelligence. When they thought of nature as an impersonal process of causation, and wished to congratulate themselves on the enlightenment of their age, they regarded primitive man as ignorant and barbarous. On the whole, they favored the belief that intelligence was an historical acquisition.

The religious writers often took the doctrine of the eternity of the world in its ancient sense, to mean that man and civilization were eternal. This supposed belief they refuted on the ground that, if man were eternal, the number of generations already deceased would be infinite, and the present generation could not exist if it had to wait for an infinity of predecessors to go before it. The argument was purely academic, for no modern thinker believed the human race to be eternal. Those who believed the universe to be without beginning had already smuggled in enough evolution to give man's origin a particular date in time. In answer to the supposed belief in the eternity of civilization the apologists pointed to the shortness of known history, the traditional belief of all peoples in a definite origin, and the recency of many important discoveries and inventions. These very facts had led Greek thinkers to the doctrine of recurrent cycles. But a millennium of Christian theology had made it impossible for any European not to see in the cosmos a unique process, an irreversible series of events. It is significant, therefore, that religious apologists, to account for the known recency of things, used the idea of progress, and sometimes the very word. "In all monuments of older times," said the Abbé Hooke of the Sorbonne, "we

observe the recent origin of the world and the progress of the
whole human race from infancy to childhood and adult life."[12]

But progress could not have for believing Christians the fundamental meaning that it came to have for the new philosophy. If
man was created perfect, no subsequent *perfectibilité* was necessary, except possibly to retrieve the loss sustained in Adam's fall.
And if man had not been created perfect, what became of the
goodness of God? Was it likely that a beneficent God would create
him benighted and frail, and leave him to grope through ages of
violence, toil and suffering, toward a hoped for perfection that
most men could never see? Or was it to be believed, by any but
atheists, that men should have to rely, for such advances as they
made, on their own efforts rather than on faculties originally
given to them by a creator?

The idea of progress was in truth not a comforting one, except
for men in whose minds the possibilities of the future outweighed
the grim realities of the past. Voltaire, with his knowledge of
history and sense of human suffering, might well have agreed with
the Christian writers in regarding it as a dubious consolation.
"This God of goodness," observed the Catholic Comte d'Autrey
(and but for the conclusion it might have been Voltaire speaking), "this God of goodness could have enlightened in one word
and one instant the whole posterity of the first man, as he enlightened at the beginning all races of animals with an instinct more
certain than our reason. . . . What, is it possible that the creator of
the world should have preferred that this people, born for instruction and for virtue, should begin by being ignorant and stupid?
He would then have willed that man should learn only by a long
series of crimes and calamities. . . . He would have willed, this
God of goodness, this almighty Being who gives to all things from
the first the full perfection of which they are capable, he would
have willed to enlighten by horrible stages the only beings able

[12] Hooke, *Religionis naturalis et moralis philosophiae principia* (1752-54),
Vol. I, pp. 57-8; F. Feller, *Catéchisme philosophique* (Liége, 1773), pp. 28-9;
J. Menoux, *Notions philosophiques sur les vérités de la religion* (Nancy, 1758),
pp. 9 ff.; Yvon, *op. cit.*, pp. 19-20; Fabry, comte d'Autrey, *op. cit.*, pp. 38-40.
"Je vous demande," says the count of Autrey, "s'il est vraisemblable que les
hommes policés aient restés soixante ou quatre-vingt mille ans sans inventer
l'imprimerie." cf. N. Jamin, *op. cit.*, p. 15: ". . . les arts, les machines trouvées
en différents temps pour les besoins des hommes sont autant de preuves de la
nouveauté du monde."

to know and adore him. This picture of Providence makes you shudder. You will say that I blaspheme against God and Nature, against analogy and reason." All this being conceded, Voltaire would perhaps have advised men to dig patiently in their gardens. Fabry d'Autrey concluded that man, though originally perfect, had brought himself to woe by the fall. He invited his readers to choose: either man's sufferings came from sin, or they were due to the slowness and difficulty of his rise from an original savagery. For him the decision could not be in doubt.[13]

Unable to accept progress as part of a divine dispensation, religious writers sought to prove it impossible. Their strongest argument was taken from the empirical psychology of their opponents. From the generally accepted fact that men could learn nothing in isolation, and that children learned by imitation of their elders, they argued that every generation must have been preceded by one able to instruct it, and that however far into the past investigation might reach, at no point would there be found a time when an ignorant and brutish society could give birth to men of intelligence.

The Protestant Formey suggested as an experiment, while admitting it to be impracticable, that a group of human beings should be isolated in childhood and left so for several generations. He was sure that they would never learn anything, and concluded that a race of men thus thrown unassisted on the earth would soon perish.

The Catholic Le Gros observed that the doctrine of *perfectibilité* was a way of asserting not a faculty of moral self-perfection but an initial emptiness of mind, both psychologically in the infant and historically in the human race. But, he said, Rousseau and other adherents to this doctrine generally thought that the first men had been physically like those of the eighteenth century. How then, asked Le Gros, granted the known interdependence of body and mind, could the first men have been mentally so inferior as the infidels maintained?[14]

These were weighty objections. Probably the *philosophes,* when aware of them, saw in them the captiousness of the unenlightened. It was, however, such logical difficulties as these that eventually

[13] *Le pyrrhonien raisonnable,* pp. 60-71, 102-3, 118.
[14] J. Formey, *L'anti-Émile* (Berlin, 1763), p. 217; C. Le Gros, *Examen des ouvrages de J.-J. Rousseau et de Court de Gebelin* (Genève, 1786), pp. 33-41.

drove serious thinkers further away from both Moses and Rousseau, leading them to embrace ever vaster reaches of time, in which the rise of knowledge from ignorance should be gradual enough to be plausible, and to adopt the idea of biological evolution, in which the earliest men should be thought physically as well as mentally different from their successors. The religious apologists of the eighteenth century saw in these same difficulties new grounds for believing in revelation. Convinced that intelligence could not arise from stupidity, they concluded that man had been originally endowed by a creator who was the source of all knowledge. From his proposed experiment, said Formey, it would become evident that the first men were created with the use of speech and with a certain body of knowledge, from which they gradually built up the arts and sciences as known in the eighteenth century.[15]

In this conflict of opinions it was clearly important to know what the first ideas of the first men would be. The *philosophes,* for the most part, believed that they had been of a practical kind. "It is clear," said Montesquieu, "that the first ideas of man would not be speculative. He would think of preserving his existence before inquiring into his origin." Montesquieu therefore set down peace as the "first law of man"; following in order after this were the instincts to seek nourishment, to reproduce, to form societies, and to love God. He excused himself by observing that duty to God, though fifth in order, was the first in importance. But his classification implied that religion and speculative thinking were refinements to which men might aspire when more pressing wants were satisfied, rather than attributes so fundamental in human nature that it would not be human without it. Religious writers vehemently protested. And not only the Christian but the Cartesian and rationalist view of human nature was impugned.

Montesquieu, said the Abbé Bonnaire, "constantly forgets that he is speaking of an intelligent being. An intelligent being, who feels that he is intelligent and that he did not make himself, seeks first of all to know his origin. That is his most natural impulse. But our author prefers to imagine that hunger would be his first sentiment. . . . The intelligent being would thus begin by being wholly animal. . . . Do you wish me to give you the true key to all this? It is that the author regards, or seems to have regarded,

15 Formey, *op. cit.,* pp. 218-28; Fabry d'Autrey, *op. cit.,* pp. 58-71.

intelligence in man as an acquired faculty or quality, with the consequence that the soul is only a progressive ordering of parts of matter."[16]

The same wide differences revealed themselves in discussions of the history of religion. The infidels, even when respectful to Christianity, offended the faithful by their theory of its origin. Orthodoxy held that man was created in Eden with knowledge of the true God. The unbelievers, when not arguing that man received this knowledge from nature, held the contrary opinion that he attained to it by a laborious growth in civilization. According to Rousseau, men in the earliest ages were unable to understand the idea of spirit, and so had peopled the world with physical divinities. According to Montesquieu, it was the increase of human intelligence that had turned men from idolatry to the Christian religion. But neither of these statements, seemingly so flattering to Christianity, could be accepted by true believers.

Montesquieu's notion implied that the triumph of Christianity was not supernatural, Rousseau's that the first men were ignorant pagans. Both placed Christianity in a sequence of cause and effect, making it a consequence of earlier conditions. Both asserted the reality of progress, holding that men moved through time from error toward truth. The church, on the other hand, taught that knowledge of truth was connate with man himself. Christians, therefore, like the *philosophes* themselves when they took the other horn of their dilemma, believed that the first man had been a theist. "If theism," said the Abbé Yvon, "was the first religion it must be the true one, which is divided into natural and revealed. Error, being only a disfigured copy of truth, must have come after it." This was the reverse of the idea of progress.[17]

Montesquieu offended further when he said that Christianity was especially suited to the climate and people of Europe. Believers, of course, held that Christianity was equally suited to the whole human race, since it was the only complete statement

[16] L. Bonnaire, *L'Esprit des Lois quintessencié* (n.p., 1751), pp. 40-3; *Nouvelles ecclésiastiques* (1749), p. 162, (1750), p. 68.

[17] Yvon, *op. cit.*, Vol. I, p. 55. Yvon, however, has the idea of progress: ". . . la raison a fait . . . des progrès . . . aussi nécessaires que la croissance des arbres et des plantes." *ibid.*, Vol. II, p. 450. On Yvon see above, p. 119. cf. *Nouvelles ecclésiastiques* (1749), p. 166; Gauchat, *op. cit.*, Vol. XIX, p. 129; Hooke, *op. cit.*, Vol. II, p. 799.

of the true relation of man to the world and to God. In attributing its success in Europe to geographical and other local conditions Montesquieu greatly narrowed its scope, and represented it as a purely human phenomenon, by no means even unique, since he regarded Mohammedanism in the same way. He set aside as irrelevant the question whether it was true or false, and in doing so, though he marked an epoch in the philosophy of history, he both outraged the religious and left many of the infidels dissatisfied. The Jansenists thought the Jesuits had been too lenient in reviewing the *Esprit des lois*. They pointed out that Montesquieu's method was to avoid judgments of value, to regard all social phenomena as equally the consequence of natural conditions, and to reduce all beliefs, customs, religions and institutions to mere facts that could hardly have been otherwise.[18] The Abbé Gauchat raised the same objections. "Not the least expression," he said, "by way of corrective, in the cause of virtue. Not a censure of vice. . . . Not a word of praise for truth, not a word for the preference that it merits. So singular an impartiality becomes a tacit approval of error and an outrage to virtue."[19]

The more advanced infidels made much the same criticism. They too found Montesquieu too phlegmatic, because, like the orthodox, they were more certain than Montesquieu of possessing a truth of their own. Montesquieu gave offense, at bottom, by using the method of science and history. He referred phenomena to the causes which he thought produced them, and judged those to be right which were in harmony, not with ethical principles, but with a general system of conditions into which he could fit them.

Attitudes toward human history and progress were made concrete in various conceptions of the state of nature and of primitive savagery. In medieval Europe, when Christians contemplated the few savages that they knew anything about, they did not think that they saw the original condition of man. In the eighteenth century this older opinion was most fully represented by the Jansenists, who regarded the state of nature as one not really natural to man, but one into which he had been plunged by the Fall, and in which he could know nothing of true virtue or religion. Catholic orthodoxy, led by the Jesuits and the Molinists, held that the state

[18] *Nouvelles ecclésiastiques* (1749), pp. 161-7 (1756), pp. 33-6.
[19] Gauchat, *op. cit.*, Vol. IV, pp. 204-5, 217-18, 237 ff.

of nature *could* have been original to man; that Adam was created with both natural and supernatural gifts, but *could* have been created with the natural only; that savages still possessed the natural gifts, which had not been impaired by the Fall; and that therefore savages could have, without knowledge of Christianity, an intelligent natural morality and a natural religion that contained part of the truth.[20] The *philosophes* went further in holding that the state of nature was positively the original state of man, and that the first man had in fact received only natural gifts.

There were, however, two tendencies among the *philosophes*. Sometimes they regarded the state of nature as one of ignorance and brutality, from which man had emerged by an historical progress. Sometimes, as in Diderot's *Supplément au voyage de Bougainville,* they represented men in the state of nature as intelligent and benign, adept at philosophical conversation, and endowed with an unerring insight into morals and theology. Jean-Jacques Rousseau brought the two tendencies together, arguing frankly, in his first two discourses, that it was the ignorance of the natural man that made him an unprejudiced thinker, and his lack of civilized refinements that made him kind-hearted and good. Thus Rousseau became the apostle of primitivism, if not of anarchy, and launched the attack on all known forms of civilization which the judicious Grimm, who was rarely so mistaken, thought too sophistical to need refutation from a serious thinker.

Catholic critics, examining the new ideas of the state of nature, denied that man possessed originally only natural gifts. But since they regarded the supernatural gifts as somewhat special, and thought, unlike the Jansenists, that much of man's life was purely natural, they were able and willing to debate with the infidels on their own terms. In the infidel philosophy it was not the assertion of man's natural goodness that they most vigorously denied. What they chiefly denied was the idea that man had not at first possessed intelligence. It was the belief that man had been at first a kind of brute, that his first impulses were produced by physical needs, that his intellect and institutions were acquired empirically in the process of satisfying bodily wants. The orthodox upheld the idea of Providence against that of Progress. They upheld also the rationalism that had reached its height in the preceding century.

[20] See above, Chap. II.

When not affected by the new modes of thinking, they meant by nature reason. The state of nature, since the Middle Ages, was, by definition, the hypothetical state in which men lived by unaided intelligence without benefit of supernatural revelation. The infidels made frequent use of this hoary conception, but added two significant innovations. They asserted that this state of nature was actually the whole original state of man, which believers denied by pointing to the revelation that had begun with Adam; and they maintained, though with many lapses into the older opinion, that man at the beginning was not a rational creature, but a being who acquired his intelligence by experience in his environment.

It was the genius of Rousseau to state clearly and eloquently what contemporaries were waiting to be told. He announced that man in the state of nature was not rational, but that the state of nature was nevertheless a standard by which society might be judged. He thus made room for two of the most powerful tendencies of the age, the growth of empiricism, which made difficult the conception of man as an essentially rational creature, and the growth of social discontent, which made necessary some ideal basis for condemning the existing order. He expressed a revolution in the idea of nature. Nature was no longer rationality, but empirical circumstance; and human nature was not primarily the capacity for intelligent knowledge, but a body of wants, instincts, impulses, and feelings.

To Rousseau's belief in the goodness of human nature orthodox Catholics did not usually object. When an anonymous critic of Rousseau, to vindicate civilization, held that men in the state of nature were turbulent, stupid and fierce, devoid of ideas, and unable to distinguish right from wrong, the *Journal de Trévoux* took a position equally removed from both sides. It maintained that men naturally possessed intelligence, conscience, and the capacity for moral development. It thus gave expression to the theology known to the Jansenists as Molinism. On this matter the orthodox stood nearer to Rousseau and most other *philosophes* than to the Jansenists or any thinkers who held nature to be amoral or bad.[21]

[21] *Journal de Trévoux* (1755), pp. 1738-9. See also J. Fumel, Bishop of Lodève, *Instruction pastorale sur les sources de l'incrédulité* (Paris, 1765), p. 39. The *Journal de Trévoux* (1751), pp. 505-26, reviewing Rousseau's *Discours sur les arts et les sciences,* praises the author's literary skill, wishes him success in the

It was when Rousseau produced the more characteristic part of his message, declaring that human nature was fundamentally emotion, that the orthodox rose in opposition. The orthodox would concede human nature to be good only when the distinctive element in human nature was held to be reason.[22] If by nature Rousseau meant reason, said Gauchat, then he might correctly argue that "the first movements of nature are always right"; but in fact he meant only native inclinations, and to argue that native inclinations were always right was to fly in the face of both revelation and experience. Rousseau's fundamental error, it seemed to Gauchat, was his attempt to understand the nature of man in terms of his physical origin, and then to base law and right on human nature thus physically defined. Laws of right were in his opinion imposed on man by a power that established his moral condition; and the proper way to understand human nature was to understand its dependence on these laws, to know, that is, not man's inclinations but his duties. He therefore proceeded to describe a state of nature acceptable to Catholics, in which man should be a rational creature able to understand moral truth.[23]

A most incisive criticism of the state of nature as conceived by Rousseau in the two *Discourses* was published three years before the Revolution by the Abbé Le Gros. Le Gros thought it an outrageous paradox for Rousseau to attribute moral quality to a being to whom he denied rational or reflective life. "How, in speaking of men whom he calls 'null,' 'brutish,' 'stupid,' 'imbecile,' can he exalt with enthusiasm 'their antique simplicity,' 'their original goodness,' 'their primitive innocence'?" How could he apply such value judgments to purely physical beings? "Has anyone ever said of an orang-outang that it was naturally 'good and happy, wise and simple'? Or spoken of its 'antique simplicity,' 'primitive innocence,' and 'original goodness'?" Rousseau complained that he was treated as a bad man for having dared to call men good. "No, Jean-Jacques, I shall not treat you as a bad man 'for having dared to maintain that man is born good.' Everyone knows that

future, and lets his ideas pass without much comment, probably seeing in them a harmless *tour de force*.

[22] Except for such deviations into sentimentalism as are suggested in the quotations on pp. 51 and 108 above.

[23] Gauchat, *op. cit.*, Vol. V, pp. 65 ff., 76-7, 85-7, 101-3, Vol. XIX, 137-55. See also Formey, *Anti-Émile,* pp. 216-25.

man comes from his Creator 'good, happy, wise, and perfect';
no one disputes this truth. What you are blamed for is your making
man come from his Creator in a state of stupidity, and yet maintaining that in this state men are good, happy, wise, and simple.
What you are blamed for is your making their goodness depend
on their imbecility, their happiness on their stupidity. What you
are blamed for is your having been guilty in all your writings of
an enormous abuse of language, and having offered us, as the
'true road to happiness,' the ignorance, imbecility and stupidity
that you have not blushed to attribute to our first parents."[24]

Le Gros spoke with a vigor which the more timid critics of
our age may think excessive, but the reasonable century did in
truth produce this monstrous irrationality. Primitivism, however,
was only one development among several. Unbelievers were pretty
generally agreed, despite frequent utterances to the contrary, that
rational intelligence was not an original faculty of the human
race. They were pretty generally agreed that human nature was
more nearly animal than had previously been thought. They were
agreed, too, when they considered the matter, that man was a
casual occupant of the universe, a physical product of natural
causes, not a soul providentially created. Sometimes, however, seeing in human intelligence an historical acquisition, they valued it
the more highly precisely for that reason, and, inheriting from
Christian theology the feeling that time is subordinate to absolute
ends, as a stream flowing beneath the light of eternity, they arrived at the idea of progress. This idea, if open to obvious ironical
objections, was perhaps no more so than any other supernatural
belief, and was at any rate a way of putting human meaning into
a world understood in terms of time and causality. To the idea of
progress, which asserted the value of civilization and of historical
development, primitivism was to all appearances the direct contrary. If many people inclined strongly toward them both, the
fact arose from their conception of nature, which allowed them

[24] Le Gros, *op. cit.*, pp. 62-6. See also Cardinal Gerdil, *Discours philosophique sur l'homme considéré relativement à l'état de nature et à l'état de société* (Turin, 1769) ; and L. Castel, *L'homme moral opposé à l'homme physique de M. Rousseau* (Toulouse, 1756). "Quoi?" says Castel, "pour connaître l'homme, vous lui ôtez tout ce qu'il a de mieux?" p. 34. For other answers to Rousseau see A. Monod, *De Pascal à Chateaubriand: Les défenseurs français du Christianisme de 1670 à 1802* (Paris, 1916), pp. 402-24.

to believe that civilization, though wholly natural in one sense, would become still more natural, in another sense, as time went on.

Like primitivism, Christian orthodoxy approved of man in his original state, but did so for different reasons, since where Adam was a rational creature, man "fresh from the hands of Nature" was unencumbered by the intellect. Like believers in progress, the orthodox thought highly of civilization, though here again the reasons were different. For the religious, civilization was the outcome of the creator's gifts. For full believers in progress, civilization, with all its arts and sciences, was man's own achievement, which he had built up painfully alone—although, to be sure, he received useful communications from Nature.

CHAPTER VIII

OBLIGATION AND LIBERTY

"THE true cause of unbelief is the severity of Christian morals. The obscurity of the mysteries is only a pretext."[1] So wrote the Abbé Trublet, and such was the opinion of all religious people, even of those who in examining the views of the infidels refrained from abusing them personally. The opinion was not the whole of the truth. Many believers were able to live about as they pleased, and many unbelievers practised most of the rational virtues.

But it would be false to regard infidelity, above all in the France of Louis XV, as a purely intellectual movement arising from considered doubt. The *philosophes* wrote not only for the thoughtful, but for the wits and fops of fashionable Paris, the *beaux esprits* and the *petits maîtres,* of whom we read little in most histories of infidel philosophy but very much in the records of the time. The new ideas spread among people whom many *philosophes* would themselves condemn, the gullible and talkative world of the drawing-rooms, who needed new subjects for sprightly conversation and saw in "philosophy" an exciting novelty of the day; persons to whom the Christian virtues of chastity and humility were usually remote, and who thought poverty and obedience the special qualities of the masses. For such people, it may be supposed, Diderot introduced the more salacious parts of the *Encyclopédie,* and among such people many *philosophes* habitually lived, as did Helvétius, whose early life contains much to amaze the innocent.

Ribald the writings of the infidels undoubtedly were, full of crude jokes and grave erudite indecencies; but the ribaldry was only on the surface. A moral revolution was in progress underneath. The infidels were in revolt against the Christian conception of man. The whole controversy was a moral one, involving the

[1] N. Trublet, *Essais de littérature et de morale* (1749), Vol. II, p. 414.

ultimate moral questions: what a man should expect from life, where he should look for his most substantial satisfactions, what authorities he should recognize as just, what definition he should give to the happiness which everyone conceded to be his proper goal. For serious thinkers the obscurity of the mysteries was no mere pretext for unbelief. The mysteries had long ceased to have any meaning for them. They were told by apologists that, since the mysteries need have no intelligible meaning, they should be content with the evidences for belief; but these evidences were either miracles, which their new faith in nature made it impossible for them to accept, or the perpetual existence of the church through the ages, which to their historical sense seemed only a series of natural events. The strongest argument of the apologists was to maintain, not that the mysteries shed any light on human nature, but that human nature was such that in the presence of wonders men must believe and obey.[2]

Many of the faithful were no doubt satisfied with this argument. Those whose faith was habitual or whose interests were chiefly ecclesiastical could thus accept as relevant to human affairs mysteries which otherwise would seem meaningless and arbitrary. Acknowledging the authority of the church, they accepted its doctrines as somehow true, with as much and as little reason as those of the infidels who thought its doctrines superstitious because they scoffed at its authority. The question of authority overshadowed all others. The dispute over the fact of revelation was too heated, in the minds of many, to allow for much critical appreciation of its content. But the content could not be neglected, nor did intelligent persons on either side limit themselves to the question of miracles. We have just seen what debates arose about the revealed doctrine of creation. We must see now some of the differences between Christians and unbelievers on the moral question of what a good life ought to be.

There was more religious feeling in France in the middle of the eighteenth century than is often supposed. The church drifted into no such sterile ineffectiveness as the Church of England of the time. If in France there was nothing like the Methodist movement, it was not only because Catholic psychology was very dif-

[2] See above, Chap. IV.

ferent from Protestant, but because the official church was not wholly neglecting its business.

The provinces were visited by *missionnaires,* authorized preachers who conducted revivals. In the mid-century the Jesuits alone evangelized more than sixty towns. The Oratorians also travelled widely. Though assignments to preach were strictly controlled by the hierarchy, many of the preachers seem to have spoken pretty freely. Like all preachers, they condemned sexual laxity, lewd dancing, suggestive pictures, and the general frivolity and irresponsibility of the times. They exposed in addition the particular sins of the age: intellectual vanity and the *recherche du bel esprit*; the worldliness of the upper clergy; the idleness and arrogance of the wealthy; luxury, extravagance, and selfishness in giving alms; the careless bringing up of children, and the corruption of children's minds with notions of rank, pride, and exaggerated etiquette. They held forth against the venality of judges, dishonesty in commerce, and the ruthless spoliation of debtors; against the oppression of the working classes, the keeping down of wages, and the beggary and brutalization of the peasants. Many of these preachers, more than most of the *philosophes,* more even than most of the revolutionaries of 1789, represented the common people as the victims of the rich and the powerful.[3]

In Paris, it appears, congregations preferred a plain moral talk, and *beaux esprits* ostentatiously left the church when the sermon dealt with theology, but in the provinces there was much interest in Christian doctrine. Occasionally the provincials were shocked by a visiting Jesuit, as at Avignon in 1759 and at Montpelier in 1761, when Father Le Chapelain expounded his views on the need of loving God.[4] But such clashes were exceptional.

The most famous of the Jesuit preachers, Father Bridaine, carried through France a gospel almost Jansenist in its sternness. He preached heaven and hell, the delusiveness of the world and the imminence of eternity, the need of instant repentance, the small number of those to be saved, the swiftness and ineluctable exactness of divine justice. He was a powerful speaker, a master of homely images and vigorous gestures, who flung himself into his

[3] A. Bernard, *Le sermon au dix-huitième siècle* (Paris, 1901), pp. 198-215, 218-26, 302 ff., 379-80.
[4] *ibid.,* pp. 237, 362. See also above, p. 44.

OBLIGATION AND LIBERTY 181

words till the sweat streamed from his brows, and whose voice, while strong enough to fill a cathedral, was so poignant and appealing that it reached the heart of every hearer. Even Marmontel, who like Rousseau preferred a religion without terrors, was so profoundly impressed by Bridaine that he remembered him to the end of his days.[5]

Many others may be named to show that religion was much alive. The Jesuit Berthier, for sixteen years editor of the *Journal de Trévoux,* was something of a mystic, and wrote spiritual works of permanent value to Catholics. The Abbé Roche, whom we have noted as a critic of Locke, secluded himself for many years in the heart of Paris. Louis Racine, son of the great Racine, wrote religious poetry inspired by the reading of Pascal. Le Franc de Pompignan, brother to the bishop of Puy, made translations of the Psalms which many held to be the best religious verse of the day, and which won him admission to the Academy, where he raised an uproar by attacking the unbelievers in his first address. In high society, the Duke and Duchess de Penthièvre were famous for their devotion. Among the people, thousands read the books of the Marquis de Caraccioli, an impoverished nobleman of Italian origin who earned his living by producing works of piety and meditation. He urged his readers to cultivate their inner lives, to give only a part of themselves to society and the world, to put aside vanity and triviality, and to discipline themselves to a Christian self-perfection.[6]

[5] On Bridaine, Bernard, *op. cit.,* p. 207; Marmontel, *Oeuvres* (Paris, 1825), Vol. IX, p. 218, and Bridaine's *Sermons* (5 vols., Avignon, 1823), e.g. "Sur l'importance du salut," and "Sur la mort" in Vol. I, and "Sur le petit nombre des élus" in Vol. II.
[6] G. Berthier, *Oeuvres spirituelles* (Paris, 1811, often reprinted) ; L. Racine, *La Religion* (Paris, 1742, often reprinted). J. J. Le Franc de Pompignan, *Poésies sacrées, psaumes et cantiques judaïques* (Paris, 1763), and *Discours et mémoire* [on entering the Academy] (n.p., 1760). Compared with what the *philosophes* said of their opponents Le Franc de Pompignan's address was relatively innocuous, but it provoked a furious reply from Voltaire in the *Quands,* the *Pourquois,* etc.; see Voltaire, *Oeuvres* (Paris, 1883-85), Vol. XXIV. On the duke and duchess de Penthièvre see d'Argenson, *Mémoires* (Paris, 1859-67), Vol. VI, p. 188, Vol. IX, p. 12: Fréron, *Année littéraire* (1761), Vol. VI, p. 215. On Caraccioli see his works, e.g. *Conversation avec soi-même* (1753), *La jouissance de soi-même* (1759), *La grandeur de l'âme* (1761), and the *Journal ecclésiastique,* which in one year passed from cool suspicion to the warmest praise of his writings: January 1761, p. 73; July, pp. 75-6, September, p. 79; January, 1762, pp. 83-6. Standing quite apart, a layman of deep religious experience, an individualist

Even the hundred and twenty-odd bishops, who owed their offices to family connections and were expected to be administrators rather than saints, could count among their number some men of genuine fervor. A handful still sympathized with the Jansenists, notably Beauteville, whose tiny diocese of six parishes was too poor to allow its occupant to be worldly, and Fitz-James, whose Scottish origin perhaps disposed him to moral rigors. A better example of piety in high places is offered by La Luzerne, bishop of Langres, a model prelate who later became cardinal, and who in 1786 issued an *Instruction pastorale sur l'excellence de la religion*. Whether or not he was himself the author, his *Instruction* was recognized as one of the best of the day. It was written with warmth and grace and a clear tone of sincerity, and the citations from the Bible and the Fathers with which such documents usually bristled were all put in an appendix at the end, so that the text remained a smoothly flowing discourse.

La Luzerne did not try to demonstrate revelation as an historical fact. He sought to show that the revealed doctrines gave the best account of man's nature. He ventured, therefore, a modest elucidation of the mysteries. "The Incarnation," he said, "shows us the dignity of our nature, and teaches us the value of our soul." In the Redemption, figured by the Eucharist, he saw the center of the Christian faith. "From high on his cross Christ embraces all times and brings them together. . . . Know, mortals, the full evil of sin, since such a sacrifice was necessary to expiate it!" He thought, like Pascal, that the dogma of sin explained contradictions in man which baffled all philosophers. The dogma of grace clarified for him both the reason for man's weakness and the true source of his strength. "Powerless in ourselves for good, we have the help of infinite power. . . . Everything in us is the gift of the Lord; our will is the effect of his, our works are his work; and this health-giving grace, this heavenly gift, beyond all our expres-

and a mystic who opposed both the *philosophes* and the Catholic hierarchy and who received no attention from either, was Louis-Claude de Saint-Martin, the "philosophe inconnu," author of numerous books, e.g. *Des erreurs et de la vérité* (Édimbourg, 1775), *L'homme de désir* (Lyon, 1790), *Le nouvel homme* (Paris, An IV). See A. Franck, *La philosophie mystique en France à la fin du dix-huitième siècle* (Paris, 1866); Sainte-Beuve, *Causeries du lundi* (Paris, 1876), Vol. X, pp. 235-78.

sions of gratitude, far from altering our liberty, enlivens and strengthens it and removes the hindrances that obstruct it."[7]

La Luzerne dwelt at length on the virtues that distinguished the Christian. Such was the temper of the age, he said, that the devout Christian needed more courage than the worldling if he was to stand by his convictions. He observed that the infidels were particularly scornful of the religious virtue of humility. He undertook to explain this virtue, contrasting it with ordinary modesty. Modesty seemed to him a praiseworthy quality, but one based usually on convenience or common sense, whereas humility arose from a profounder feeling, our sense that in ourselves we are nothing, that our good qualities are not really our own or the result of any merit of ours, that we hold them from God and should always remember the source from which we have freely received them.

He noted also that the infidels, objecting to the Christian doctrine of emotional suppression, held that a discreet satisfaction of the passions would remove from them what was "dangerous to virtue." He thought this belief a superficial one; for, he said, advancing an argument familiar to all rigorous moralists, passion was by nature insatiable, and was inflamed, not allayed, by indulgence. Christianity, according to La Luzerne, provided the most effective of all moral codes because it took jurisdiction not only over outward acts, but over the private thoughts and most intimate feelings of its believers. "It forbids not only sin but all that may lead to it. The Christian fears the danger of falling almost as much as the fall itself. To abolish perjury, Christ reproves unnecessary oaths. To prevent homicide, he represses the movements of wrath. To stop adultery, he prohibits the desire for it; the desire itself is a crime, the look an adultery. . . . Who then is this amazing lawgiver that dares to give law to thought? Who but a God could dictate the admirable commandment, *Thou shalt not desire*?"[8]

These sentiments, if they by no means exhausted the subject of Christian morality, expressed what was most peculiar to it and what distinguished it from stoical or humanitarian ethical sys-

[7] C. G. de La Luzerne, bishop of Langres, *Instruction pastorale sur l'excellence de la religion* (Paris, 1786), pp. 30-3.
[8] *ibid.,* pp. 50-64.

tems. The ideal Christian life was a life of humility and abstinence, of trust in God and detachment from the world and its pleasures. It was this ideal that the *philosophes* opposed. They were not original in opposing it; it had been often opposed in the past; but they differed from such earlier rebels as the neo-pagans of the Renaissance in furnishing a broader philosophical basis for their opposition, and in offering a more complete and more thoroughly reasoned ethical teaching in its place.

The *philosophes* taught that morality should depend on man's nature. This was their first principle, which they advanced as a recent discovery, and by which they proposed that law, right conduct, and proper forms of government should be known. But Christians had long asserted the same principle. The difference was on the specific question of what human nature was.

Religious believers held to a theory which infidels described as supernatural. They thought of man as a being created by God and subject to his judgment, who by his free will was capable of deviating, but whose true object in life was to conform himself to the realm of absolute righteousness from which he had come. Man, as Bossuet had said, in obeying the laws of God obeyed the laws of his own nature.

Philosophes, on the other hand, determined human nature empirically. They emphasized the facts of human behavior. What they perceived clearly in men was not their relationship to an objective world of absolute ends and values, but their actual needs, wants, feelings, inclinations, and ideas. They observed that men sought pleasure and shrank from pain, that they enjoyed the goods of this world, that they were restive under an authority that crossed their wishes, that they lived in society and could suffer or profit from their forms of government. With these facts of human nature they hoped to build an ethical system. They would (if successful) deduce the *ought* from the *is,* the ideal from the actual, where Christianity, in the ages of ignorance, had struggled to assert the ideal by denying, repressing, vilifying the actual, holding that man was ideally the image of God, but actually a being fallen into sin.

The *philosophes,* unlike the Christians, were thus willing to endorse human nature as they found it. Christians argued that human nature must be changed before reaching perfection; even

Molinists never dreamed that men could reach heaven by their own natural faculties. The *philosophes* thought that men would best realize their *perfectibilité* by being themselves, by shuffling off the error, prejudice, and fictitious virtues that were no part of their nature, and by getting rid of wrong education, unjust government, unintelligible religious beliefs, and unnatural and mistaken ideas of every kind. These, according to the infidels, were the true sources of evil.

This theory of evil was emphatically denied by orthodox Catholics, who often replied to it on rational grounds without appealing to the dogma of sin. "Nature does not make us bad," said Bergier moderately, "because badness, properly speaking, supposes freedom; but nature gives us lively and impetuous passions, which incline us to become bad. These passions are the primary source of the errors and vices of individuals in society. It cannot be said that error is the cause of passion, but the passions, since they blind us, cannot fail to produce errors; it is hence poor reasoning to attribute passions and vices to the bad constitution of society, which is their effect and not their cause." He concluded that religion remedied evil at its source, by giving a check to the passions, and that the philosophers who combined a program for the reform of society with an "obstinate apology for the passions" were guilty of a palpable absurdity. The Abbé Richard, giving the same argument, enumerated the causes of evil more explicitly: "pride, greed, ambition, vanity, envy, lasciviousness and the love of sensual pleasure."[9]

Religious writers were quite correct in calling the infidels apologists for the passions. To vindicate the emotional life against Christian doctrines of repression and abstinence, to give men the right to enjoy their natural feelings, to represent their appetites as bodily needs and legitimate parts of their personalities, all this was one of the chief aims of the philosophic campaign, and was the contribution made to romanticism by these thinkers whom the romantics so detested. It led sometimes to extreme statements. "Happiness is an agreeable sensation . . . truth and virtue are mere ideal goods [*biens d'idée*], extrinsic causes. . . .

[9] N. Bergier, *Examen du matérialisme* (Paris, 1771), Vol. I, pp. 470-1; C. Richard, *Défense de la religion, de la morale, de la vertu, de la société* (Paris, 1775), p. 1.

Reason must be given nature for its guide, and men should not deprive themselves of what gives them pleasure. . . . Debauchery is not a stain upon glory, and moral corruption is not incompatible with the greatness and felicity of a state. . . . Great souls are those which know how best to hate. . . . A union founded on tenderness is more pure, more healthy, and more to be respected than marriage." These are a few of many quotations gathered by Mme. de Genlis, when she wished to prove that the philosophy of the *philosophes* was one of moral degradation.[10]

Diderot, as early as 1746, announced the new morality at the beginning of his *Pensées philosophiques.* "Only the passions, and the great passions, can raise the soul to great things. . . . Sober passions make common men. . . . Restraint destroys the grandeur and force of nature."[11] He was more outspoken in a document that he did not publish. "It is wrong to attribute the crimes of men to their passions; their false judgments are at fault. The passions always inspire us rightly, for they inspire us only with the desire for happiness. It is the intelligence [*esprit*] that leads us badly and makes us take false roads. Hence we do wrong only when we judge badly, and it is reason, not nature, that deceives us. . . . Ah! what would morality be, if it were otherwise? What would virtue be? We should be insane to follow it, if it took us from the road to happiness." He concludes that the roads to virtue and to happiness *must* be the same—to think otherwise would be *affreux,* too frightful.

The source of his agitation is evident. What he really believes is that happiness comes from passion. What he wants to believe is that it comes also from virtue. To forego happiness, or to deny the passions, is unthinkable to him (that would be "insane"), but he hopes plaintively to have virtue too. The situation is not changed if we note that among both the French and the English of the eighteenth century passion often meant simply emotion. Christians did not usually find themselves in this particular difficulty, because they did not mean by happiness a pleasant state of the emotions.[12]

10 Stéphanie, comtesse de Genlis, marquise de Sillery, *La religion considérée comme l'unique base du bonheur* (Paris, 1787), pp. 175-88.

11 *Oeuvres* (Paris, 1875-77), Vol. I, pp. 127-8.

12 *ibid.,* Vol. II, p. 88, n. 1. There is room for much difference of opinion in the interpretation of Diderot's moral ideas. For contrasting views see Carl Becker,

In not publishing everything he wrote, Diderot was relatively discreet; perhaps he was uncertain. It was Helvétius who shouted the praises of passion from the housetops. "The passions are in the moral world what motion is in the physical. . . . He who to be virtuous had constantly to overcome his inclinations would be a dishonest man." Civilization and all great achievements, according to Helvétius, came from "strong passions," of which the two strongest were the love of glory and the love of women. Therefore the wise Lycurgus, in old Sparta, had arranged that in public festivals half-naked girls should mingle with the men, seeking out the valiant and spurning the cowardly. "It is to be doubted that the young warrior would be drunk with virtue?" Sparta would have been still more virtuous if Lycurgus had gone further, and if "the young heroes had felt in the same instant the double intoxication of love and of glory." Or consider the enlightened customs of Malabar, where there are no false women, where "if all the women are true it is because they satisfy all their fancies without scandal, and have a thousand lovers."[13]

Needless to say, the religious were appalled. Helvétius's book was not only put on the papal index; it was forbidden even to those who had a general permission to read infidel writings.[14] The Protestant Formey, replying to Diderot's *Pensées*, spoke for all Christians and for many rational infidels. He declared that to say a man was animated by his passions was like saying that he walked with his feet; it was true, but told nothing of the direction in which he was going. The force of the passion could not

"The Dilemma of Diderot," in the *Philosophical Review*, Vol. XXIV (1915), pp. 54-71; E. Faguet, *Le dix-huitième siècle* (Paris, 1894), pp. 288 ff.; F. Brunetière, *Histoire de la littérature française* (Paris, 1912), Vol. III, pp. 364-5; P. Hermand, *Les idées morales de Diderot* (Paris, 1923).

[13] *De l'Esprit*, in *Helvétius: Collection des plus belles pages* (Paris, 1909), pp. 113-15, 55.

[14] F. Reusch, *Index der verbotenen Bücher* (Bonn, 1883-85), Vol. II, p. 906. Soon after the publication of *De l'Esprit* in 1758, the *Encyclopédie* was also put in this class of works that could be read only by special permission from Rome, and in the following years the same policy was used with some other *philosophe* writings. On Helvétius see also *Indiculus propositionum extractarum de libro cui titulus De l'Esprit* (Paris, 1758); *Nouvelles ecclésiastiques* (1758), pp. 181-8, 201; A. Chaumeix, *Préjugés légitimes contre l'Encyclopédie* (Paris, 1758). Chaumeix was so horrified by Helvétius' book that he interrupted his critique of the *Encyclopédie* long enough to write two volumes against Helvétius, which are included in the *Préjugés légitimes*.

fix the value of the object; the value of the object, judged rationally, should determine the force to be allowed to the passion. Diderot's readers, said Formey prophetically, "overlooking, like the author, the object that arouses the passion, will believe that exuberances, extravagances, convulsions, are themselves the principle of the grand and the sublime." When Diderot, thinking in mechanical terms, observed that the passions must be in "unison" so that fear balanced courage, prudence pleasure, etc., Formey dismissed the idea as pure sophistry, holding that a person so pulled upon by his emotions would be torn in all directions at once, and would have neither object in living nor consistency in character. Formey, like Gauchat in this connection, maintained that life could be ordered only by reason.[15]

The plain fact is that these infidels wished to do what they pleased and yet have their acts bear the honorific title of virtue, thus differing from Christians, who held that virtue was sometimes painful, and from more thoroughgoing unbelievers who care little whether they be called virtuous or not. If the *philosophes* of the generation of Rousseau and Diderot were agreed in anything, it was in their belief that true virtue was pleasant, that what men ought to do was a form of what nature prompted them to do. And if the religious apologists were successful in anything, defending as they were a losing cause, it was in exposing this notion as untenable by a rational mind. Rational minds, however, or minds willing to invoke reason as the arbiter of their doubts, became increasingly fewer as the Age of Reason dissolved into an age of sentiment.

The philosophers, from the pious Rousseau to the dreaded atheist Holbach, commonly identified virtue with feeling. Hol-

[15] J. Formey, *Pensées raisonnables contre les pensées philosophiques* (Berlin, 1749), pp. 5-15; Gauchat, *Lettres critiques, ou Analyse et réfutation de divers écrits modernes contre la religion* (Paris, 1755-63), Vol. I, p. 107. See also Ilhahart de La Chambre, *Abrégé de la philosophie* (Paris, 1754), Vol. I, p. 100: "Dieu aime nécessairement l'ordre; il ne peut par conséquent nous avoir donné l'existence sans exiger de nous l'observation de ce même ordre éternel. . . ." The infidels would accept this statement in general terms, but would mean by "order" the empirical order of observed phenomena, in which their own feelings, desires and emotions would be included; where the orthodox had in mind a moral and rational order above the world of phenomenal experience. Ilhahart gives the orthodox Catholic view that Christian morality is in harmony with pure reason, and that revelation establishes the cult and adds supernatural hopes and duties. *ibid.*, Vol. I, p. iv, and all of Vol. II.

bach stated the theory concisely. "The immediate will of a
God, invariably announced to us by men capable of self-deception
or of deception of others, cannot be regarded as the basis of our
duties." This argument disposed of revelation, and was equally
valid against absolute theories of ethics, since it reduced them
to private opinions. Our duties, Holbach continued, "are more
immediately and more solidly founded on the essence of man,
on the nature of a feeling being [*d'un être sensible*], on the connections of such a being with others of the same species." Here
human nature was established empirically, in terms of the subjective feelings which according to the sensationalist psychology
were alone real; and purely selfish subjectivism was overcome by
relating men, not to any absolute, external or divine laws, but
to other men whose feelings were the same. "As soon as there
exist beings essentially lovers of happiness, capable of feeling
it, and necessary to one another in procuring it essentially, duties
are established among them, and reason suffices to indicate the
means for arriving at this common end of their desires." So duty
and reason descend from the heavenly heights; duty is derived
from the urge to happiness, and is made a social obligation; and
reason, relieved of the task of judging ends, becomes a practical
tool for finding the best methods of satisfaction. ". . . To say
that without the idea of God we cannot have moral sentiments
is to say that without the idea of God we could not feel." There
were Catholics also, as we have seen, who thought that without
the idea of God men might have moral values, but they claimed
to establish these natural values by reasoning, not by feeling.
They might have written this sentence of Holbach's, changing
only the final word.[16]

Departing from these principles, Holbach got himself into
complications which his critics were quick to expose. He held
firmly, as Bergier noted, to three convictions: that the society of
France of his time was wrong and vicious; that men draw their
tastes and ideas of good from the society in which they live;
that virtue is what gives the most satisfaction to society and to
the individuals who compose it. Assuming all this, said Bergier,

[16] The passage from Holbach is quoted by M. Pelisson, "La sécularisation de
la morale," *Revue française*, Vol. XLV (1903), p. 406, from the *Recueil philosophique* published by Naigeon in 1770. On the relation between belief in God and
belief in moral values see above, p. 40.

we must get the most satisfaction from our present corruption; we could not change without renouncing our happiness. And when we consider that Holbach also thinks men are determined by their physical constitution, his moral exhortations, said Bergier, become absurd. "If everything in man is a necessary effect of his temperament and the play of his organs, then the problem of governing him belongs to physics and medicine; morality is a chimera, and our censor's complaints are an absurdity." So the conservative Bergier supplied the conclusion which Holbach, reputed to be the most daring free-thinker in Paris, would not draw from his own principles.[17]

Holbach, like the rest of the infidels, was persuaded that men would be virtuous by nature, since true virtue gave the satisfactions that it was their nature to seek. But unfortunately nature, when regarded as the actual world of experience, gave no simple message. "Nature," said Bergier, "tells the kind, just, and indulgent man to be good, compassionate, benevolent . . . the violent and cruel man to be inhuman, intolerant, and without pity. . . . The man who commits crime by taste and temperament is no more reprehensible than the one who does a good act on the same principles; he is no more worthy of blame or punishment than one who because of his organization prefers bitter and sour foods to sweet." How then will Holbach define the good? "Will he call virtue 'that which is in harmony with Nature'? If by this we understand the nature of man in general, the phrase is meaningless; nature is not exactly the same in all individuals; the nature and the temperament of a man are the same thing. If we wish to speak of the particular nature of each man, the nature or 'essence of a bad man is to do harm'; to do harm is then for him an act of virtue. Will the author teach that virtue is 'what is in accord with our desires'? But the passions are desires, and the desires of a bad man are often crimes. Virtue, then, is to be 'what procures us happiness,' but the bad man finds his happiness in crime, and virtue is often unhappy here below. The author has defined virtue as 'what is constantly useful to man living in society,' but when a good man is unhappy in society his virtue is of no use to him. In any case the author admits that in a corrupt society virtue is rather an obstacle than a means to happiness."

17 Bergier, *Examen du matérialisme,* Vol. I, pp. 232-3, 243.

Bergier concluded that infidels of Holbach's school had really no grounds for establishing a moral system, and that their final recourse was always to contrast their maxims with the principles of Christianity, which they represented as bloody, savage, ascetic, and superstitious. Sound moral theory, he thought, must be based on the theological ideas: God, the distinction of body and spirit, free will, obligation, and eternal rewards and punishments.[18]

The *philosophes* obtained the advantages of theology by appealing to an absolute humanity. Finding that individual men might be mistaken in their views of right and wrong, they invoked the judgment of man in general. Diderot in particular took this course. He deplored the fact that Helvétius should call ideas of right and wrong mere local and variable conventions. Helvétius, he said, "seems to me not to have an exact idea of what is meant by probity relative to the whole universe. He makes it a word devoid of meaning, which he could not do had he considered that anywhere in the world the man who gives drink to the thirsty and food to the hungry is a good man, and that probity relative to the universe is only a feeling of benevolence that embraces the human race in general, a feeling that is neither false nor chimerical."[19]

Thus the primary virtue was benevolence, and it received an absolute value as more than a convention from the fact, or supposed fact, that men universally approved of it. Humanity was

[18] *ibid.*, Vol. II, pp. 314-21, 329-31. "Il est évident que confondre l'honnête avec l'utile, la vertu avec le bien physique, le devoir avec les passions, l'obligation morale avec les désirs toujours renaissants de notre coeur, c'est détruire la morale au lieu de l'établir, c'est former le code des brutes et non celui des hommes." See also F. Pluquet, *Examen du fatalisme* (Paris, 1757), Vol. III, pp. 423-5; C. Richard, *La nature en contraste avec la religion et la raison* (Paris, 1773), pp. 118-19.

[19] *Oeuvres*, Vol. II, p. 270. See Diderot's statement in the *Encyclopédie*, Vol. V, p. 116, art. "Droit naturel (moral)": "Mais si nous ôtons à l'individu le droit de décider de la nature du juste et de l'injuste, où porterons-nous cette grande question? Devant le genre humain; c'est à lui seul qu'il appartient de la décider, parceque le bien général est la seule passion qu'il ait. Les volontés particulières sont suspectes; elles peuvent être bonnes ou méchantes, mais la volonté générale est toujours bonne, elle n'a jamais trompé, elle ne trompera jamais." This is the metaphysical basis for Rousseau's doctrine of the general will, published a few years later in the *Contrat social*. On the importance to the *philosophes* of the idea of "man in general," see the illuminating pages by Carl Becker, *The Heavenly City of the Eighteenth-Century Philosophers* (New Haven, 1932), pp. 86 ff.

a sentiment of sympathy; it was also mankind, or what mankind had in common. It was a feeling, a virtue, a geographical fact and a metaphysical abstraction; and it is no wonder that a word so full of potential mystification should have saved the philosophers from the hazards of their own logic. Benevolence, of course, was an old Christian virtue. The *philosophes* somewhat altered the idea, making it not a commandment but an inclination, and teaching, for the recalcitrant, that men in particular *should* be humane because men in general *were* humane, thus keeping up the appearance of deducing values from facts, and duties from actual behavior.

Religious people, like others, felt the wave of humane feeling that swept over the latter half of the century. But some of them remained critical of the uses to which humanity was put by their opponents. Bergier, as has just been seen, denied that moral ideas could be derived from an idea of man in general. Chaumeix, criticizing Diderot, was equally skeptical, taking the purely nominalist ground that the "human race" was an abstraction without real existence. The dramatist Palissot also mocked the new ardors. In his play *Les Philosophes,* a feminine intellectual, Cydalise, explains the effects of her conversion to philosophy, concluding as follows:

> *Enfin mes sentiments ont pris un autre essor.*
> *Mon esprit, épuré par la philosophie,*
> *Vit l'Univers en grand, l'adopta pour Patrie,*
> *Et mettant à profit ma sensibilité,*
> *Je ne m'attendris plus que sur l'Humanité.*

To which Damis, the timeless Tory, answers that people who love humanity profusely love nobody very much:

> *Je ne sais, mais enfin dussé-je vous déplaire,*
> *Ce mot d'humanité ne m'en impose guère,*
> *Et par tant de fripons je l'entends répéter,*
> *Que je les crois d'accord pour le faire adopter. . . .*
> *Et pour en parler vrai, ma foi, je les soupçonne*
> *D'aimer le genre humain, mais pour n'aimer personne.*

Humanity, mixed with patriotism, produced the "fraternity" of the French Republic, whose revolutionary watchword was almost formulated by the Paris wits as early as 1770, in derision of "philosophy."

> *On appelle aujourd'hui l'excessive licence*
> *Liberté*
> *On prétend établir, à force de l'insolence,*
> *L'Égalité*
> *Sans concourir au bien, prôner sa Bienfaisance,*
> *Se nomme Humanité.*[20]

It was Rousseau who spread most widely the new cult of humanity, sensibility, and emotion. His differences with the other philosophers were less profound than he thought. Certainly he was leading no "reaction" against grim and chilly rationalism, for after 1750 there was little such rationalism left, at least in the minds of the arch-infidels, Diderot, Holbach, and Helvétius.

What Rousseau did was to refine the raw views of these thinkers. Unlike them, he was a creative artist, and so built up, from similar materials, a charming world in which ladies and poets could roam and dream, a world of passion where all the passions were gentle, a world of spontaneous impulse where the supreme impulse was the dictate of conscience. He was reverent, he yearned to believe, he hated the smartness and vanity of Paris. These qualities, which estranged him from more truculent unbelievers, made him the less repugnant to orthodox Christians. Religious writers often quoted Rousseau to refute Voltaire. They explained, in criticizing Rousseau's books, that many of his ideas were worthy of great respect. They approved of his piety, his fervors, his hymns in praise of moral beauty. But circumspect Christians thought him the more dangerous for these very merits. They deplored the fact that a thinker otherwise so estimable should deny revelation, question the divinity of Jesus, and approximate men, as they thought, to the brutes.[21]

Rousseau's ideas were complex and inconsistent, but he held, on the whole, that men were naturally warm-hearted and sym-

[20] Chaumeix, *op. cit.*, Vol. II, p. 69; Palissot, *Oeuvres* (Paris, 1788), Vol. II, pp. 61-2; Fréron, *Année littéraire* (1770), Vol. V, p. 288.

[21] Fréron, *op. cit.* (1761), Vol. II, pp. 328-30; F. Feller, *Catéchisme philosophique* (Liége, 1773), p. 24; Caraccioli, *La religion de l'honnête homme* (Paris, 1766), p. 135; L. Crillon, *Mémoires philosophiques* (Paris, 1777), Vol. II, p. 50, n. 2; Formey, *Anti-Émile* (Berlin, 1763), p. 209; Jamin, *Pensées théologiques* (Paris, 1769), p. 23.

pathetic, and that they tended to lose these qualities when they became civilized and enlightened. We have seen how orthodox critics objected to his association of moral goodness with the absence of mental refinement. They complained that such doctrine made virtue depend not on any specifically human qualities but on "a purely animal commiseration." They feared anarchical consequences. "There are then in the state of nature neither laws, morals, nor virtues, because sympathy [*la pitié*] takes their place. . . . Sympathy becomes an affection which men are not even tempted to disobey. This in effect reduces law and virtue to an internal and irresistible inclination."[22]

In the *Emile* Rousseau argued substantially the same theory. The young Emile, brought up according to his nature, was taught nothing of morals or religion and was to judge these matters wholly for himself on arriving at the age of reason. The significant feature of this theory was not its rationalism but its absolute individualism (which Catholics called anarchy), and its assumption that a young man, knowing nothing of the moral, religious, or philosophical ideas of civilized mankind, would be concerned about these questions and would decide them intelligently, and that he would be open-minded, well behaved, orderly, generous, and trustworthy—because he was born that way, and had never been perverted from his nature.

The orthodox regarded this notion as visionary. It seemed to Bergier that Rousseau, to prove his point, had been obliged to conceive of a child so remote from any being ever known or seen that what he really proved, if anything, was the necessity of revelation. "This dreamer," said Formey, "pursues his chimera without ceasing; giving us a pupil of his own fashioning, he not only forms him, he creates him; he takes him from his own head, and still thinking he follows nature, strays further from it at every moment." This was precisely the opinion of Grimm.[23]

But the infidels, if they thought that feeling and emotion should not be repressed or distorted, did not preach an unregulated pagan license. They had two principles of order, two author-

[22] Gauchat, *Lettres critiques*, Vol. V, pp. 91-3. See also above, pp. 175-6.

[23] N. Bergier, *Le déisme réfuté par lui-même* (Paris, 1771), Vol. I, pp. 66-70, Vol. II, pp. 37-66; Formey, *Anti-Émile*, p. 182; Grimm, *Correspondance littéraire*, Vol. IV, p. 343, Vol. V, pp. 114-15, 121-4.

ities, the laws of nature and the welfare of society. By these principles the excesses of liberty and individualism were to be checked. Religious apologists rejected both as inadequate. They had two chief arguments: that both were unstable, variable, relative, and dependent on human opinion; and that neither, as understood by the *philosophes,* made any provision for man's relation to God, or for the private virtues of individual character.

Catholics themselves, for the most part, had believed in natural law since the Middle Ages, but they understood it as a moral law or law of right reason, and they held that it was in accord with and contained in Christianity. For the *philosophes* natural law meant first of all the regularity of natural phenomena. As a moral conception or test of right and wrong, the idea of natural law was a vestige from theology; and it is not surprising that the infidels, having rejected theology, had difficulty in telling what concrete duties the natural law prescribed. The orthodox, confident that the true natural law taught the Christian virtues, complained that the conception of the infidels was intolerably vague.

They therefore riddled with their criticism such a work as Voltaire's *Poème sur la religion naturelle,* finding it chiefly a negation of Christianity, with a positive doctrine too hazy to be practicable or even to be intelligently criticized. Gauchat scoffed at the verse in which Voltaire summarized his faith:

> *Adore un Dieu, sois juste, et chéris ta Patrie.*

A convenient system, retorted Gauchat; it requires no acts of worship, no repression of temptation, no observance of inner virtues, no effort at detachment, purity, or temperance, "virtues that merely tyrannize the heart, without helping our neighbor." The Abbé Nonotte declared that Voltaire's natural religion was made up of innocuous generalizations. He contrasted Voltaire and his followers with Cicero, who, in appealing to natural law, had thought that it forbade pride, vengeance, falsehood, and resentment, and commanded kindness, patience, chastity, honesty, and moderation. A natural law so specific, said Nonotte, would be too severe for the modern infidels to become its votaries.[24]

[24] Gauchat, *Lettres critiques,* Vol. IV, p. 61; Nonotte, *Dictionnaire philosophique de la religion* (n.p., 1773), p. 575.

Sometimes the apologists argued that the natural law had no such existence as the infidels imagined—that it was not really to be found in the practices of non-Christian peoples. On other occasions, as we have seen, it was common for them to take the contrary view. The inconsistency was a serious weakness, but was not wholly irreconcilable, for what Catholics generally believed in either case was that the natural law had been preserved most fully in the church. They could, therefore, when necessary, point to the barbarous and savage customs of the heathen, and to the fluctuating and erratic doctrines of pagan thinkers, to show the inadequacy of natural law alone. "Where then is it established, this natural religion that we hear of endlessly? Nowhere on earth. It is in the heads of our philosophers, and different in each head. We defy them to form a fixed symbol that may serve as a rule of faith."[25]

Or it was possible to retort to the infidels that what they mistook for nature was the Christianity that they disavowed. The infidels, said Gauchat, "instructed from infancy in the principles of Christianity, learn from birth the greatest truths. These ideas, with which they grow up, seem natural to them." Hence they believe their nature to be excellent, and revelation an imposture. In a general sense, it is no doubt true that the *philosophes* imputed to nature the fruits of a millennium of Christian civilization. But it enraged them to be told so, as well it might, for such criticism threatened the foundations of their beliefs. It was to overthrow Christianity and Catholic authority that they idealized nature and natural law; and if this "nature" was only Christianity reflected, if nature was only ingrained habit, as Pascal said, then the whole argument based on it would collapse.[26]

The other principle of order to which the new thinkers deferred was the general welfare, or what they often called the public felicity. This proved to be a more lasting principle than nature. Men who could believe in no other absolutes could find something absolute in human society. If man was not a soul created for eternity, if all to be had from life must be found in the living of it,

[25] P. Boudier de Villemert, *Pensées philosophiques sur la nature, l'homme et la religion* (Paris, 1784), Vol. I, p. 112.

[26] Gauchat, *Lettres critiques,* Vol. XIX, p. 195; Diderot, *Oeuvres,* Vol. II, pp. 91, 96.

if all values were subjective and not fixed by a superhuman reality, if the worst evils were pain and suffering and undesirable
states of consciousness, if the course of time unfolded a progress
but no directing providence, if man's peculiar excellence was not
that he was free to obey a creator but that he could understand
and manage his environment, if all men were in the same pre-
dicament and were the more dependent on each other's assistance
because they could not depend upon God's, and because their most
pressing need was not personal salvation but the improvement
of their common circumstances of living—all of which was the
upshot of the *philosophe* teaching—then morals were mundane,
secular, and social, and the best man was the one who did most for
the general good. "I shall call virtues of prejudice," said Helvétius
speaking in effect for all the leading *philosophes* except Rousseau,
"all those whose exact observance contributes in no way to the
public happiness."[27]

This outcome of the infidel ethics was deplored by orthodox
Christians. The Assembly of the Clergy, in official session in
1775, condemned as a vulgar error of the day the idea that "virtue
consists in doing good to men," and attributed it to its true source,
the loss of faith in an eternal law and sovereign intelligence presiding over the world.[28] Christians asserted that men had three

[27] *De l'Esprit* in *op. cit.,* p. 52.

[28] *Avertissement de l'Assemblée Générale du Clergé de France . . . sur les
effets pernicieux de l'incrédulité* (Paris, 1776), p. 15. The tendency to the socializing of ethics was so strong that religious writers themselves sometimes suc-
cumbed to it. Paulian, for example, in his *Dictionnaire philosophico-théologique*
(Nimes, 1770), declares in the article "Philosophie" that the philosophers are
mistaken in thinking virtues "productions politiques," but holds in the article
"Morale" that morality is the "science de société civile," and cites as an ex-
emplary moralist Descartes, whose moral theory consisted chiefly in the observance of custom. P. F. La Croix, *Traité de morale* (Carcassonne, 1767), outlines
a moral system scarcely distinguishable from that of the infidels. By far his
longest section is on duties to society, which he introduces with three principles :
"I. Tous les hommes sont naturellement égaux. II. Ils ont chacun leurs droits.
III. Il est en nous un sentiment naturel d'humanité. . . ." (p. 36.) There is a
formal analysis of *bienfaisance,* pp. 105-6. The principles of the felicific calculus,
as developed by Bentham, are to be found in Maupertius, *Essai de philosophie
morale* (Berlin, 1749). Maupertuis, applauded by the orthodox as a philosopher
who was also a Christian, argues that pleasures and pains are quantitative, that
they may be mathematically calculated, and that happiness is a large sum of
pleasures, abstractly evaluated by their duration and their intensity. "In general," he says, "the estimate of happy or unhappy moments is the product of

kinds of duties—those to God, themselves, and their neighbors. Many infidels would perhaps accept these three categories. But by the first they meant that men should recognize the existence of a Supreme Being, and on the matter of duties were most keenly alive to the duties that this Being owed to them. "A religion," said Marmontel, "that announces to me a propitious and kindly God is the true one, and anything repugnant to the idea and sentiment that I have conceived cannot be this religion."[29] As for duties to themselves, the infidels usually meant that they owed it to themselves to be happy. Religious and personal duties they thus transformed into rights, claims upon God and nature to make them happy; and the only real duty that they recognized was the duty of respecting the rights of others.

Religious thinkers, in reply, rejected the view often advanced by the *philosophes,* that men received duties only with the formation of society. Where the *philosophes* demanded the rights "anterior" to society, orthodox Christians emphasized the obligations. This difference in theory was significant in practice. It was, in effect, the difference between the individualism of Christianity and the individualism of modern democratic and industrial society.

Bergier made the point clear when, in 1789, the year before he died, he tried to stem the Revolution by demolishing the idea of the social contract. The philosophers, he said, have asserted that men in the state of nature are like animals, living apart from one another, and having no moral obligations. "Hence they have decided that there is neither natural right nor natural duty. How, indeed, could these be founded on a nature that arose by chance from chaos?" How, indeed? But Bergier erred in imputing so much logic to his opponents, who, in reality, did believe in a natural right. "Just as one animal owes nothing to another, so a man owes nothing to his fellows unless he engages himself by a social compact. But whence comes the obligation to observe

the intensity of the pleasure or pain by its duration." (p. 5.) See also the deistic Protestant Mlle. Marie Huber, *La religion essentielle de l'homme* (Amsterdam, 1738), pp. 89-90, 120-7.

[29] Marmontel, *Bélisaire,* in *Oeuvres choisies* (Paris, 1824-27), Vol. V, pp. 158, 162. Quoted with horror by the *Nouvelles ecclésiastiques* (1768), pp. 33 *ff*. When Justinian observes that God is terrible, Bélisaire replies, "Terrible aux méchants, je le crois; mais je suis bon."

this supposed compact? The philosophers no doubt will say, from the interest of each individual and from the fear of being punished by society. We defy them to find any other basis for any moral obligation whatever. Hence a man is not bound by a duty whenever he judges that he has no interest in observing it or nothing to fear in neglecting it."[30]

The religious most often opposed this socializing of ethics by reaffirming their own principles. They held that men were bound by obligations even in solitude, since it was the nature of each individual to look for salvation in another life. The man who failed to do so, according to the Abbé Humbert, betrayed his nature; he was like fire without heat, a non-being, who should justly return into nothingness. The obstacle to salvation was sin, of which, in the words of another, there were "three principal roots, namely, impurity which makes man a beast, pride which makes him a false divinity, and greed which makes him an idol." "The misery of man," said the *Journal ecclésiastique,* "is that he takes for his true good what flatters his inclinations and desires here below. His true good is what God desires of him. And what does God ask of him during life? That he judge himself, keep his eyes always open on his acts, and pardon himself none." "Faith is here in harmony with reason," said Forbin: "man would be a god if the infinite good toward which he tends were to be found infallibly in whatever objects his intelligence might present to him. . . . Whatever he did would be his supreme good, a state suitable only to the Deity, for the true good can only be in the eternal and changeless order, and hence man cannot reach it without God."[31]

The *philosophes,* however, would be willing to admit that the goods they sought need not be eternal. If some of them recommended belief in a future life, it was not because they wished men to prepare themselves for eternity, but because they wished them to behave themselves in society. The more matter-of-fact among the faithful understood the doctrine of immortality in this same practical way. Life eternal, for most people, had paled into vague

[30] N. Bergier, *Quelle est la source de toute autorité?* (Paris, 1789), p. 44.

[31] P. Humbert, *Pensées sur les plus importantes vérités de la religion* (Besançon, 1742), p. 2; F. Saint-Adon, *Vérités sensibles de la religion* (Paris, 1768), p. 24; *Journal ecclésiastique,* November 1764, pp. 149-52; G. de Forbin, *Accord de la foi et de la raison* (Cologne, 1757), Vol. II, p. 51.

"future rewards." These future rewards were not so much ends to be sought in themselves, as mysterious compensations for refraining from natural pleasure. Where for men of deep religious belief the world was an offshoot of eternity, for many people in the eighteenth century "future rewards" were an appendix to life, a nebulous projection from the natural world.

It was only sensible, in these circumstances, for the *philosophes* to look for more natural incentives to good conduct. There were in general two schools. One, dominated by Rousseau, held that men were good by native spontaneous inclination. The other, which claimed to be more realistic and was most fully represented by Helvétius, held that nature must be managed by art, that men must be supplied with special inducements, that they would more willingly promote the public welfare if in doing so they enjoyed private pleasures. For this school also, good conduct was the consequence of a natural inclination; but the natural inclination was to be aroused by the legislation of an ideal society. Hence, in the ideal society, everyone would be free, doing only what he desired to; and yet everyone's acts would redound to the public advantage.

The two schools were not always distinguishable, and need not be distinguished. Together, they helped to produce such diverse fruits as the utilitarian ethics, the utopianism of Fourier, the belief that the pursuit of private profit would best assure the public abundance, and the closely related belief, often expressed in the eighteenth century, that men who sought personal fame and immortal glory would perform acts highly useful to society.

To the religious it seemed that such thinkers were trying to found virtue on vice, to deduce benevolence from selfishness, to replace obligation by irresistible impulse or private calculation of advantage. Frederick the Great, for example, aroused the ire of the Jansenists by his definition of virtue as "a happy disposition of the mind, which has many faculties, one of which impels us to fulfil duties to society for our own satisfaction."

The apologist Chaudon denounced the whole of the philosophical altruism as an inflated egotism. The infidels, he said, teach that we should love all men except those who hate us; that we need not love our parents unless they are good to us, nor our fellow citizens unless we choose to belong to their country, since

no man is born a subject of any state; that we should refrain
from harming others, unless we are by nature so perverse as
to enjoy hurting them; that we should relieve the poor if we
take pleasure in doing so, but cannot be obliged to against our
wishes, since pleasure and pain are the sole springs of action,
and no man can be made to undergo pain. " 'To whom, then, do I
owe humanity?' 'To those who contribute to your pleasure and
happiness.' "[32]

The public welfare, like the natural law, could not in itself be
a subject of dispute, for everyone was persuaded that his own
views were fully in harmony with it. The argument of social
utility was one of the commonest that defenders of religion could
use. Many felt, like Stanislas, former king of Poland, that religion was valuable in preserving order, rank, property, and
social classes.[33] They affirmed that the infidels taught atheism
and anarchy.

Competent apologists were more specific in their charges; not
content with pure assertion, they offered reasons to show why
the philosophical ideas were antisocial. Their most general reason
was that the infidel moral system rested on selfishness, on what
they might have called individualism had the word then existed.
"Any doctrine that does not detach men from themselves," said
the bishop of Puy, "which limits their desires and hopes to the
present life, which assigns no rule for their actions except their
pleasure or personal advantage, is the scourge of society."[34]

According to the Abbé Denesle, the very fact that everyone
could claim for his own ideas the sanction of natural law and
social utility rendered these sanctions meaningless, "a prejudice
as stupid as any other," mere wilful affirmations of opinion; and
from the philosophers' belief that all human acts were only natural phenomena in the physical universe it would soon follow that
laws against theft were the mere invention of the rich, those
against rebellion the creation of the powerful, those restraining

[32] Frederick the Great, *Dialogue de morale à l'usage de la jeune noblesse*
(Berlin, 1770), p. 1; *Nouvelles ecclésiastiques* (1771), p. 22; L. Chaudon,
L'homme du monde éclairé (Paris, 1774), p. 267.

[33] Stanislas Leczinski, *L'incrédulité combattue par le simple bon sens* (Nancy,
1760), pp. 50-1.

[34] Quoted by Fréron, *Année littéraire* (1763), Vol. VII, pp. 68-9. Fréron
heartily approves.

children the work of selfish fathers and mothers, "and so with all others." Hence the very conception of law and right would disappear, or would be used only as a cloak to force.[35]

The arguments of social conservatism, based on natural law and on the public welfare as understood by the religious, were brought together by a certain Roussel, otherwise unknown, in his book on *La loi naturelle.* He began, in his preface, by asking whether the philosophers reached their doctrines, as he said they should, from the study of the "first Being," the origin of the world, the nature of man, morals, and society. On these matters, he observes, they are at odds among themselves. They cannot agree on the question of God's existence. Some make man spring from the void, some from the sea, some from the earth. They all deny the freedom of the will, and so, he says, teach palpable absurdity. They reduce moral values to conventions, regard virtue and vice as arbitrary distinctions, and identify reason with the desires, which they call needs. They have no theory of authority, their social contract is a myth, and their assertion that governments were originally set up by the people is not true. Their theory of education is based on a mistaken conception of human nature; for education must really teach, not merely allow the child to go his own way.[36]

Proceeding to the first page of his text, Roussel, like Montesquieu at the beginning of his great work, gave a definition of law. It was significantly different from Montesquieu's. Law, said Roussel, is "a rule established by a legitimate authority." Montesquieu had defined law as the proper relation between objects, thus leaving the seat of authority undefined, or placing it by implication in the actual behavior of phenomena. "The natural law," Roussel added further on, "expresses what we are by origin in telling us what we ought to be." Roussel's natural law was thus primarily moral. Man's origin was to be inferred from his moral nature, rather than, as the *philosophes* would be more inclined to think, his moral nature from his natural and historical origin.

[35] Denesle, *Examen du matérialisme* (Paris, 1754), Vol. II, pp. 13-14; T. Pichon, *Les arguments de la raison* (Londres, 1776), p. 139.
[36] Abbé Roussel, *La loi naturelle* (Paris, 1769), pp. vii-xviii.

Roussel thought that in the natural law of some of the *philosophes* desire took the place of duty. "Whatever is not in nature," say our new sages, "is contrary to reason; whatever contradicts our inclinations is not in nature; man acquires at birth an inviolable right to liberty, property and pleasure; he owes it to himself to be happy." These ideas Roussel considered anarchical. If, he said, the philosophers wish us to believe that the people once chose their kings and magistrates, they should offer more evidence and less declamation. Even if their social contract existed it would be absurd; it would be no contract, for there would be no one to judge or punish its infringement; one of the parties, the people, would decide all disputed questions, and could break the contract at will without putting itself in the wrong.[37]

Roussel noted the various devices by which the new thinkers sought to discredit the existing order in France. "Why should a Frenchman be concerned to point out the barbarous freedom of savages, the manners and morals of Indians, the rudeness of ancient republicans who soaked their hands in their children's blood to assure the public tranquillity?" Why should they preach, as a serious educational theory, that children should be taught nothing of what men have believed in the past? A man is not the more open to natural ideas for having had no ideas forced on him in childhood. Not all received opinions are groundless "prejudices." Some represent the acquired wisdom and accomplishment of the race. "He who wished to divest himself of all prejudices in this sense would be a man who regarded himself as alone in the world, at the moment when the world came from the hands of its creator."[38]

Roussel thus showed, at least to the satisfaction of those who agreed with him, that the philosophy of the infidels was an elaborate apologetic for individual wilfulness. For positive doctrine, he had little to offer but unrelieved conservatism. "Man," he said, "is necessarily born subject to the Supreme Being, to reason, and to public authority. These three links must never be broken." In short, it was man's nature to be dependent, and he became more dependent as his life became more complex. "To escape all

[37] *ibid.*, pp. 1-24, 84, 89, 119-20.
[38] *ibid.*, pp. 249-53, 271, 226-7.

social dependence a man would have to become a savage; to wish to do so, he would have to be crazy."

Combining Christianity and conservatism, Roussel advised men to accept their lot. "The laws displease us because we refuse to conform to them. If we make it our chief concern to conform to the laws and to attach our happiness to them, their burden will be light and we shall become more aware of their value."[39] This was to argue that there was no real injustice, that men's grievances were self-produced, that discontent arose from obstinacy and waywardness, or from what theologians called original sin. Such arguments were not likely to impress the *philosophes*.

The differences between the *philosophes* and the intellectual conservatives was profound. The *philosophes* were empiricists. They meant by natural law a systematic statement of what actually happened. By reasoning, they meant regulating thought by observed facts, or by sensation and feeling. The intellectual conservatives, especially the defenders of religion, were metaphysically rationalists—rationalism in this sense being perfectly harmonious with belief in revelation. They meant by law a cosmic rule of right and wrong, which established rightness both in the moral sense, by prescribing what men should do, and in the logical sense, by prescribing how men should think, and how the world, as the product of an intelligent creator, must rationally be constructed. Law was the expression of a superhuman rightness in things, the voice of God, to which human laws and human behavior must conform.

The *philosophes* could not feel law as an obligation imposed from on high. They were deferential, indeed, to nature and the natural law, but they included themselves in nature, and thought that the natural law legitimized the empirical facts of their existence, their needs, wishes, impulses, and capacities for enjoyment. Law, natural or divine, was not for them a rule to which men must force themselves; it was a cosmic authorization for them to do what gave them happiness in the world. It was a charter

[39] Roussel, *op. cit.*, pp. 162-3. Bergier's *Quelle est la source de toute autorité?* (Paris, 1789), is a good statement of the philosophy of conservatism, and may be compared with the works of Burke, de Maistre and others who opposed the French Revolution.

of liberty, under which men as individuals need observe only the rights of each other, and men as a whole, free from obligations not fixed by themselves, had the right to master the world and do with it as they pleased, and to make such changes in their government and society as they might suppose would be useful to these ends.

CHAPTER IX

NATURE AGAIN

IT HAS been seen in the second chapter, and at intervals since, that orthodox Catholics believed in the existence of a natural law, a natural religion, and a state of nature in which men could know right and wrong. It was from Catholic theology that these ideas passed into the minds of the infidels, where they became fundamental to the new intellectual system, and offered a means of discrediting, as "unnatural," the Christian revelation, the church, and many of the existing institutions of France.

These uses of the idea of nature had not been foreseen by the theologians who worked it out, and were not approved by Catholic thinkers of the eighteenth century. Most of the orthodox, seeing a familiar idea put to strange uses, were outraged and indignant. Too close to the idea of nature to criticize it on principle, they were usually content to maintain that the infidels were mistaken in what they held to be natural, and that in any case the natural, though valid, was insufficient, and must be supplemented by a supernatural revelation, through which alone the full rewards of heaven were to be attained.

There were, however, some thinkers who examined directly and consciously the whole of the philosophers' idea of nature. Stray fragments of this criticism have appeared in the two preceding chapters. It was the most fundamental criticism that opponents of the philosophers could make, for the idea of nature was the most fundamental of the philosophers' beliefs, being the master idea that raised their philosophy from a mass of demands and assertions to the level of a reasoned system of thought. No idea of the time was more pervasive or accepted with less question. None was more firmly fixed in the prevailing climate of opinion. To seize upon the idea, objectify it, and submit it to critical scrutiny, while on all sides thinkers were passing it trustfully about, was to escape partly from the intellectual climate, to enjoy some measure of mental independence. If to be ahead of one's time is a merit, certain of the conservative thinkers of the eighteenth century must be admitted to a share in it, for in doubting the philosophers' idea of nature they used arguments which are nowadays often heard.

But before describing these arguments we must raise a question which it seems that no one then faced distinctly. What was the difference between the "nature" of Catholic theology and the "nature" of eighteenth century philosophy? On this depends the related question, whether the orthodox, with their own ideas of nature, could attack those of the *philosophes* without flagrant inconsistency. An answer to these questions has been suggested in the last paragraphs of the preceding chapter. The philosophers, at least by comparison with their opponents, were empiricists. Profoundly affected by the growth of science, they meant by nature the actual physical world, and by natural law a description of how phenomena really behaved. The "nature" of theology was not primarily empirical; it was normative, concerned less with what actually existed than with what rightfully should exist. It was a regularity placed in the world by a supreme authority, God, who was supremely rational and supremely just. This theological nature could not be other than rational—hence the vagaries, much deplored in modern times, of the schoolmen who sought to deduce knowledge of the physical universe from considerations of abstract logic.

The *philosophes,* on the other hand, though they hoped that nature and reason were the same, when forced to choose one of the two, chose nature. Reason, as they said, must take nature for its guide. And by nature they meant the facts of experience. Could the philosophers have remained pure empiricists, no difficulty or confusion might have arisen. But no one can remain a pure empiricist, passively content with whatever happens to exist; least of all could the philosophers, with their passionate belief that much of what existed should be done away with.

So the philosophers, to meet their own needs, reached a conception of nature which was in part that of science, holding that the natural is the actual, and in part that of theology, holding that the natural is the right and the just, which unfortunately are often

purely ideal. To keep together these somewhat disparate conceptions, they sometimes tended to think, like Pope, that "whatever
is, is right," that the actual and the ideal are identical. More often,
as time went on, they embraced in one form or another the idea
that "man is good," that human feelings, needs, and desires are
not only objective phenomena but are morally praiseworthy in
themselves, conforming to natural law in both senses of the word.
It is to be feared that at this point the philosophers fell into much
the same difficulties as the medieval schoolmen. Where the schoolmen hoped to establish the empirical order by deduction from an
ideal rightness in things, the *philosophes* took the opposite course,
hoping to find an ideal rightness by consulting the facts of experience.

Each method was awkward in the field to which it was unsuited.
The schoolmen never learned much about the physical world, and
the *philosophes,* in the theory of values, could scarcely distinguish
between a virtue and a pleasant experience, between a good man
and simply "man."

It may be concluded that Catholic thinkers, whatever else may
be said of their views, were at least not inconsistent when they
rejected the philosophers' idea of nature. What they rejected was
the belief that nature, and especially human nature, were to be
known by empirical, physical, or historical facts. It was on this
ground that Le Gros, Gauchat, Castel and various others criticized
Rousseau. Gauchat expressed the Christian idea clearly. "Even if
anatomy," he said, "making all conceivable progress, should positively know the first elements of the beginning of our species, how
could it decide a moral question on its nature? It is as if, from
moral or metaphysical notions of the soul, we tried to deduce the
fibers and properties of the body. That would form a curious
treatise in medicine." For Gauchat the question of nature was a
"moral question," and he therefore thought it beside the point
for Rousseau, when inquiring into the nature of man, to ask
whether men were originally hairy and four-legged.[1]

The difficulty was that the two conceptions of nature, the normative and the empirical, could never be kept apart. In theological
thinking, the essentially moral conception had supported many

[1] G. Gauchat, *Lettres critiques* (Paris, 1755-63), Vol. V, pp. 72 *ff*. On criticism
of Rousseau see above, pp. 173-7.

particulars alleged to be historical: Eve's temptation, Adam's fall, the Jewish prophecies, the incarnation, the founding of a supernatural church. In philosophical thinking, that is, in the philosophy of the *philosophes,* the empirical conception of nature had produced many moral affirmations, of which the goodness of nature was the chief. And since the *philosophes* entertained a dual idea of nature, drawn from theology as well as from science, they sometimes argued in terms suspiciously like those of the old scholastics, fitting and adjusting their facts to suit a higher rightness best known to themselves. The ensuing confusion was extreme. Critics of the philosophers perceived this confusion almost as soon as the great books of philosophy were written.

In 1751, for example, five years after its appearance, the Abbé Bonnaire wrote a critique of Montesquieu's *Esprit des lois.* Though called by the Jansenists as irreligious as Montesquieu himself, Bonnaire was a professional and apparently an orthodox theologian.[2] His book, though given over mostly to details, contained a criticism of principle that is often made today. "When our author assures us," said Bonnaire, "that his principles are drawn from the nature of things, this assertion means that it is thus that he imagines them. Good faith obliges him to admit that things are not always as he imagines them, but he defends himself by saying that they should be so in order to be perfect." (This relates to the famous passage where Montesquieu, after discussing the three kinds of government and their respective principles, declares that the principles are not always to be found in reality, but would be found in governments perfect in their type—thus revealing that in this connection his idea of nature was normative rather than empirical.)

"This idea," continues Bonnaire, "seems to me pretty much like the idea of one of our prominent doctors, who, forced to admit that bleeding is not a happy remedy for smallpox, added that the malady should accommodate itself to the treatment. The principles of the three governments are not really as the author describes them, but they must become so under penalty of permanent imperfec-

---

[2] *Nouvelles ecclésiastiques* (1752), p. 54. D. Mornet, *La pensée française au dix-huitième siècle* (Paris, 1929), p. 203, speaks of an Abbé Bonnaire who died a "déiste solennel et notoire," but it is doubtful whether this is the same Bonnaire. This Louis de Bonnaire who criticized Montesquieu wrote a number of works of theology and devotion, and died in 1752.

tion. He imposes law, claims to refashion nature itself." This view may be contrasted with that of most of the *philosophes,* who thought Montesquieu too staidly factual, too inclined to see in nature what actually was, rather than what ought to be.[3]

From Voltaire also, and from his critics, we may draw a curious example of the same straining to fit brute facts into an ideal nature. The fact in question was the ceremonial prostitution in ancient Babylon reported by Herodotus, who declares that each lady of that city, once in her life, went to the temples to offer herself to strangers. Voltaire, in his *Philosophie de l'histoire,* rejects this fact, holding that so disgraceful a custom would be unnatural to a civilized people, and that "what is not in nature is never true." Of Voltaire's reasoning on this point we have two criticisms, one by the orthodox Larcher, the other by Grimm.

Larcher is vaguely aware that to call a fact unnatural is no way to dispose of it, but he makes little of this argument. He contends that Herodotus's statement is true, because such customs show how pagan superstitions pervert the mind. His reasoning is thus like Voltaire's; he settles the question of fact at the convenience of his theory; but where Voltaire can stand no blackening of the nature of civilization, Larcher can allow no whitening of paganism. On the other hand, Grimm, who counted himself a *philosophe* but has left many shrewd comments on *la philosophie,* saw at once the whole mass of assumptions on which Voltaire's conclusions rested. "What is not in nature is never true? But unfortunately the most abominable practices are in the nature of man." And he adds that anyone who wishes to understand the history of the human mind must not lightly dismiss the beliefs and customs of other times and places. He thought Voltaire's *Philosophie de l'histoire* superficial, impatient, and propagandist. To support his opinion, he outlined a conception of history that Ranke and Lecky would not have disowned.[4]

[3] L. Bonnaire, *L'Esprit des Lois quintessencié* (n.p., 1751), Vol. I, pp. 99-100. See also Montesquieu, *Oeuvres* (1 vol., Paris, 1835), p. 204.

[4] Voltaire, *Oeuvres* (Paris, 1883-85), Vol. XI, pp. 35-6; P. Larcher, *Supplément à la Philosophie de l'histoire* (Amsterdam, 1767), pp. 87 *ff.*; Grimm, *Correspondance littéraire* (Paris, 1877-82), Vol. VI, pp. 272, 278. Voltaire seems to have taken seriously his "apologie des dames de Babylone." He alludes to the question and snipes at Larcher in many of his writings. See the index to his *Oeuvres,* under *Larcher* and *Babyloniens.* His concern for the purity of the

Grimm, indeed, perhaps because he was not a Frenchman, is notable as a man who lived for years in close association with the philosophers, conversing often with Diderot and sharing many of his opinions, and who nevertheless was able to view his colleagues as at a distance, consider their ideas objectively, smile at them as apostles of a new faith, and, on occasion, pour upon their heated utterances a cold wash of common sense. He could not believe in the social contract, or in *capucinades sur la vertu,* or in the *Bon sens* of Holbach, which he called atheism for ladies' maids and wig-makers, dangerous chiefly for the danger of boring the reader.[5]

But what Grimm most often objected to in the prevailing philosophy was its picture of nature and the state of nature. "To have a correct idea of life among savages a man must have lived long among them, and, in describing their life, be more concerned to tell the exact truth than to satirize our own."[6] More than this, on the state of nature, could hardly be said so briefly. He was equally incisive in his comments on nature itself. He condemned severely De Lisle de Sales's *Philosophie de la nature.* This author, he observed, " 'questions' nature ceaselessly; he says that we must 'hearken to its oracles,' 'follow its impulsions.' . . What miserable gibberish! And yet I am persuaded that M. de Lisle honestly imagines that he has said something. But what is nature? Is it not everything that is? And does not what exists exist of necessity? How can anything be contrary to nature? If we leave these children to prattle, they will bring into philosophy a kind of mystical talk that has no meaning. But," he adds optimistically, "it is not to be feared that they will succeed. *Ma foi,* we are too far advanced toward reason to come back to gibberish, even gibberish that has a philosophic air."[7]

Babylonian ladies may be compared to his attitude to the Jews, whose women he says must have copulated with goats, since a law prohibited this practice. *Oeuvres,* Vol. XIX, pp. 522, 535, Vol. XVIII, p. 22, Vol. XXV, p. 60, n.

[5] Grimm, *op. cit.,* Vol. VI, pp. 427-8, Vol. X, pp. 175-6.

[6] *ibid.,* Vol. III, p. 58. See also Vol. IV, pp. 131-9.

[7] *ibid.,* Vol. IX, p. 49. See also Vol. III, pp. 53 *ff.,* 154. Grimm is a shadowy figure whose ideas are difficult to determine because much of his *Correspondance* was written by others. From 1753 to 1773 he did most of the work himself, but Diderot is known to have taken part. It is unfortunately not always possible to distinguish Diderot's contributions by external evidence. In a remarkable passage in Vol. II, pp. 492-8, concluding with an "Essai d'un catéchisme pour les enfants,"

Grimm was a good deal of a skeptic, who, though he once confessed to feelings of piety on hearing religious music, can by no stretch of the imagination be classed with the religious thinkers of the time. Yet the fact is, since skeptics were few,[8] that to find people who agreed with him on the matter of nature he would have done well to look among the orthodox. Certain of the orthodox perceived, as clearly as Grimm, that the philosophers' idea of nature was twofold, sometimes embracing everything actual, sometimes including only the right and the good. They noted also that these two conceptions were held together by a new kind of dogma and mystery. The same difficulty existed in Christianity, where the problem was to explain how God, who willed everything actual, yet willed only the right and the good; but in Christian theology the problem received an answer in the dogma of sin, according to which man, helped by the devil, produced evil, and caused the actual world to be different from the ideal.

The Abbé Duhamel, in 1751, thought he detected an unconscious and unacknowledged dogmatizing in the new philosophy. He pointed especially to the philosophical poems of Pope and to some of the earlier and more optimistic writings of Voltaire, in which he found the opinion that since everything arises from natural law, "whatever is, is right." Yet Voltaire held much to be wrong. He berated the Christian Pascal. "But after all," said Duhamel, "why this annoyance with Pascal? He was a part of the world as much as Voltaire and all other beings. He was the kind of man that he had been made, that he had to be because of a most perfect combination of general laws. His existence was right, because in the

we find warm sensibility, copious moralizing and veneration of nature, all of which, while familiar enough in Diderot's writings, is out of keeping with the views expressed in those parts of the *Correspondance* cited in notes 4, 5 and 6 above. A sequel to this passage, containing an "Essai d'un catéchisme pour les princes," occurs in Vol. III, pp. 215-20. See also Vol. III, pp. 258-9. If it could be shown that these passages were the work of Diderot, we should have added reason to regard Grimm as a rather skeptical and tough-minded thinker.

[8] The only pure skeptic of this period known to the present author is Louis de Beausobre, son of a Protestant clergyman living in Prussia, who, in his *Pyrrhonisme du sage* (Berlin, 1754), denies the possibility of certain knowledge, empirical, rational, pragmatic or revealed. He declares, p. 75, that the philosophers deify nature. "S'ils n'ont pas de cette nature qu'ils veulent déifier une idée plus claire et plus juste que nous n'avons de l'être suprème, ne sommes-nous pas en droit de retorquer contre eux l'argument, et nier l'existence de la nature?" This is substantially the position taken by Bergier against Holbach. See below.

new systems whatever is is right [*tout est bien*]. If he was a 'fanatical dreamer' he only followed his natural inclination; if he was a 'severe and somber madman' it was because of his dominant passion, and this passion, according to Pope and Voltaire, comes from the animal spirits:

Selon que les esprits répandus dans le corps,
Sont plus ou moins nombreux, plus faibles ou plus forts.

. . . What, then, does Voltaire mean? Would he reform a world already perfect? Can he conceive of one more perfect than this? But then what becomes of his principle? No doubt the world would have been more perfect if Pascal had thought and spoken like Voltaire, and if such 'fanatics' had never existed. . . . If the world is the *best of all possible worlds,* why does not Voltaire leave it as it is?"[9]

Voltaire lost his optimism as he grew older, largely because of dilemmas like those suggested by Duhamel; but Duhamel declared that not even Pope or the Voltaire of the early Voltairean writings really believed that everything was right. They both, he said, smuggled in the idea of sin, to reconcile an ultimate rightness of things with an undeniable wrongness of actual conditions. Both, he asserted, ascribed the disorders of the world to a fall from a state of innocence. He quoted Pope's contrast of the natural and the degenerate man, which concluded, in the version best known in France:

Et malgré ses remords dans le crime affermi,
L'homme trouva dans l'homme un farouche ennemi. . . .
La nature indignée se fit entendre.

"Here is the fall of man into sin. The Christian religion is mistaken in teaching this truth; human reason, in teaching it, is correct. It is no longer to be believed that our miseries come from the criminal disobedience of our first parents. We are now taught that they come from man's having shed the blood of animals and eaten their flesh [Pope's explanation of human ferocity, in the passage in question]—a new kind of crime, far more reasonable."

And Duhamel adds further on: "Note these important words, *La nature indignée se fit entendre.* It is no longer God, but nature

[9] J. Duhamel, *Lettres flamandes* (Lille, 1751), pp. 21-2. The epithets describing Pascal are quoted from Voltaire.

that punishes crime. But marvel especially at the logic of what Pope says. Man in the state of innocence, as the English poet describes him, was the same as he is today. The proof is that today he is as he comes from the hands of God. And yet man today has *degenerated* from his first state."

It seemed to Duhamel that by this inconsistency the philosophers took over the idea of sin without admitting it—that they held man to be both good and bad, and the world both right and wrong, at the same time and without explanation. He did not perceive that the nearest philosophical equivalent to the Christian doctrine of sin was the idea of "prejudice," by which man, naturally good, was held to have fallen into a mass of unnatural ideas and artificial institutions which caused his woe. Perhaps in 1751 this idea was not yet common enough to attract a critic's notice.[10]

Conservative thinkers were especially aroused to a thorough criticism of the idea of nature by Holbach's *Système de la nature*. Published anonymously in 1770, this book was one of the last of the notable *philosophe* writings, significant in giving bold and systematic expression to ideas already familiar. In a sense, it marked an epoch. Contemporaries, after about 1775, sometimes thought that the *philosophes* were losing their popularity; and Meister, then writing Grimm's newsletters, gave as one cause the publication of Holbach's book, which he said estranged many sympathizers by pushing the new ideas to an extreme.[11]

Observers were surely deceived if they thought that philosophy was going out of favor. They perhaps had in mind only the Encyclopedist philosophers, who in the 1770's were growing old or dying off, but whose ideas were constantly reaching larger numbers of people. In this process of dissemination the numerous writings of Holbach were important. If they repelled some rising youngsters like Goethe, they were no doubt furtively read in the circles which are often a generation behind the leaders of thought —as Grimm said, among the ladies' maids and wig-makers who could still find in them a not yet antiquated thrill. In one respect, indeed, the scandalous blasphemies of Holbach might encourage

10 Duhamel, *op. cit.,* pp. 60 *ff.*

11 Grimm, *op. cit.,* Vol. XI, p. 496, Vol. XII, pp. 205 *ff.*; Linguet, *Annales civiles,* Vol. I, p. 63; Mme. de Genlis, *La religion considérée comme l'unique base du bonheur* (Paris, 1787), p. vii.

the new fervors made popular by Rousseau. Readers of both authors would learn to venerate Nature.

The attack on Holbach was one of the most successful maneuvers in the whole campaign against the infidels—successful, that is, in a logical and academic sense, for if it could not stop the practical consequences of his negations, it at least showed that his positive doctrine was untenable by the unaided reason. Holbach's positive doctrine was unquestionably vulnerable. It is hard to see how any critical reader, then or now, could fail to observe his palpable contradictions, could fail to note, for example, how he insisted with equal assurance that nature was an unmoral machine and a benign power that made for righteousness. But Holbach only said plainly what the philosophers were generally disposed to believe, and the criticisms made of his *Système,* so far as they were valid, were valid against much of the infidel philosophy. His critics, aware of this fact, assaulted his book the more unmercifully.

We need consider only one work, Bergier's *Examen du matérialisme,* one of the best pieces of critical writing of the century. The argument in which Bergier had most confidence was one that arouses little interest today, since today we have no very clear notion of matter; it was the familiar argument based on the Cartesian dualism, holding that matter, being inert in essence, must receive motion from another source, which Christians and deists were agreed in calling God. It was one of the chief merits of Holbach that he tried to overcome this dualism by arguing that matter was essentially active. To argue thus, it then seemed to the faithful, was to take a long and perhaps final step toward atheism. Bergier therefore combated the idea with great vigor, and in doing so, as we have seen, detected what was undoubtedly an unresolved difficulty in Holbach's book, namely the doctrine that while matter as a whole was animated and active, each particle was passive, dead, inert and movable only by impact from another particle.[12]

Bergier noted also at the outset how Holbach, declaring that nature was the universe and the universe only matter in motion, insisted that nature must not be personified. "But this is nevertheless what he does throughout his work. Everywhere he puts nature in the place of God, attributes to it not only force, energy, action,

[12] See above, pp. 142-3.

but laws, rules, foresight, and goodness, although he assures us at the same time that he does not. By this continual abuse of terms, the reader of the book is disoriented from beginning to end."

According to Holbach, said Bergier, all our acts and thoughts are the effect of nature in us, yet our troubles arise from our denying, flouting or deviating from nature. "Such is the luminous doctrine into which we are to be initiated. But if man ignores [*méconnaît*] nature it is nature itself that forces him to ignore it, and not all the reasonings and harangues nor the whole book of the author will make nature retrace its steps."[13] And again: "We cannot suspect the author of inadvertence when he repeats at the end of the chapter that there can be no real disorder in a nature where everything follows necessarily the laws of its own existence; he assures us elsewhere that all is of necessity as it is, and that hence there is no positive good or evil. After this discussion he proceeds to teach that the distinction between virtue and vice is founded in the nature and necessary relations of things. The reconciliation of all this is beyond our intelligence."[14]

Bergier was especially annoyed at the facility with which Holbach, while denying the existence of God, ascribed the divine attributes to the material world. He noted Holbach's opinion that men formed the idea of God by negations of their own experience, representing God as infinite, eternal, and immutable; but he thought it even less convincing for Holbach to ascribe these same qualities to matter, particularly since he pronounced matter to be ultimately unknowable. "The incomprehensibility of God, he says, should convince men that they should not concern themselves with the question, that it is madness to reason about it; consequently, it is also madness to reason about matter or concern ourselves with it, since it too is incomprehensible." Atheists denied God, said Bergier, because they had an anthropomorphic idea of him. "They reproach us with having formed the Deity on the model of man, and themselves use such a notion to conclude that the Deity would not be happy if he took an interest in our acts or were offended by our crimes. They reason about the goodness, wisdom, and justice of God according to their idea of these same qualities

13 *Examen du matérialisme* (Paris, 1771), Vol. I, pp. 3-6.
14 *ibid.*, Vol. I, p. 112, citing the *Système de la nature* (1770), Vol. I, pp. 69, 85, and Chap. IX.

in men; and it is on this faulty comparison that all their objections fall. . . . The justice of men consists in rendering to others what is due them, divine justice in requiring of each what he has been given."[15]

Bergier exposed other inconsistencies, which were not all absolute contradictions, but which called for more analysis than Holbach had given them. Holbach, he said, explains religion as the outgrowth of a natural sentiment, and also as the product of the chicanery of priests. He attributes the belief in God to primitive ideas of nature, and also to the cunning policy of early lawgivers. He declares that the gods were engendered by fear, and that atheism arises from a fear of a strange and powerful divinity. He holds the inclinations of nature to be invincible, but inveighs against men for having yielded to the natural inclination to form a religion. He maintains that since the world constantly changes there can be no immutable God, but says that material atoms must be fundamentally immutable. He affirms determinism on one page, denies it on another; reasons from essences which calls unknowable; argues that men's acts result from blind necessity, yet thinks that good and evil may be imputed to human beings and that human nature may be reformed.[16]

Two volumes packed with quotations, with renewals and repetitions of the same attack, with examples drawn from all parts of the book to show the same persistent illogicalities, with rephrasings of its high-flying language into plain statements that could be rationally judged, constituted Bergier's reply to the "System of Nature," and formed on the whole the most effective indictment that the French church of the time ever made of certain important beliefs of the infidels. Before such a catalogue of difficulties Holbach himself, if he read the book, must have quailed. "We do not hesitate," said Bergier at the end, "to repeat the observation made at the close of our first volume, that the *Système de la nature,* far from favoring the progress of unbelief, is perhaps the decisive blow to disconcert its projects; and that the mon-

---

[15] *ibid.,* Vol. II, pp. 79, 139, 145-56; Vol. I, pp. 48-9; Vol. II, pp. 94-5.
[16] *ibid.,* Vol. II, pp. 461-2.

strous errors brought together in this work are the fairest trophies that philosophy could have raised to the glory of religion."[17]

This parting judgment, coming from Bergier, was something more than the hopeful dictum of an infatuated piety. In the widest sense no doubt it was mistaken, for irreligious thinking continued to spread. But it contained an accurate prediction. The *Système de la nature* proved in time to be the last great work of aggressive infidelity produced by the *philosophe* school. After Holbach, popularizers continued to make known his ideas, but a religious reaction also set in, which the Revolution made more rapid and more fervid. There emerged in the nineteenth century, dominating its mental air, not certainly religion in the old sense, but a hankering after religion, a nostalgia for a faith no longer possible to leading minds, a reminiscent and warm religiosity, to use the accurate if unkind term, which had no patience with theology or any intellectual statement of belief, but which gave currency to the esthetic Catholicism of Chateaubriand, and caused even such pronounced anticlericals as Guizot and Renan to admire what they conceived to be the pure teachings of Jesus. Such is the historical fact. Whether it came about because of logical defects or inadequacies in the thought of Holbach and the *philosophes* would be hard to show.

As for Bergier's *Examen du matérialisme,* the disinterested reader cannot fail to note that, however strong as a reply to Holbach, it proved nothing whatever about the truth of Christianity. Bergier, indeed, did not intend that it should. That task he undertook in other writings. But he did feel, and all believers then felt, that to cast doubt on the philosophy of the infidels somehow made orthodox religion more easily credible. Apologists often maintained that the doctrines of the infidels were mysteries, that the infidels, having no rational grounds for believing as they did, were in fact as credulous as the faithful. The Abbé Bonhomme, in a series of poetical epistles comparing Christianity and deism, addressed to Voltaire, stated as his purpose:

[17] *ibid.,* Vol. II, pp. 473-88. For other criticism of the idea of nature as used by Holbach see Fréron, *Année littéraire* (1772), Vol. VII, p. 315; Grimm, *op. cit.,* Vol. X, pp. 194-5; G. von Holland, *Réflexions sur le Système de la Nature* (Paris, 1773), Vol. I, p. 3; P. Pinault, *La nouvelle philosophie dévoilée* (Paris, 1770), pp. 79-80, 105 *ff.*

> . . . *je veux te montrer que crédule toi-même,*
> *Tu trahis la raison, tu démens ton système.*

And he gave this advice:

> *Aveugle, vous riez de l'aveugle Chrétien;*
> *Comme lui, croyez tout ou ne croyez plus rien.*[18]

He even used the arguments of Hobbes and other atheistical thinkers to show the impossibility of belief in deism. This method of apologetic, though not uncommon, was highly dangerous. It sought to push the infidels farther toward absolute negation than they wished to go, on the assumption that, horrified by the prospect, they would come back chastened to the fold. It offered the choice between blind faith and universal denial, between skepticism and the humble acceptance of revealed truths. To prove Christianity, it proved that men could not rationally believe anything at all.

This element of skepticism ran through much of the religious thinking of the time. Skepticism and the appeal to pure faith are by no means uncongenial. Both, restricting the scope of reason, deny the possibility of critical or discriminating belief. The surrender of the mind is equal, whether men profess to believe "nothing" or are willing to believe "all." And on the really fundamental question, whether man may trust his own mind to conduct him through the world, it was the religious believers of the eighteenth century, not the infidels, who were fatally touched with doubt.

It is important, however, to draw distinctions. To say that religious thinkers made no effective use of reason would be wholly unwarranted, as much of this book has been designed to show. They used reason, often very skilfully, to examine the views of their opponents. They were at their best when taking the offensive, engaged in destructive work, demolishing the positive doctrines that were set up against them. The same may be said also of the infidels. It may be that reason is a destructive tool. For defensive and constructive purposes, as we have seen in the fourth chapter, believers were suspicious of pure reason and looked rather to what they held to be empirical fact. They preferred not to discuss the

[18] Bonhomme, *L'Anti-Uranie, ou le Déisme comparé au christianisme, épitres à M. de Voltaire* (Paris, 1763), pp. 50, 54. See also N. Jamin, *Pensées théologiques* (Paris, 1769), pp. 233 ff.; La Luzerne, *Instruction pastorale sur l'excellence de la religion* (Paris, 1786), pp. 21 ff.

rationality of revelation, and chose to represent it as an historical event, an act of God's will which, whether or not reasonable, natural, necessary, or probable, had in fact taken place.

Hence the positive arguments affirming the truth of religion fell upon questions of evidence, and the content of religious teaching, removed to a plane "above reason," passed beyond the reach of the human understanding. The apologists, indeed, when engaged in this part of their work, outdid themselves in declaring that the dogmas of Christianity were utterly, darkly, and impenetrably mysterious.

But the human mind cannot flourish on a diet of pure mystery. This lesson is to be read in the history of theology, for theology is the attempt to harmonize religion with rational thinking, and has been in decline since the days of William of Occam, when the idea got abroad that revelation was not necessarily rational, and that the objects of religious belief were not necessarily consistent with human reason. In time, particularly with the coming of the Jesuits, these objects of belief were relegated to a definitely supernatural sphere, and many of the questions of importance to theologians, as to all thinking men, were held to be soluble within the limits of the natural intelligence. The effect, it appears, was to make the doctrines which were specifically and peculiarly Christian, that is, the revealed doctrines, seem far more mysterious, more baffling, and more arbitrary than Augustine or Aquinas ever supposed them to be. The *philosophes* of the eighteenth century are the better understood when seen against this theological background. In the thirteenth century it would have been madness for Europeans to reject the revealed doctrines, for in doing so they would have rejected reason itself, and invited intellectual confusion. In the eighteenth century, to reject the revealed doctrines meant rejecting only what was generally admitted to be unapproachably mysterious, and left intact the sphere of rational nature, usable as a moral standard of rightness, which, thanks mostly to theologians, had grown up in the meanwhile.

It is time to summarize the argument of the preceding chapters. We began by considering the dispute between the Jesuits and the Jansenists, a matter whose importance in the eighteenth century has not always been recognized by historians. In the course of this dispute the orthodox church, led by the Jesuits, assigning religion to a special supernatural sphere, marked out large areas of life for the operation of reason, natural law, and free will, areas within which man was not really a fallen creature and in which original sin did not apply. The church in this way anticipated many beliefs of the *philosophes,* at the cost, however, of making revealed religion seem a somewhat arbitrary addition to the natural world. Its existence could not be demonstrated by reasoning, and apologists therefore turned to the record of history. Some, like Jean Hardouin, perceiving that purely historical method could not prove a supernatural revelation, appealed frankly to church tradition, in which the truth about the past was to be known independently of written records. Others, like the Abbé Houteville, more numerous and more orthodox, tried to prove revelation as an historical fact by purely historical methods, using the Bible simply as a documentary source; but they were never able, by such methods alone, to show that the miracles on which true Christianity was supposed to be founded were any different from miracles alleged in support of other forms of belief. They had to conclude that true miracles were those that corroborated true doctrine, thus invoking the very revelation which they were attempting to demonstrate. At bottom their argument, like that of the other school, rested on tradition and on faith.

Revelation, with its corollary of the authority of the church, was the most important issue on which Catholics and unbelievers were divided. Sometimes it was apparently the only issue; Prades, the friend of Diderot; Hooke, professor at the Sorbonne; Loménie de Brienne, a radical undergraduate in 1751 and later archbishop of Toulouse, together with many professors and students throughout France, shared in the most fundamental ideas of the philosophers. At the same time important spokesmen of the church criticized and rejected these ideas. They frequently opposed the reigning theories of Locke and Condillac, which saw in the human mind a mechanical play of sensations. They argued in reply that the mind was unitary, self-acting and irreducible, and that the soul was therefore neither material nor mortal. Orthodox theorists, not sharing in the philosophers' conception of infinite time and natural causality, and upholding the Christian doctrine of creation, objected to such evolutionary ideas as were beginning to appear; and, believing that man was created a rational being, were unable to agree that human intelligence was an historical development—were unable, that is, to accept fully the idea of progress.

In the field of ethics, despite the tendency to laxism among Jesuit moralists, Catholics did not normally concede as much as *philosophes* to liberty. Where *philosophes* held that man is by nature free, Catholics believed him to be by nature under obligation, required to conform to the will of a creator. In part, this difference involved a difference between two conceptions of nature.

It seems fair to conclude that the orthodox of the eighteenth century offered an intelligent criticism of the philosophy of enlightenment. If they could not overthrow it, they could at least lay bare some of its assumptions and implications. If they could not predict its consequences, they are hardly to be blamed, for neither could anyone else; and to our disillusioned age the dark forebodings of the orthodox, the prophecies of chaos to follow on the decay of religion, seem to have contained about as much truth as the vision of the philosophers, who looked forward to indefinite progress in the paths of reason. Could they all come back to life in the middle of the twentieth century, it would not be the conservatives who would be the most surprised.

The orthodox thinkers do not deserve quite so deep an oblivion as they have fallen into. Neither should their merit be exaggerated. They had many weaknesses, quite apart from whether their ideas were valid or correct. None of them had the gifts of expression of Rousseau or of Voltaire. As conservatives they were all condemned to repeat what had been heard before; they could not hope to be brilliantly original. Committed to a position which they held to be timelessly true, they had little to attract a world in rapid change. They lived in a world that was visibly growing, in wealth, in population, in productive capacity, in scientific knowledge and in the refinements of civilization; and for all these developments, the real concern of men of the eighteenth century, they gave a much less satisfactory explanation than the *philosophes*. Their ideas were not especially useful to the kinds of people who were coming into power, property-owners, merchants, lawyers, scientists, and government officials, the bourgeoisie which produced and which was produced by the civilization of the time. They were thus left stranded, some possibly on the heights of eternal verity, others in the jungles where obsolete opinions are debated, and all of them isolated from the main onrush of events. The French Revolution, transmitting the principles of the *philosophes* to the nineteenth century, sealed their doom. After the Revolution the *philosophes* seemed in retrospect to be giants, their adversaries mere pygmies. Today, now that the faith in progress, liberty, and a beneficent natural order is being questioned, we can consider with more patience the criticism which this faith received when it was formulated.

BIBLIOGRAPHICAL NOTE

I have not thought it necessary to list here all the materials I have used. Full bibliographical indications have been given in the footnotes, and the editions are specified. Adequate details are given with the first citation of every work in each chapter.

Good bibliographies for the relevant eighteenth century writings are easily available. Albert Monod, *De Pascal à Chateaubriand: Les défenseurs français du christianisme de 1670 à 1802,* Paris, 1916, lists about six hundred titles for the years from 1740 to 1790. He includes only writings classifiable as defenses of Christianity against unbelief, and omits devotional works, theological works other than apologetic, and works in Latin. For the writings of theologians the standard bibliography is H. Hurter, S.J., *Nomenclator literarius recentioris theologiae catholicae,* 3rd ed., 5 vols., Oeniponte (Innsbruck), 1903-13. Volume IV is on the years from 1664 to 1763, Volume V on the years from 1764 to 1894. Hurter's treatment is selective, not exhaustive; for the theologians that he mentions he gives brief biographical notes and summarizes and evaluates their work. For the writings of Jesuits on all subjects, see A. de Backer, S.J., and C. Sommervogel, S.J., *Bibliothèque des écrivains de la Compagnie de Jésus,* 3 vols., Paris, 1869-76. In M. Picot, *Mémoires pour servir à l'histoire ecclésiastique pendant le dix-huitième siècle,* 2nd ed., Paris, 1816, the entire fourth volume is a catalogue of eighteenth century writers, orthodox, Jansenist, and *philosophe,* whose works bear on the church history of the time. In the third edition of Picot, 7 vols., Paris, 1853-54, this catalogue is distributed through the separate volumes. Obscure writings overlooked by bibliographers or not known to be extant may often be found named or reviewed in contemporary periodicals. For this purpose, on the subject of this book, the *Journal de Trévoux* and the *Année littéraire* are especially useful.

There are a number of recent studies of French Catholic thinkers in the eighteenth century. None has the same scope or purpose as the present volume. On formal apologetic the standard work is that of Monod named in the preceding paragraph. It is remarkable for the completeness with which it fulfils its aim, but fails to set the apologists against their background of Catholic theology. Monod's view of the apologists tends to be negative. He regards as concessions to the *philosophes* many developments which I have represented as arising from Catholic theology itself, such as the attitude of eighteenth century Catholics toward nature and reason, the distinction between morality and religion, and the relaxation of the idea of original sin. Monod's readers are likely to conclude that the criticism of the *philosophes* was feeble and inept.

On the internal development of religious thought in the period there is an able study by Bernhard Groethuysen, *Die Entstehung der bürgerlichen Welt- und Lebensanschauung in Frankreich. I Band: Das Bürgertum und die katholische Weltanschauung.* Halle, 1927. Groethuysen avoids the error of regarding the *philosophes* as the positive and the orthodox as the negative pole in the intellectual currents of the time. His interpretation of the Jesuit-Jansenist controversy is substantially the same as mine, but he perhaps carries it too far, representing the Jansenist-Augustinian view as the dominant form of Christianity before the seventeenth century, and the Jesuit-rationalist view as a definite innovation. Groethuysen labors under a heavy burden of German *Historismus,* seeing in the *Bürgertum* a unique historical phenomenon with a *Weltanschauung* which had never existed before and will not exist in the future, and attributing to this *Weltanschauung* the decline of fear of God, the loss of the sense of sin, and latitudinarian ideas of various kinds, which I quite agree are characteristic of modern bourgeois culture, although I cannot see that they are necessarily peculiar to it. Nevertheless, Groethuysen's contribution is a valuable one.

Henri Bremond, *Histoire littéraire du sentiment religieux en France, depuis la fin des guerres de la religion jusqu' à nos jours,* 12 vols., Paris, 1921-36, is a monumental work, but was left by the author at his death with the eighteenth century practically untouched. Victor Giraud, *Le christianisme de Chateaubriand,* 2 vols., Paris, 1925-28, contains in its first volume a few pages on contemporary opponents of the *philosophes,* but is of slight value for this subject. Pierre-Maurice Masson, *La religion de Jean-Jacques Rousseau,* 3 vols., Paris, 1916, is as nearly definitive as any work of historical scholarship is ever likely to be; it deals ably with the religious milieu in which Rousseau grew up and wrote. François Cornou, *Élie Fréron: Trente ans de luttes contre Voltaire et les philosophes du dix-huitième siècle,* Paris, 1922, is only incidentally an analysis of ideas; centering about a man whose reputation has suffered from the triumph of his enemies, it gives a vivid picture of literary feuds in eighteenth century Paris.

Of these recent works, however, I have not made much use except to trace the sources on which my own study is almost entirely based. I owe more to some of the older monographs cited in the footnotes. My greatest obligation is to a book only indirectly connected with the subject, Carl Becker, *The Heavenly City of the Eighteenth Century Philosophers,* New Haven, 1932. I doubt whether Professor Becker would agree with all I have said about the *philosophes* or their opponents. It is to the *Heavenly City,* nevertheless, that I owe, besides other more intangible debts, the belief that the philosophy of the *philosophes* was itself a faith, and that to understand the thought of the eighteenth century we must understand what the various parties meant by nature and human nature. The emphasis on this interpretation is the chief point in which my book differs from its predecessors on the subject.

INDEX

INDEX

d'Alembert, 7, 13, 18-19, 119, 122, 128, 131, 139
Âme des bêtes, 114, 147-54, 165
Andras, 14
Animals, *see Âme des bêtes*, Evolution
Anthropomorphism, 157, 216
Antoine, 43 n., 92 n.
Aquinas, 79, 220
Archias of Corinth, 81
Assembly of the Clergy, *see* Clergy
Atheism, 142, 168, 211, 215, 219
Augustine, 30, 38, 43, 53, 90
Autrey, *see* Fabry
Auxerre, 45, 49 n., 125
Avignon, 180

Babylon, 210
Bacon, F., 18
Baius, Baianism, 24, 29, 33
Barruel, 151
Bayle, 60, 61, 79-80, 117, 141
Beaumont, archbishop of Paris, 78, 123
Beausobre, L. de, 15, 212 n.
Beauteville, bishop of Alais, 43, 75, 182
Bebescourt, 109
Benedict XIV, 86
Benedictines, 13, 60, 108
Benevolence, 191-2; *see also* Sentimentalism
Bentham, 197 n.
Bergier, 21, 46, 59 n., 82, 87; on miracles and revelation, 96-102, 130, 138 n., 141 n., 142-3, 157, 159 n., 164 n., 185; on moral obligation, 189-92, 194, 198, 204 n.; on Holbach and idea of nature, 215-18
Berkeley, 131
Berruyer, 68-76, 96 n., 102, 105
Berthier, 18-19, 65 n., 181
Besançon, 96
Bible, authority of, 63 *ff*., 82, 85, 97, 165; *see also* Genesis, Moses
Billardon de Sauvigny, 118
Blonde, 29 n., 36

Bollandists, 60
Bonhomme, 121, 127, 218-19
Bonnaire, 170-1, 209-10
Bonnet, 112-17, 141 n.
Bossuet, 53, 54, 184
Bougainville, 164 n.
Boullier, 20 n., 139, 152 n.
Boulogne, 15
Bourges, 46
Brancas, archbishop of Aix, 43, 44 n., 49
Bridaine, 180-1
Brienne, archbishop of Toulouse, 13, 14, 120, 221
Brotier, 128 n.
Bruno, 111
Buffier, 19, 143-4 n.
Buffon, 6, 106, 135, 152 n.; evolutionary ideas, 163 *ff*.
Bullet, 82
Burke, 204 n.
Busenbaum, 42, 46
Butler, 83

Cabrespine, 44
Caen, 61
Calas, 15-16
Calmet, 81
Calvinism, 29, 39, 46, 93
Camier, 40-1, 49
Caraccioli, 181, 193 n.
Carra, 163.
Cartesian dualism, 136 *ff*., 215; *see also* Descartes
Cartesians in eighteenth century, 139-47, 166, 170
Casnedi, 46
Cassini, 34 n.
Castel, 176 n., 208
Caylus, bishop of Auxerre, 49 n., 127
Censorship, *see* Press
Changeux, 157-8
Chassaignan, 109 n.
Chateaubriand, 218

Chaudon, 89, 128 n., 152 n., 200
Chaumeix, 20 n., 152 n., 164 n., 187 n., 192
Cicero, 195
Civilization, 11-15, 171, 176-7
Claparède, 21 n.
Clarke, 83
Clergy, Assembly of, 10, 13, 43, 85 n., 91, 96, 97, 128, 197
Cochet, 139, 145
Coleridge, 140
Collet, 38
Condillac, 124, 131, 135, 153, 221
Condorcet, 131
Conscience, 40-1, 46-7, 51, 174
Conservatism, 202-4
Copernicus, 110
Cosmology, 110-17, 160 ff.
Creation, 153, 156-66
Crillon, 21 n., 193 n.
Cuppé, 108 n.
Cycles, recurrent, 160, 167
Cyrano de Bergerac, 162

Deforis, 5-6
Deism, 61, 110, 145, 161, 215
Denesle, 137 n., 138 n., 201, 202 n.
Denyse, 55 n., 81 n., 87
Descartes, 14, 110, 113, 136-7, 147, 197 n.; see also Cartesian
Desforges, 16 n.
Determinism, 142, 190, 213-14, 216-17; see also Free Will, Predestination
Diderot, 8, 19, 41, 51, 78, 81, 83, 97, 106, 114; on Prades affair, 118-28, 131, 160, 163, 173, 178; moral theory, 186-8, 191-2, 211
Dogmas, see Mysteries
Dogmas of philosophes, 212
Duclos, 18
Dufour, 141 n., 152 n.
Duhamel, 69 n., 128 n., 212-14
Dupréaux, 15 n.
Dutoit-Mambrini, 109 n.

Education, 9, 49, 153, 194, 202
Empiricism, 77 ff., 89 ff., 103, 145, 148, 160 ff., 174, 184, 189, 204, 207; see also Sensationalist psychology
Encyclopédie, 18-20, 97, 107, 117 ff., 131, 135, 138, 139, 163, 178, 187 n.
Encyclopédie méthodique, 97

Equality, 126 and n., 133-5, 193, 197 n.; see also Rights of man
Eternité du monde, 159 n.
Eternity, 157 ff., 199; see also Immortality
Ethics, see Moral theory
Ethiopians, 163
Evil, origin of, 185 ff.; see also Moral theory, Sin
Evolution, 112-17, 149, 152-3, 161-6, 167, 170; see also Âme des bêtes

Fabry, comte d'Autrey, 159 n., 164 n., 168-9
Faith, 20-2; see also Reason and faith, Revelation, Mysteries, Supernaturalism, Tradition
Fanaticism, 6, 15, 81, 87-8, 212-13
Fangouse, 59, 141 n.
Fatalism, 142, 159; see also Determinism
Fathers of church, authority of, 67, 71
Feller, 165 n., 168 n., 193 n.
Fitz-James, bishop of Soissons, 29 n., 43, 49 n., 75-6, 182
Flangebouche, 96
Fontenelle, 110
Forbin, 158-9, 166, 199
Formey, 169-70, 187-8, 193 n., 194
Fournier, 81
Fourquevaux, 36 n.
François, 93, 137 n.
Frederick the Great, 200
Free Will, 29-33, 36 n., 46, 74, 142 ff., 184; see also Determinism, Moral theory, Predestination
Fréret, 96
Fréron, 7, 15, 20, 105, 137 n., 139 n., 152 n., 181 n., 193 n., 201, 218 n.
Frevier, 64 n.
Fumel, bishop of Lodève, 36 n., 94 n., 174 n.

Galien, 36
Galileo, 6
Gamaches, 91
Gauchat, 21, 54, 63, 84 n., 85, 90, 152 n., 159 n.; on evolutionary ideas, 164-6, 171 n., 172, 175, 188, 195-6, 208
Gaultier, 69 n.
Genesis, 81, 111, 116, 130, 156 ff.; see also Bible, Cosmology, Moses
Genlis, Mme. de, 186

Geology, 160 ff.
Gerdil, 176 n.
Germ theory, 106, 113-15
Girondists, 163
God, ideas of, 29-30, 40, 44, 107, 108, 110, 143-5, 156, 161, 180, 189, 198; see also Image of God
Goethe, 214
Goodness of man, 51, 73, 173-5, 199 ff., 208; see also Sentimentalism
Gourlin, 43, 75, 127
Grasse, de, bishop of Angers, 49 n.
Griffet, 64 n., 86 n.
Grimm, 7 n., 16, 28, 85 n., 119 n., 139 n., 173, 194; on idea of nature, 210-12, 214, 218 n.
Gros de Besplas, 21 n.
Guizot, 218
Guyon, 32 n., 36 n., 69 n.

Hardouin, 65-76, 102, 221
Hartzoeker, 106
Hayer, 138 n., 139-40, 148 n.
Heaven, 32, 108, 180; see also Immortality
Hell, 108, 180
Helvétius, 14, 17, 122, 125, 128, 131, 134, 160, 178, 187, 191, 197, 199
Herodotus, 210
Hiero of Syracuse, 82
History, 53 ff., 81 ff., 160, 167 ff., 172, 210
Hobbes, 219
Holbach, 97, 119, 130, 142, 157, 160, 163; on moral theory, 188-91, 211; on nature, 214-18
Holland, von, 218 n.
Homiletics, see Preaching
Hooke, 40-1, 51, 57 n., 92, 123, 126 n., 167, 171 n., 221
Houteville, 54, 80-1 87, 97, 221
Huber, 198 n.
Huet, 118
Humanity, humanitarianism, 191 ff.; see also Sentimentalism
Humbert, 199
Hume, 85, 131-3, 134 n., 140

Ideas (universal), 144-5; see also Innate ideas
Ilhahart de La Chambre, 137, 152 n., 188 n.
Image of God, 35, 107, 151, 184

Immortality, 136, 149, 155, 158, 199-200; see also Heaven, Hell
Incarnation, 91-2, 111, 182
Index (papal) of Prohibited Books, 27, 187
Innate ideas, 104, 129, 136 ff., 143-7, 170
Inquisition, 27, 33 n.
Intolerance, see Tolerance

Jamin, 59 n., 159 n., 168 n., 193 n., 219 n.
Jansenism, 9, 12, 15, 24-52, 73-6, 92-4, 97, 100-1, 120, 128-9, 142, 165, 172, 174, 200, 209
Jesuits, 9, 14, 17-20, 28-52, 65-76, 90, 93, 120, 124, 128-9, 145-6, 164, 172, 180-1, 220-1
Jews, 59, 87, 97, 211 n.
Julian the Apostate, 27, 58

Kant, 129, 136

La Barre, 16
La Baume-Desdossat, 105
La Baumelle, 7, 16 n.
La Croix, C., see Busenbaum
La Croix, P., 141 n., 197 n.
La Flèche, 14
La Luzerne, bishop of Langres, 182-3, 219 n.
Larcher, 210
Lavater, 112
Laxism, 49, 222
Le Chapelain, 180
Lecky, 210
Le Franc de Pompignan, J.-G., bishop of Puy, 14, 85 n., 91 n., 201
Le Franc de Pompignan, J.-J., 181
Le Gros, 56 n., 125, 169, 175-6, 208
Leibniz, 79-80, 136
Le Moyne, 45
Lesser, 106
Liberalization of doctrine, see Modernist tendencies
Liberté, égalité, humanité, 193
Lignac, Le Large de, 103, 137 n., 139-41, 143-5, 152 n., 159 n., 164 n.
Linguet, 7 n., 15-17, 20 n., 164 n.
Lisle de Sales, de, 211
Locke, 41, 113, 124, 131, 139, 147-50, 153, 221; see Sensationalist psychology

Louis, A., 138
Louis, dom, 108
Louvain, 44
Lycurgus, 187

Maillet, de, 162-4
Maistre, de, 204 n.
Malabar, 187
Malebranche, 136-7, 138 n.
Malesherbes, 17, 128
Malpighi, 106
Malvin de Montazet, archbishop of Lyons, 26, 49 n., 74, 84
Marmontel, 7, 16 n., 117-18, 181, 198
Martyrs, 87-9
Materialism, 142, 153, 162, 215-18; *see also* Determinism, Soul, Self
Maupertuis, 197 n.
Mazarin, *collège*, 139
Mechanism, 142-3, 152
Meister, 214
Mendelssohn, Moses, 112
Menoux, 168 n.
Metz, 153
Mey, 120 n.
Mirabeau, comte de, 16 n.
Mirabeau, marquis de, 16 n.
Miracles, 27, 61, 82-102, 124, 179
Mirepoix, 125
Modernist tendencies, 10-20, 30-52, 61, 68 *ff.*, 82, 97, 106-29, 152-3, 164 n., 197 n.
Mohammed, Mohammedanism, 86, 87, 88, 100, 127, 172
Molina, Molinism, 31 *ff.*, 49, 72, 174
Molinos, 33
Monestier, 137 n., 139, 145-6
Montauban, 125
Montesquieu, 78, 170-2, 202, 209-10
Montpelier, 180
Moral theory, 29-53, 178-205
Morality and religion, separation of, 39 *ff.*, 43, 45
Moreau, 21 n.
Morellet, 16 n.
Moses, 56, 64, 78, 93, 99, 116, 165-6; *see also* Genesis, Bible
Muschembroek, 106
Mysteries, 79 *ff.*, 89-92, 104-9, 159, 178-9, 182, 220
Mysticism, 181

Natural law, 28-34, 39-40, 93, 195-6, 202-5
Natural morality, 8, 50-1, 173
Natural religion, 28, 75, 78, 173, 195
Nature, 28-34, 51-2, 142, 174, 190, 206-19; *see also* Supernaturalism, Natural law, etc.
Nature, state of, 31, 36, 126 n., 167, 172-7, 198, 211
Needham, 160 n.
Newton, 11, 85, 110
Nieuwentyt, 106
Nonotte, 81, 95, 159 n., 195

Occam, 79, 220
Occasionalism, 136-7
Oratorians, 14, 180
Origen, 95
Origins of man, 162 *ff.*, of intelligence, 167 *ff.*; *see also* Evolution, Creation

Paley, 83
Palissot, 16 n., 130, 164 n., 192
Para du Phanjas, 56 n., 85 n., 152 n.
Paris, abbé, 128 n.
Pâris, abbé, 92, 94, 100
Parlements, 9-10, 68, 105, 125
Pascal, 26, 28, 47, 61, 181-2, 196, 212-13
Paulian, 57 n., 128 n., 197 n.
Pelagianism, 32, 34
Pelvert, 29 n., 96 n.
Penthièvre, 181
Perfectibility, 114, 133, 167, 169, 185; *see also* Progress
Personality, 149; *see also* Self
Pichon, 152 n., 202 n.
Pierquin, 109
Piety, 181-3
Pinault, 218 n.
Plato, 139, 156-7
Pluche, 106-7
Pluquet, 21, 137 n., 159, 191 n.
Polignac, 137 n., 152 n., 164 n.
Pompadour, Mme. de, 128
Pope, Alexander, 208, 212-13
Port-Royal, 25
Prades, 117-31, 153, 221
Preaching, 14, 180-1
Predestination, 30
Preestablished harmony, 136-7
Prémontval, 149

Press, freedom and control of, 16-17, 18; *see also* Index, Parlements
Primitivism, 134, 173-7; *see also* Nature, state of
Probabilism, 47-8
Progress, 58, 119, 161, 166-77; *see also* Perfectibility, Evolution
Protestants, 10, 19, 25; salvation of, 46, 65, 70, 73, 78, 136
Providence, 106-7, 155, 166, 169, 173

Quesnel, 25

Racine, L., 181
Ranke, 210
Rationalism (as opposed to empiricism), 79-80, 170, 173-5, 204
Raynal, 15, 131, 164 n.
Reason and faith, 79-80, 103, 219-20; *see also* Skepticism
Reason, right, 40, 42, 43, 51, 79-80, 188, 207; *see also* Nature
Renan, 218
Revelation, 34, 52, 61-2, 77-102, 138, 153, 179 *ff.*
Rhodez, 44
Richard, 138 n., 141 n., 185, 191 n.
Richérisme, 26
Rights of man, 108, 126 n., 197 n., 198, 203; *see also* Equality, Humanity
Robinet, 161-2, 166
Roche, 139, 148-50, 181
Romanticism, 138, 146, 151, 185; *see also* Sentimentalism
Rouen, 49, 69
Rousseau, 18, 39, 41, 46, 51; on revelation, 78, 85, 87, 96, 98-9, 107, 128; on equality and psychology, 134-5, 169, 171; on state of nature, 173-6, 181, 188, 193-4, 197, 199, 208
Roussel, 138 n., 202-4
Roussel de la Tour, 49 n.
Royou, 164 n.
Rulié, 81 n.

Saint-Adon, 199 n.
Saint-Germain l'Auxerrois, 139
Saint-Lambert, 12
Saint-Martin, 182 n.
Saint-Sulpice, 14
Self, 131-2, 140-54; *see also* Soul, Sensationalist psychology
Sennemaud, 96 n., 164 n.

Sensationalist psychology, 104, 113, 124, 128, 130-54, 169, 189; *see also* Empiricism, *Tabula rasa*
Sentimentalism, *sensibilité*, 51, 108, 151, 188-92
Shelley, 147
Simon, Richard, 60
Sin, 35-8; philosophic sin, 41-3, 73-5, 134, 169, 184, 199; *philosophe* equivalent, 212-14; *see also* Moral theory
Sinsart, 138 n., 152 n.
Skepticism, 15, 69, 103, 132, 211-12, 219
Smith, Adam, 134 n.
Social contract, 198-9, 202-3
Sorbonne, *see* University of Paris
Soul, 113-14, 136, 147; *see also Ame des bêtes*, Self.
Sparta, 187
Spinoza, 60, 117
Square thoughts, etc., 137
Stanislas Leczinski, king of Poland, 201
State and church, 8-10, 128-9
Suarez, 58, 64
Supernaturalism, 32-3, 34, 38, 44 n., 50, 52, 76, 77-102, 115, 171, 173, 176, 184, 220-1; *see also* Revelation, Creation, Miracles, Soul

Tabula rasa, 133, 146, 150; *see also* Sensationalist psychology
Talma, 15
Telliamed, 162-4
Terrasson, 110-12
Tertullian, 95
Time, 155 *ff.*
Tolerance, toleration, intolerance, 5 *ff.*; *see also* Press
Torné, 90
Toul, 14
Toulouse, 14, 16, 145, 221
Tradition, 53-75, 88, 101-2
Trent, Council of, 24, 33, 39, 63-4, 75
Trévoux, Journal de, 18-19, 49, 64 n., 93, 128, 143, 164, 174, 181
Troya d'Assigny, 96 n., 152 n.
Trublet, 83, 178
Turgot, 14
Tutiorism, 48

Unigenitus, 25 *ff.*, 33, 39, 43

University of Paris, 9, 14, 26, 40, 51, 58, 68, 92, 117-29, 152 n., 153, 167; *see also* Hooke, Prades, Le Gros, Cochet, Pluquet
Utilitarianism, 191 n., 197 n.

Valentia, 64
Valla, 60
Vernes, 21 n.
Villemert, 159 n., 196 n.
Villiers, 138, 164 n.

Voltaire, 7, 8, 14, 58, 86, 117, 119 n., 125, 128, 131, 139, 143 n., 164, 168-9, 181 n., 193, 195, 210, 212-13, 218
Vulgate, *see* Bible

Warburton, 78
Wordsworth, 146
Worlds, plurality of 110-17, 153

Yvon, 57 n., 117, 119, 159 n., 164 n., 168 n., 171